HOW CAN TALKING HELP?

HOW CAN TALKING HELP?

An Introduction to the Technique of Analytic Therapy

Roy M. Mendelsohn, M.D.

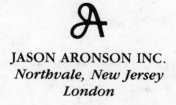

JASON ARONSON INC.
Northvale, New Jersey
London

Production Editor: Judith D. Cohen
Editorial Director: Muriel Jorgensen

This book was set in 11/14 Garamond by Lind Graphics of Upper Saddle River, New Jersey, and printed and bound by Haddon Craftsmen of Scranton, Pennsylvania.

Library of Congress Cataloging-in-Publication Data

Mendelsohn, Roy M.
    How can talking help? : an introduction to the technique of
analytic therapy / by Roy M. Mendelsohn.
        p.   cm.
    Includes bibliographical references and index.
    ISBN 0-87668-503-3
    1. Psychoanalysis. 2. Psychotherapy. 3. Psychoanalysis—Case
studies. 4. Psychotherapy—Case studies. I. Title.
    [DNLM: 1. Psychoanalytic Therapy.   WM 460.6 M537h]
RC504.M395   1992
616.89'17—dc20
DNLM/DLC
for Library of Congress   91-35243

Manufactured in the United States of America. Jason Aronson Inc. offers books and cassettes. For information and catalog write to Jason Aronson Inc., 230 Livingston Street, Northvale, New Jersey 07647.

*To the children
who have taught me most
about the value of words*

Contents

Preface

Over the years many different curative factors have been identified in psychoanalytic treatment. Advances in psychoanalytic theory have led to changes in technique and have enlarged the range of treatable psychological disturbances. There is now more information about those aspects of the treatment environment that lead to progress, and it has become possible to be more specific in determining what is most likely to be curative with a given patient.

The ultimate proving ground for any theory of mental functioning is its effect on the patient. Psychoanalysis places a patient's validating responses at the forefront, particularly their unconscious significance. Constructive growth is established based on a translation of a patient's unconscious communications. It is a complex task, however, to distinguish between the forces designed to maintain pathology and distortion and those forces that lead toward healthy functioning. The effort to make their distinction is often amply rewarded, for it can then be possible to find ways to intervene successfully with even the most serious disturbances, especially those that had been considered untreatable, unmodifiable, or for whom psychoanalytic treatment had either failed or been disruptive.

Effective treatment relies on an understanding of the underlying trouble. This requires a satisfactory integrative theory offering flexible guidelines that can be extended into the exploration of unknown territory. The way a positive element of the treatment is formulated depends a great deal on whether the patient's difficulties are seen as the result of (1) an intrapsychic, primarily infantile instinctual conflict, (2) a disorder in the composition and unfolding of a nuclear self, (3) a disturbance in the representation and integration of the mental impressions of self and object, or (4) a deficit, defect, or hypertrophy in the defensively distorting functions of the ego. Each perspective contributes to the overall picture, deepening a therapist's grasp of what is needed to enable constructive growth.

Enlarging the frontiers of psychological disturbances depends on an accurate appraisal of what is required of a therapist at each step along the way. This goal can only be accomplished if the treatment conditions are empathic with, and strengthening to, the psychic constellations in the unconscious system that facilitate constructive growth. These intrapsychic processes may be extremely deficient, vulnerable, and intermittently or totally split off from continuity of experience. Under such circumstances, a much-needed source of validation is largely unavailable, and thus the most important unconscious communications are unlikely to take place within a verbally symbolic sphere. Instead, they are diverted into behavior or remain as a silent presence, so that the resulting gaps can only be filled in by a therapist's sensitive reading of the nonverbal aspects of the therapeutic interaction. When this occurs, as it almost always does in the primitively organized personality, an inordinate emphasis is put on a therapist's subjective intuitive and empathic responses for discerning what is necessary to further psychological growth.

In order to comprehend fully a patient's internal experiences, a therapist must be able to achieve a high degree of empathic immersion in them. Their archaic nature can then readily elicit regressive identifications, anxiety-laden fantasies, and troublesome early memories. The discrimination between empathy and countertransference can be problematic. This area of therapeutic functioning is at the frontier of expanding sound, psychoanalytically derived principles of treatment to reach more serious psychic disturbances. One vital element involves a therapist's ability to become more sensitively attuned to the meaning of all subjective reactions. It is then possible to be more discriminating in the sometimes confusing task of separating out the indications of unconsciously empathic responsiveness and of countertransference.

The treatment dilemmas that arise in entering unknown territory may sometimes call for interventions that seemingly reach beyond the realm of sound psychoanalytic principles. Here a therapist's personality and mode of functioning become central to the outcome. This factor can be more subtle in addressing the treatment needs of a well-structured personality; it is often downplayed or unrecognized. In addition to being accurate in identifying unconsciously empathic and inappropriate countertransference-based responses, a therapist must recognize a patient's strivings to attain integration through the enactment of infantile and preverbal traumas. These require support, but it is imperative to distinguish them from the destructive forms of acting out that are antithetical to growth. An interpersonal environment conducive to trial-and-error methods of learning has to be created, for it is the cure that determines the cause. This underscores how crucial it is to become more aware of the early indicators of incipient errors. Subsequently, it may be possible to absorb the detrimental influences of a mistake and even turn its negative features into therapeutic gain.

This is a book about the intimately intertwined positive forces at work in a psychotherapeutic relationship. Depending on the situation, some are clearly evident in the forefront, whereas others operate silently in the background. Chapter 1 gives an overall view of how these growth-promoting qualities overlap; it identifies the conditions that determine which is most prominent at a given moment. Chapter 2 examines the role of interpretations leading to insight. Chapter 3 highlights the effects of constructive positive identifications with the therapist and therapeutic attitude, describing the means by which they are encouraged. Chapter 4 explores profound regressive experiences, distinguishing between benign and malignant forms, and points out when they are necessary to enable continuity of experience. Chapter 5 discusses the problem of providing new actual experiences to fill in the gaps in psychic functioning; it presents an expanded view of the concept of insight. Chapter 6 details the significance of a therapist's subjective responses, defining the role of empathy and countertransference. Chapter 7 outlines the patient's contribution, illustrating the distinction between acting out and reenacting preverbal experiences and infantile traumas. Finally, Chapter 8 gives a summary statement to pull together more concisely what furthers growth in a psychotherapeutic process.

1

The Growth-Promoting Properties of a Therapeutic Interaction

The Interdependency of Constructive Influences
Interpretation, Management, Regression,
   and New Experience
The Relationship of Separation-Individuation to
   the Conditions of Psychoanalytic Treatment
The Basic Psychoanalytic Principles and the
   Qualities of a Good Object
The Assessment of Therapeutic Needs

The Interdependency of Constructive Influences

A 5-year-old boy began his treatment by stating, "I felt like I had the headache and my parents were getting the aspirin." He was referring to my meeting with his parents on several occasions prior to seeing him. This statement showed a great deal about him, though the most significant part of his trouble would not be apparent for some time, since he had no way of putting it into words. Nevertheless, what he said immediately indicated that he was acutely aware of some internal suffering, he was ready to do something about it, and he could be psychologically minded. In addition, he was able to use humor and irony in expressing the sense of rejection he felt. This was quite surprising to me after having heard his history from his parents and after seeing him in the waiting room. He had been sitting quietly in an upright position dressed in a jacket and tie, looking extremely worried and serious.

Thus, right from the outset, the prospect of entering a potentially helpful relationship was opening up a sense of hope for him, which was allowing feelings to emerge that he usually held tightly in check.

He had been referred because of his parents' deep concern about his depression, lack of vitality, often-repeated statements of not wanting to live, and unyielding, somber mood. He had no friends, always appeared tense, and was easily frustrated. His parents were engaged in an active battle around the advisability of seeking help, with the mother desperately wanting it for her child and the father equally adamant in insisting that it was unnecessary. Several sessions were spent trying to clarify the nature of their disagreement. The mother expressed an intense feeling of guilt dating from the time when she was depressed for approximately one month when he was 8 months old. After this time both parents felt he had changed. He gradually seemed to lose his enthusiasm, which was replaced by a look of sadness. She was eager for her child to have the help she thought she could not provide and believed she was implicated in ways that were vague and hard to define. After these introductory sessions, the father was able to recognize the narcissistic insult he experienced in acknowledging his son's difficulty. He could see his resistance was a defense against his own vulnerabilities, sought treatment for himself, and felt able to support his child's needs.

An appointment was then made, and the boy readily came into the office. He showed constriction in his every movement and exhibited what looked like very poor muscular coordination. He was eager to talk and after his initial comment went on to describe his frustration at my meeting with his parents while he had to wait for his sessions. He spoke at length of his unhappiness, of feeling unloved, and of being awkward and inept at everything he undertook.

During the early months of daily sessions he looked forward to coming and was remarkably verbal. The stiffness and rigidity in his posture slowly gave way and his whole countenance changed. He began to show a wide variety of affective expressions consonant with his vivid portrayals of feelings toward family members. He struggled mightily to idealize his parents, but only thinly disguised the towering rage that pressed for expression just beneath the surface. When he spoke of his mother being like a queen in his eyes, what emerged was a picture of a distant regal figure having all of his care arranged by others, only deigning to bid him good night when he went off to sleep. The descriptions of his father were meant to convey the idea of sharing play activities, but what came out was the image of a very busy, narcissistic, infantile man. Moments of contact were characterized by giving in to the child's every whim only to leave abruptly when any need was expressed.

His reaction to my interpretive comments about the defensive function of his idealizations, and my pointing out the underlying hostility, was quite startling. Each time I began to talk he sat almost transfixed as though avidly listening and taking in every word. It appeared to reflect a hunger for contact, and particularly for communication directed specifically to him. It was surprising to see a 5-year-old child listening to an interpretation that went beyond just a few words. At first slowly and then escalating in intensity, regressive elements began to enter into his entire manner of functioning. He became provocative in his behavior, leading to angry and irritable physical attacks on my person. Much of this was accompanied by loud and almost maniacal laughter. There were also brief episodes of loss of bowel control and fecal smearing. Along with this profound regression his lack of coordination disappeared and he demonstrated that his basic physical endowment was really superior. It seemed as though his skeletomuscular inhibition was an attempt both to express and to control overwhelming aggressive impulses through constant tension, and the release from conscious control was responsible for the muscular improvement.

My words, which had been so welcome in the initial sessions, gradually were perceived as a source of injury. It reached a point where even the slightest indication that I was about to talk was enough to trigger shouting or some explosive behavior. I was now no longer seen as an ally but as a dangerous figure and one who had to be overcome or subdued. Any attempt to offer transference interpretations of the unfolding regression were not only unsuccessful but could not even be articulated enough to be taken in. At the same time, separations from me aroused extreme anxiety, often to the point of panic. It looked as though he couldn't stand me yet couldn't be without me. It was evident that something powerful and regressive was taking place, although the origins were obscure. A specific theme, however, of someone or something being tied up was frequently repeated. He fantasized being in a boat pursued by hundreds of bigger people intent on subduing him and tying him up in retaliation for a theft. There were many fantasies in which he emphasized his tremendous power and strength, all involving breaking loose from bonds or from a burglar who was climbing in his window to pin him down. He also imagined himself as the world's greatest wild-horse tamer, chasing wild horses and tying them up if they tried to escape.

Toward the end of the second year of treatment the theme of being tied up was lived in the therapy. Previously he had generally indicated gratitude, despite his mild protests, when he was out of control and physically restrained. Now even "accidental" contact precipitated intense hatred: "You hurt me and won't let me go. I hate you. I can't stand it. I'm leaving. I have to get out of here. You're trying to tie me down." When he sat he felt himself completely immobilized and screamed that he was tied up and couldn't move. The significance of this material remained unclear and I found it extremely difficult to determine how to provide the safety and containment for its meaning to surface. The regression continued unabated. He often became uncontrollable, either acting wild or insisting on smearing his feces. At these moments I had no obvious alternative other than to hold him as gently as I could, which offered no real answer and only fed whatever was raging within him.

After much deliberation and soul-searching, including consultative and supervisory help, I wondered whether his reaction to any verbalization was an implicit unconscious direction. I had the idea that it might be expressing his need for total silence in order to bring forth the underlying experience. I proceeded to conduct the relationship with this in mind and was rewarded by a change in his behavior. The meaning was still not clear, but it was indicative of his attempt to carry some internal experience into a communicative modality. Each session began with my silence as he entered, looking wild and knocking over objects in the room. He then stopped as though expecting a response, which was not forthcoming. After a while he also fell silent, appearing pensive and preoccupied. He began to collect pieces of string and knotted them together, rolling them into an expanding ball. He became obsessed with this activity, which extended into the external world. Much of his time was spent searching for more string, and the ball got larger and larger. At this juncture there was a frantic request from his family to meet with me because he was creating havoc in his environment. I simply asked him how he felt about such a meeting, and he silently but vigorously nodded his assent. In the session just prior to the meeting, he came in with his ball of string and kept going in and out of the office, looking confused. Finally he asked a flood of questions, making it apparent that he was seeking to define the boundaries of my office. He wanted to tie up the entire office with me in it, but was frustrated in figuring out how to begin. I realized his behavior was motivated by an emerging unconscious fantasy and remained silent so it could unfold. Later I spoke with his parents, who felt helpless in dealing with his frantic and driven behavior. They wanted my help in understanding what was happening. I could only tell them there was much I did not yet understand, but I added I felt I was on the right track. Something important seemed to be on the verge of coming into view. I alluded to his attempts to tie me up, at which point his mother turned pale and gasped as she recalled some of the details of the time of her depression.

An extremely close relative had been killed in an accident while riding a horse, and she had spent the next month at the nearby home of this relative's mother. She was annoyed by her child's demands so she strapped him into a baby chair and left him each day. She returned periodically to attend to his physical needs, usually feeding him while he remained strapped in the chair. She felt very guilty and had forgotten about it until reminded by my description of his behavior.

In the subsequent session with the boy, I started to relate what I had learned, only to be interrupted as soon as I connected his behavior to his mother. He insisted on learning about it directly from her. That evening his mother told him in great detail, and afterward his whole way of functioning in the therapeutic relationship changed. He was curious about his internal reactions, especially noticing how many of his fantasies and feelings had a similar flavor. He was either tied down and filled with helplessness and rage or, conversely, frantically investing all of his energy into tying down and controlling someone else while filled with aggression and glee.

Looking back over the earlier sessions I realized how much this preverbal experience had subtly influenced the entire course of his psychosexual development. It was incorporated into his perceptions, fantasies, and reactions in a manner characteristic of each stage.[1] I also recalled the initial period when he had sat transfixed, listening to my words. Although his hunger for contact was certainly one aspect, it also may have contained some elements of the sensation of being tied down while being fed. My interpretive efforts, although initially welcome, later clearly interfered with the unfolding of this regressive preverbal trauma. His explosive response at any attempt I made to speak appeared to be a combination of his transference anticipation of being tied down once again, and of his need for my complete silence so he could fully express the dimensions of this preverbal experience. In this situation almost total silence was necessary to resonate with the way the relationship with his mother was registered. Only then could it be re-created in the immediacy of the transference. He had managed to achieve higher levels of psychic organization so that it did not require some concrete action on my part to enable representation of the trauma. There was no gap in psychic function to be bridged and he did have the capacity to symbolize and to internalize interpretive interventions. The traumatic preverbal event had influenced all further developmental expansion, including the way in which the stimuli of the internal and external worlds were perceived and to which he adapted. It was also silently exerting its effects in the transference. Although he had attained considerable progress in psy-

---

[1]**Alvin Frank** referred to the unremembered impressions of early childhood as unforgettable, so profound is their effect. This important article called attention to the way in which highly cathected inaccessible memory traces of traumatic intensity facilitate maladaptation through their direct fixative influence on subsequent stages and tasks. These mental events can be inferred through deductions based on alteration of ego states, symptoms, symptomatic behavior, character alteration, and the reproduction of early impressions by reliving them in the psychoanalytic situation (Frank 1969).

chic structuralization, it had continued to color all facets of his intrapsychic and interpersonal functioning.

Within the arms of a benign therapeutic regression the full extent of this patient's preverbal trauma could be revealed and a pathway created for its recovery. It was necessary, however, to depart somewhat from a verbally interpretive modality, for almost total silence and an absence of concrete actions were the required ingredients, even in the face of his out-of-control behavior. Had my emotional attitude been one of defensive withdrawal, it would probably have been so parallel to the trauma of the infantile experience that it is unlikely it could have been included within the integrative work of the treatment. Fortunately there appeared to be a strong therapeutic alliance, which gave me the time and space finally to grasp how his unconscious direction for me to remain silent was expressed. Much depended on my ongoing search to identify unhelpful countertransferences and stay open to empathic intuitive responses. Ultimately my silence had the effect of an interpretation, in that the patient's unconscious communication was both understood and acknowledged. The range and degree of this child's disturbance, operating in conjunction with the considerable advancements in psychic structuralization, highlighted the different elements having a constructive influence that were necessary before a successful outcome could result.

Although sensitive empathic interpretations were important throughout, they stood at the forefront only at the outset of his treatment and in the later phases when the impact of what had been unspeakable had entered the realm of symbolic communication. Initially, therefore, an interpretive grasp of his underlying rage allowed him to feel sufficiently contained and held, so that a door was opened to a regression that escalated to a point where it seemed to be out of control. At such moments management considerations became a primary focus of attention, but they had to be applied carefully so that there was room for the enactment of his preverbal trauma. During this phase the makeup of the underlying therapeutic alliance was most in evidence, for under the sway of a profound regression there was no connection whatsoever between his observing ego and my therapeutic functioning. The alliance that did exist was clearly between those forces deeply buried within his personality that were seeking to find a growth-promoting experience and my capacity to receive and respond to these unconscious communications in a way that was in tune with what was needed. The overall management of the framework, in combination with the strength of the alliance, fostered constructive and positive identifications with both my approach and attitude. This was reflected in the way he was able to be introspective about and to integrate infantile instinctual strivings following the period when his preverbal trauma was reconstructed.[2]

In this situation the reconstruction was given by his mother. The fantasy ramifications, however, became a part of the transference, and were included in the interpretations that were most helpful. It was also necessary for the regression to reach a deep enough level before the preverbal trauma could be expressed. My initial impression that the regression was out of control was only partially accurate. I did not have a full grasp of its meaning and hence could not offer the conditions he required in the relationship. It was striking to observe how once I began to understand the significance of his need for silence, the regression was no longer out of control but rather

---

[2]**Harold Blum** investigated the effects of reconstructions and found that the historical reconstruction of real experience and real traumatic episodes remained significant and could reorder the misinterpretation of internal and external reality (Blum 1977).

enabled a full living out of his preverbal experience. The end result was a new solution in that he was now able to achieve a penetrating grasp of what he had gone through. He could see and integrate the impact it had upon him by understanding the origins and significance of the fantasies that were constantly operative to affect almost every aspect of his life.

Thus at different stages his treatment included interpretive help to undo defenses and to foster the integration of unconscious fantasies; sensitive management of the treatment framework to create conditions of safety, thereby fostering constructive identifications; and a profound therapeutic regression that was deep enough to reach and incorporate experiences that were preverbal in nature and could not be articulated. This early trauma had to be fully enacted, and in the process it facilitated the flow of unconscious and conscious experience. The treatment relationship provided an opportunity to repeat the original event, while representing a new and different outcome that had a positive effect on his entire mode of functioning. In this situation there were no obvious gaps in psychic functioning that had to be bridged, although the inhibitions it created were alleviated. All of these factors were interwoven and overlapping, as each depended upon the other for the conditions of the treatment to match his therapeutic needs.

Interpretation, Management, Regression, and New Experience

Over the years advancements in psychoanalytic treatment have primarily emerged from a study of its failures, the very places where the process has been obstructed. Through questioning the nature of the obstacles, much has been discovered, involving both the patient's transference and the therapist's countertransference. At first the emphasis was on neurotic constellations, which were remarkably responsive to interpretations of unconscious content. These were individuals who essentially had negotiated separation and individuation successfully, thereby establishing the mental foundation necessary for development to progress and self-expansion to continue. Any pathological consequences that arose could be most effectively alleviated through the influences of a verbally communicative treatment modality emphasizing insight. A therapist's interpretation of pathological distortions, emanating from unconscious infantile, primarily instinctual, conflicts and repeated in the transference relationship, resulted in an enlargement of self-knowledge, enabling the integrative forces in the personality to achieve new solutions to infantile dilemmas. Although it gradually became apparent that the nature of the treatment relationship within which interpretive interventions were offered was vital, it could be provided within the usual familiar conditions of psychoanalytic treatment.

Clinicians coming in contact with more serious disturbances came to realize that success could only be accomplished when the significance of the actual interaction could be appreciated. Concommitantly the crucial importance of the personality of a therapist was recognized[3] and along with it the effects created

---

[3]**Myron Hurwitz** was interested in the nature of the impact the person of the analyst and his theories has upon a patient, and its importance in determining the course and outcome of the treatment. He noted that those analysts whose theoretical point of view excludes the reality of a personal impact are not likely to take this factor into account. Analysts who take this view appear to value insight above all else and tend to see the cognitive analysis of the oedipal conflict to be the sign of a

by the manner in which the conditions of the treatment were applied and how the interaction was conducted rose to the forefront. The holding and containing properties of a secure treatment framework became evident, as did the need to distinguish between those patients who required varying degrees of flexibility and those who required a firm unyielding stance. Within this context one could see that although interpretive efforts led to integration through insight, it could only take place when a patient felt securely held and safe enough to instigate a benign regression. This had the result of fostering positive, constructive identifications. At the same time the advantages and disadvantages of a profound regression began to become apparent. Many controversial questions arose as to when such regressions were essential and when they were a product of some deficit or defect in the treatment situation itself.

---

successful analysis. Their tendency is then to consider the possibility of nonverbal components in the effectiveness of treatment as being nonanalytic in nature.

Separating distortions from "reality" is a most complicated task. It is vital for the analyst to differentiate those reactions of the patient to the real, consciously or unconsciously perceived aspects of the analyst from those responses to inner stimuli. After the reality of certain dimensions of the analyst have been clarified and accepted the transference use of these characteristics can be demonstrated. The impact on the analysis such a clarification can make centers on the strengthening or undermining of the patient's capacity to test reality, to trust, to temper both parties' grandiosity, and to aid in lifting repression. When preoedipal and preverbal factors are included as important in their own right, the sense of something missing is then not viewed as neurotic oedipal longing but as a failure to include earlier, more archaic issues. Addressing very early and primitive developmental concerns organizes them, puts them into words, and in this way helps to master them (Hurwitz 1986).

When a regression, no matter how extreme, opened up a pathway for reaching otherwise inaccessible infantile experiences, the consequence was positive, as continuity of experience within the personality was attained. A regression could get out of control, serving no identifiable useful purpose, since healthy elements in the personality were eroded and pathological defenses supported and strengthened. Recognizing the differences between these benign and malignant forms of regression became essential, with important implications for determining a therapist's contribution to each. However, through the therapeutic work with these narcissistic disorders, the powerful input of preverbal experiences was revealed, and potential avenues for including them within the realm of therapeutic influence emerged.[4] Again there was much controversy as to whether unusual measures had to be introduced in order to address these primitive experiences sufficiently, or whether they could be integrated within a firm, unyielding psychoanalytic framework. In general those preverbal experiences that had accreted to more advanced psychic structures were best handled without modifications or deviations from the secure conditions of a verbally interpretive modality. On the other hand those that existed split off from such advanced

---

[4]**Hans Loewald** has written extensively on the significance of the psychoanalytic situation. He thought the psychoanalytic process was the arena par excellence for studying the underlying psychic activity that enters into the organization, maintenance, and growth of the individual mind. It repeats and reveals the essential features of the formative stages of psychic development. This understanding is being supplemented and deepened by the more recent recognition of the impact of preoedipal disturbances on the analytic process. When modifications of technique are called for they are no less psychoanalytic because they take into account insights into, and requirements of, more primitive stages of development and mental disturbances (Loewald 1970).

structures did seem to require actual experiences, often of direct contact with a therapist, before enough internal structure could be formed to allow symbolic functions to make use of a verbally communicative relationship. (Mendelsohn 1991)

The impact of preverbal traumas can be extreme, having an effect on all advancing stages of development and even upon the emerging form and shape of internal thought and language. These influences are then repeated in the nonverbal aspects of an unfolding transference relationship.[5] On most occasions they operate silently, with their healing taking place in a subtle and often unnoticeable fashion. There are times, however, when the preverbal experiences have been so traumatic that they become a predominant feature of the transference. They cannot be articulated, so that a therapist has to be open and willing to be guided by the patient's unconscious perception of what the treatment relationship must offer in order to integrate

---

[5]**Anne Marie Weill** has been concerned with the more subtle, nonverbal aspects of the treatment relationship and felt that the effects of some preverbal experience could easily go unrecognized. She called particular attention to those individuals who manifest a continued self-depreciation, a holding on to affects that are negatively and painfully tinged, which she thought might well psychologically represent a holding on to the symbiotic state of non-well-being. She speculated that organismically experienced, neuronically incurred memory traces exert their influences by kindling phase-specific problems. Thus a child with an emerging self core that is drenched with aggressive drive derivatives will have a more-than-average rapprochement crisis. In some patients dynamic thinking about oedipal and even preoedipal rapprochement sources of pathology has to be led even further back into the preverbal sphere. The significance of a failure in the symbiotic phase is paramount, and any ensuing rapprochement difficulty and later psychopathology are then superimposed and intertwined (Weill 1985).

their disruptive effects. Under these circumstances the differing aspects of the treatment that have a constructive influence tend to stand out at one time or another, as the others recede into the background, or sometimes all are simultaneously present in the forefront of the transference. Having these factors highlighted suggests that they may all be operative in any treatment relationship, and in all likelihood an overlapping interplay of these constructive influences must be present for a psychotherapeutic venture to be curative.

The Relationship of Separation-Individuation to the Conditions of Psychoanalytic Treatment

A psychoanalytically conducted therapeutic relationship is designed to facilitate the flow of projective identifications, thereby fueling the transference through a free-associative process and enabling the unfolding of a benign regression. Within the context of the resulting interaction there is a constant interchange of transference and countertransference reactions in both parties. The therapist is responsible for maintaining the proper working conditions through management of the framework, appropriate silences, and interpretations empathic with unconscious communications and experience. A therapist's emotional responsiveness and unconscious understanding are communicated in this way, having a profound influence on the patient's transferences. To the extent that the therapist introduces elements into the interaction derived from transference experiences, which are in some measure inevitable, the patient in turn could be said to have a countertransference reaction. It is by virtue of this admixture that material becomes available for guiding the therapist's conduct, and when interventions are empathic with the patient's unconscious perceptions of what is required to promote growth, therapeutic progress is manifested.

Those individuals who have negotiated separation and individuation during the developmental years have continuity of experience well structured within the personality, and symbolic processes are functional. The primary mode of communication is therefore readily and optimally embodied within the realm of verbal dialogue. This is in contrast to more primitively structured individuals. Here verbal interpretations are either too distant or incapable of being internalized. Active participation in concrete experiences of involvement may therefore be necessary, and immediate responses may at times be imperative. It is in this area that unusual measures may be indicated. However the ensuing therapeutic interaction is then exposed to a greater risk of contamination, since a therapist's behavior may feed an unconscious fantasy or resonate with and repeat early infantile traumas. This potentiality makes it mandatory to develop some guidelines for determining when such measures are called for, and for validating whether it is appropriate. One major criterion involves attaining as clear a picture as possible of what specific experience is necessary for the process of separation and individuation to be completed.

The earliest phases of psychological development are occupied with the task of building up a mental representational world with a sufficient degree of firmness to enable advances in self-individuation and self-differentiation to take place. There is much evidence to suggest that the psychological symbiosis of postuterine life represents a developmental advance. Before it is possible for the lack of differentiation to evolve that is essential for internalizing the experiences furthering mental structuralization, enough empathic resonance with an external object must be present.[6]

Body ego experiences and their object-impression counterparts are mentally represented within the containing arms of a symbiotic relationship, and a system of self-representations possessing varying qualities is consolidated. The nature and function of these disparate self-experiences, and the manner in which they coalesce into good and bad entities, has been previously described (Mendelsohn 1987a). It is not until good self-experience has been sufficiently represented to be structuralized that it is possible to initiate an individuating process. This crucial developmental task goes hand in hand with the healing of splits in the self and ego, ultimately leading to the evolution of continuity of experience within the personality for the first time. Self-observation becomes functional, with its unifying and organizing effects, and the influences of an object are then available for furthering self-expansion by serving a multiplicity of regulatory, guiding, and defensive functions. Up to this point in development, the impressions of an object have been inadequately consolidated, poorly differentiated, and basically unavailable for strengthening self-experience. Now they provide the intrapsychic wherewithal for constructive identifications and prohibitive or regulatory influences.

The intrapsychic achievement of locating the impressions of a separate good object's influence, and structuralizing the

---

[6]**Daniel Stern** is known for his remarkable research work with young infants. He elaborated upon the recent findings that challenged generally accepted timetables and sequences evolving from a psychoanalytic point of view. These findings suggest that the capacity to have merger or fusionlike experiences as described in psychoanalysis is secondary to and dependent upon an already existing sense of self and other (Stern 1984).

connection, makes it possible to form a foundation that is manifested in vitally significant changes in psychic functioning. These changes have important implications for determining the therapeutic interventions needed to facilitate psychological growth. The individual moves from the primacy of body ego experiences as the major factor instigating reactivity to the predominance of mental constellations of internal thought, language, and fantasy. The shift from living within the body to living within the mind has an effect upon all subsequent interactions. Although interpersonal interventions continue to be important the individual is no longer dependent upon them for regulation, which can be taken over by inter- and intrasystemic operations. The effect of the primary process on mental activity is less openly in evidence, and there is an increasing appearance of greater coherence in thinking and language as the secondary process assumes dominance.

The structural linkages uniting and differentiating an ever-expanding system of self-representations, based on body ego experiences, and an object-representational system, based upon their object-impression counterparts, results in projective identifications possessing clearly demarcated boundaries between the self and object. There is then a background sense of a differentiated self with gender identity, in contrast to the lack of a unified sense of self and difficulties in separating what belongs to internal experience and what is provided by an external object. The effects upon impulse activity are also noticeable, in that direct impulse discharge is less prominent. The ego displays increasing success in serving as a mediator. This is manifested by the proliferation of instinctual derivatives, allowing containment of instinctual wishes and enabling intrapsychic conflict to be the most significant feature of any emerging difficulties.

The nature of anxiety also changes from a fear of annihilation and loss of an object's influence, to the loss of an object's love, and on to the signal anxiety of castration. This is accompanied by a change from internal experiences of total organismic distress, in which soothing and comforting by an external object become essential, gradually moving toward an increased capacity for self-soothing and for the elaboration of a vast array of defensive maneuvers. The defenses change from the more chaotic, disorganizing effects of splitting mechanisms to those abetting repression and increasing the capacity for regulation in a relationship. Affective experiences move from being simple and extreme, either positive or negative total responses, to the increased unfolding of nuances with depth and richness.

Split self and object images have evolved into whole self and object images, and the urgency and demand for need-gratification equally changes to a more discriminating ability to be selective. Self and object constancy are established. Along with it is a greater internal sense of confidence, increased frustration tolerance, and the anticipation of the potential for eventually achieving gratification. This is accompanied by a shift from the search for anaclitic experiences with an external object to the ability to experience gratification through under-standing. Transferences also change from a chaotic repetition of primitive, archaic, narcissistic stages to more stable, object-related experiences. The internal demand for a dyadic relation-ship moves toward an expanded, variegated object world, and eventually to the emerging capacity for oedipally determined object relationships.

The Basic Psychoanalytic Principles and the Qualities of a Good Object

Experiencing the attributes of a good object is central if growth is to be promoted. Therefore the principles that guide the conduct of a therapeutic relationship must be woven together to present the combined qualities of a good object within the context of the total person. This would unite the good-object properties of optimal gratification, optimal frustration, and those of a transitional object in such a way that what was being unconsciously sought by a patient to discover a road to health could be both identified and provided. In turn it would have the effect of evoking and amplifying the representations of good self-experience at the foundations of the patient's personality, which elicit a containing and holding influence. Conditions of safety are created in this manner, making it possible for disruptive and regressive infantile experiences to enter the treatment relationship through the vehicle of the transference. Previously inaccessible psychic content can then be exposed to the integrative effects of insightful self-introspection, fostered by interpretive help, while constructive positive identifications are taking place.

When the basic psychoanalytic principles of free association, abstinence, anonymity, and neutrality are defined by their essential nature, they can be applied to be in accord with the psychic organization of a patient's personality (Mendelsohn 1987b). The responsibility for a patient's adaptation to a therapeutic environment then shifts from the patient to the therapist. The task is to conduct the interaction grounded upon an understanding of what is growth-promoting in the relationship.

The principle of free association is designed to facilitate the expression of the psychic contents in the deeper layers of the personality, and the therapist's role is to participate in such a way that this process unfolds. Interpretive interventions are the exclusive modality of communication in addressing the cohesive personality, whereas management considerations assume primacy with more primitively structured individuals. The principle of abstinence is designed to obviate against reinforcing pathological defenses, and the therapist's role is to desist from participating in a manner that has this effect. The principles of anonymity and neutrality are designed to further the free flow of projective identifications fueling the transference. These principles direct a therapist to filter out inappropriate projections and impositions, so that there is no interference and room remains for appropriate emotional responses to be an integral part of the interaction.

This definition of the basic psychoanalytic principles is founded upon an expanded view of the transference, including both unconscious perceptions and fantasy distortions. It provides the theoretical groundwork for adapting the ground rules and boundaries of the treatment so as to fit with what is required by a given patient to achieve ongoing progress. A broader range of psychopathological states can then be given the opportunity for utilizing psychoanalytic treatment to gain structural change. For some this means finding a solution to infantile, primarily instinctual conflicts, while for others it may mean healing developmental deficits, defects, or arrests. In addition there may be some for whom impossible infantile dilemmas, involving preverbal traumas, have left gaps in psychic functioning. Through offering the specific concrete experiences in a relationship that represent a new and successful outcome, heretofore lacking mental representations can be laid down that enable separation-individuation to be negotiated. The gaps then are filled in, allowing processes of symbolization to become viable and allowing treatment to advance.

When the principle of free association is defined as the patient's responsibility to report all available mental content without exercising censorship or judgment, it operates upon an unsound foundation. Such an undertaking is impossible to accomplish, for the myriad of thoughts, fantasies, sensations, and mental impressions that pass through a person's mind cannot all be articulated, much less identified. Although those selected are significant, they clearly depend upon using judgments and censorship. Such a false premise echoes with the traumas of early development, particularly with severely disturbed patients exhibiting archaic transferences. In addition, this principle is often referred to as the fundamental rule, and is presented as an instruction or suggestion. In that case the conditions of the treatment will depend upon submitting to the unwarranted authority of a therapist, or may be experienced as a seduction. When this kind of input is incidental to the primary intrapsychic difficulties of the patient it may not have as powerful an impact as when it resonates with early trauma. It still introduces a dimension of emotional meaning that is antithetical to the principle itself.

The principle of abstinence was originally meant to guide a therapist in refraining from participating in gratifying unconscious instinctual wishes with the idea that the motive to gain an understanding of unconscious forces would thereby be diluted or even eliminated. The subsequent frustration was then seen as necessary to bring infantile impulses more clearly into view, where they could be exposed to the integrating influence of interpretive interventions. This conception, however, failed to make the distinction between regressive wishes, based upon fantasy, which cannot be gratified, and regressive cravings, based upon developmental experiences antithetical to growth and at the foundation of pathological defenses, which can be gratified. The end result would be reinforcing a pathological defense within which regressive wishes are embedded. Though it leads to the same end point of rendering unconscious instinctual wishes inaccessible to integrative work, the reasons are significant. First, defining abstinence as desisting from the reinforcement of a pathological defense encourages a more penetrating understanding of the composition of pathological defenses and recognizes both the existence and makeup of healthy defenses. Second, it calls attention to those features of the treatment framework that may have this effect. Finally, it eliminates deliberate frustration as an accompaniment of a therapist's emotional stance. Undue or unnecessary frustration only encourages an adversarial atmosphere, whereas the optimal frustration of refusing to participate or foster a pathological interaction enhances the containing properties of the relationship. This principle requires an explicit, discrete delineation of the patient's defensive organization and emphasizes the importance of determining those that are pathological. Attention is thereby focused upon the effect of the conditions, principles, ground rules, and boundaries of the treatment.

A patient's unconscious perceptions, expressed through derivatives, of what is growth-promoting in a relationship can be included in determining how the principles of treatment will be applied. A therapist's ability to manage the overall framework is thereby expanded. There is greater flexibility in extending the boundaries of a therapeutic relationship for those who must gain specific experiences to enable processes of symbolization to be functional, and hence ultimately to make use of a primarily verbal modality of communication. Patients exert pressure upon a therapist to alter the ground rules and boundaries of the treatment in a variety of ways and for different reasons. The treatment framework contains vital unconscious meaning, and it is always a serious undertaking to consider engaging in modifications. What may be seeking reinforcement of a pathological defense in one individual may be expressing a desperate need for a new experience with another. Identifying the specific composition of a pathological defense and how it is manifested in a relationship paves the way for a therapist to discern more accurately what emanates from a healthy attempt to heal a developmental deficit. When approached with this perspective, the firmness and containment of a psychoanalytic treatment framework can be maintained, replacing potential rigidities with flexibility without compromising its principles.

The principles of anonymity and neutrality were designed to allow a patient's transference wishes and expectations to unfold without contamination by the actualities of the immediate interaction, and specifically by a therapist's unique and idiosyncratic style of functioning. It has long been recognized that a therapist's personality is an integral part of the relationship and that it is impossible to function as a mirror reflecting back only what is projected. The emotional distance involved in any stance attempting to do so would only create an obstacle toward making the therapeutic properties of the relationship viable. Furthermore, to treat the facts of a therapist's persona as elements to be excluded involves an emotional atmosphere of prohibition, which tends to echo with intrapsychic forces working against self-exposure. The existence of the actuality obscures the transference components of the prohibition, rendering its recognition relatively inconsequential as long as that position is held. This does not mean that such information is openly provided, since unnecessary self-revelations can only serve narcissistic interests and are potentially burdensome and overstimulating. It does mean they do not have to be hidden. The essence of these principles is to enable projective identifications to flow freely and fuel the transference without interference from a therapist's projections and impositions. It is therefore incumbent upon a therapist to filter out personal reactions, utilizing them in the service of a deeper unconscious understanding of the patient. A firmly grounded basis for including the therapist's emotional responsiveness can thereby be incorporated, allowing the transference–countertransference interchange to be subject to therapeutic understanding.

A free-associative process has all the qualities of optimal gratification, in that those forces in a patient's personality seeking to be heard and understood are encouraged, so as to achieve greater self cohesion, a stronger sense of personal identity, and increasing autonomy and independence. In conjunction with the optimally frustrating experience of not having pathological defenses strengthened, necessary regulation and restraint are provided. Anonymity and neutrality insure that there is an avenue to utilize the therapist in whatever way is dictated by the demands of a patient's personality, thus having the features of a transitional object. Once the proper conditions have been established for the conduct of the treatment there is a match between the way psychoanalytic principles are applied and the specific attributes of a good object for a given patient. The door is then open to identify features of the ensuing interaction that work against growth, and to offer the appropriate interventions that will serve to further therapeutic progress.

The Assessment of Therapeutic Needs

When cohesiveness and continuity of experience are sufficiently well structured in the personality during the developmental years, the necessary intrapsychic ingredients are present for healthy psychological processes to become functional. Continuing self-expansion may still be rendered severely impaired or obstructed, usually from the effects of infantile instinctual conflicts. These are then expressed in symptoms, inhibitions, or the distortions produced by the formation of character pathology. Nevertheless all of the required building blocks have been laid down, and under the proper conditions they can be made available for the therapeutic task of undoing pathological influences. Myriad defensive and adaptive functions are developed on a relatively solid mental foundation of stability, so that there are no deficiencies in the sense of personal identity or the capacity for integration. Consequently, the projective identifications utilized to engage in object relationships, which are manifested in transference-based experiences, are fairly well differentiated. A psychotherapeutic situation offers the circumstances for pathology to be re-created in the treatment relationship, where the light of reason and understanding can provide what is necessary to further growth.

The relationship in which the required insight and integration transpires is of course a significant factor. It also may play a role in healing any residual developmental deficits and arrests through the constructive identifications arising out of the therapeutic interaction and the way it is managed. The primary focus of the treatment, however, centers around expanding self-awareness and increasing self-knowledge by the synthesizing and integrating effects of enlarging the vistas of self-experience. The communicative modality is primarily verbal, as interpretive interventions are a therapist's major instrument for eliciting change. Interpretations must be in tune with unconscious communications, presented within a firm framework of psychoanalytically determined ground rules and boundaries. This framework maintains the background atmosphere of safety required for regressive experiences to emerge into consciousness. Aspects of human experience that are nonverbal in nature, determined by early developmental interactions incapable of being articulated, enter into the relationship but in ways that are at best difficult to ascertain. They are usually only identifiable by vague body sensations, or through a therapist's intuitive deductions concerning behavior.[7]

An essential feature of any treatment is the bond of mutual purpose that has to exist between patient and therapist. This is essential in order to sustain the relationship under conditions in which intense infantile emotions, both positive and negative,

---

[7]**Mark Kanzer** has also paid close attention to how patients express themselves nonverbally through such means as physical sensations, symptoms, affect, and manner and style of communicating. A psychoanalytic process has to be uniquely adaptive in order to facilitate the pursuit of the verbal and the nonverbal, and the reconstruction of the preverbal (Kanzer 1961).

are elicited. This therapeutic alliance is based upon a connection between the patient's unconscious perceptions of the qualities in a relationship needed to promote growth and a therapist's management of the treatment, appropriate silences, and relatively accurate interpretations. The existence of cohesiveness and continuity of experience in the personality enables unconscious perceptions to be expressed primarily through derivatives, usually in narrative form. They add an important dimension that aids a therapist in the complex and difficult task of validating the degree to which the reading of unconscious experiences and communications has been appropriate and well timed. Although the activity of unconscious perceptions may also be expressed in a variety of other ways, including behavior and action, they are generally amenable to recognition and acknowledgement in a verbally communicative sphere.

The difficulty in determining the specific attributes that make a therapeutic response growth-promoting is enormously compounded when addressing individuals showing a lack of cohesiveness and absence of continuity of experience. Archaic ego states, developmental deficits and arrests, unstable narcissistic transferences fueled by poorly differentiated projective identifications, and a primitive psychic organization in which splitting interferes with continuity of experience all contribute to make the reading of unconscious perceptions highly unreliable. Determining specifically which factors are mutative to achieve therapeutic change requires a greater reliance on subjective responses and a more precise evaluation of a patient's personality structure. To complicate the matter further, there is a large element of uncertainty as to how to be precise in defining concepts such as empathy, countertransference, acting out, and enacting infantile and preverbal traumatic experiences in the therapeutic relationship. Distinguishing between these interrelated phenomena, both in theory and in their actual clinical manifestations, is an imposing task.

Empathy usually refers to a therapist's capacity to enter a patient's internal world in a transient manner for the sole purpose of understanding the unconscious significance of the particular experience.[8-11] Yet it may become intermeshed

---

[8]**Ralph Greenson,** long a proponent of the value of introducing human, caring qualities into the therapeutic interaction, regarded empathy as the analyst's way of "emotionally knowing" the patient. Empathy meant an experience was shared with the feelings of another person on a temporary basis, with the main motive to achieve understanding. Identification, which is closely related, is essentially an unconscious and permanent phenomenon, whereas empathy is preconscious and temporary. Thus the working model of the patient within the analyst is not merely a replica of the patient, but one that is close enough not to distort and distant enough to be of help. It is also different from the model of the patient within the patient, and contains insights and interpretations that have not yet been given and are close to the patient's consciousness (Greenson 1960).
[9]**Stanley Olinick,** who had done some of the early work on the origins of empathy, stressed the regressive features of an empathic experience, particularly if it was to be utilized in the service of another. The analyst is required to suspend temporarily and partially the usual reality orientation in order to gain access to subliminal and preconscious functioning, and though it creates a vulnerability to the patient's input, it is indispensable to therapeutic work. This trial identification is essential for the understanding of a patient and includes the process of empathy. The resulting empathic experiences must be validated beyond their immediate sense of certitude (Olinick 1969).
[10]**David Beres** and **Jacob Arlow** did a great deal to further our understanding of empathy, and noted its two distinguishing characteristics. First, it is a transient identification, and second, the empathizer preserves separateness from the object. The function of empathy relies on a variety of supplementary ego functions and is more than an immediate affective response. Empathic communication is fundamental to analytic work, but it must be supplemented with disciplined attention in the form of consistent self-observation. Intuition is the immediate knowing or learning of something without the conscious use of rea-

with, and indistinguishable from, a countertransference-based response elicited by the relationship. In addition, it is vital to distinguish between countertransference phenomena that facilitate unconscious perceptiveness, thereby amplifying empathic resonance, and those that interfere with ideal therapeutic functioning.[12-14] In therapeutic work with more primitively

---

soning. Along with empathy it plays a basic part in grasping unconscious processes in the minds of others (Beres and Arlow 1974).

[11]**Michael Basch** is one of a number of psychoanalysts espousing a self psychological point of view who have demonstrated in a deep and penetrating way the role of empathy in a therapeutic interaction. He described the long period of listening, examining personal reactions, and then bridging the gap by constructing suitable analogies between the patient's associations and the analyst's experience that is often required before becoming attuned to the patient's affective communication. Thus the immediate feeling of affective communion and recognition between patient and analyst may either not exist or be suspect. Empathy does not have to begin with the affective component, but can be entered at the interpretive or experiential phase of the process (Basch 1983).

[12]**Ernest Wolf,** also from a self psychological perspective, showed how empathic perception can be reduced by repression and disavowal, can be enhanced by attention-focusing processes, or can be distorted in the service of defense. Similarly, countertransference may sharpen, dull, or distort empathically derived data (Wolf 1983).

[13]**David Berger,** in his excellent book on clinical empathy, illustrated the ways in which a therapist may move unwittingly into defensively generated states of countertransference by becoming overly sympathetic or by drawing back from the patient. In an overly sympathetic state the therapist may be drawn into a prolonged identificatory position, and in an intellectually distant state the therapist may attend to the patient's communications only as an outside observer (Berger 1987).

[14]**Paula Heimann** was one of the first clinicians to clearly

organized patients a great of intrapsychic content is incapable of being communicated in a verbally symbolic modality. Much will then depend upon a therapist's ability to allow subjective reactions and responses to be a source of information and a guide for introducing helpful interventions.[15] It has become

---

delineate how a therapist's countertransference reactions could be put to good use, and were a necessary component of the treatment. She believed that a therapist's emotional responses could help to focus attention on the most urgent elements of the patient's associations and also served in selecting interpretations. When well understood, countertransference is not only part of the analytic relationship, but it is the patient's creation and a part of the patient's personality. She cautioned, however, that this approach could not represent a screen for the analyst's shortcomings, nor should the analyst impute to the patient what belongs to the analyst. The expectation that an analyst can function consistently without manifesting any evidence of intrapsychic conflict or being drawn into unhelpful regressive identifications is not only unrealistic but fails to recognize the potential value of such incidents when they arise (Heimann 1950).

[15]**Joyce McDougall,** focusing on primitive, nonverbal communication, had this in mind in reflecting upon the probability that what has been submitted to primal repression cannot be communicated, except through "signs" registered by a therapist's countertransference feelings. Part of the pitfall of these countertransference affects leaving signs in the analyst are that they consist of more than the unique reflection of an inner emotional state, or of unconscious reactions to the patient's monologue. It may very well not deal with the repressed, but with a primitive communication not decodable in the usual way. If at such times the analyst persists in seeking repressed content, in replying aggressively, or in turning away in silence, then the analyst is acting out. An attitude of expectant silence, which to the neurotic spells hope and opens the psychic space wherein long-buried desires may once more come to light, offers little but desolation and death. Everything that has been

evident that countertransference can be present in the absence of empathy, but empathy requires countertransference in its broadest sense in order to be a viable experience.[16] In this context it is essential for each therapist to become intuitively acquainted with the individual clues suggestive of a disturbance in ideal therapeutic functioning.[17,18] In its original meaning

---

stifled by primal repression remains potentially active and actual, since it is inevitably ejected into the outer world. Everything that has been silent becomes a message in action, and it is this action communication that may install itself within the analytic situation. It may then be possible for the analyst to render the action symptom apt for expression through language (McDougall 1979).

[16]**Hanna Segal** is well known for her understanding of countertransference phenomena. In this article she underscored the fact that countertransference is always unconscious, and when it is in a good functional state there is a double relationship to the patient. One is receptive, containing, and understanding of the patient's communications; the other active, producing or giving of understanding, knowledge, or structure to the patient. Infantile experience is not excluded, since the capacity to perceive and contain infantile parts of the patient depends on the capacity to contain the infantile parts of ourselves. We give part of our mind to the experience, but also remain intact, using professional skills to assess the interaction. We are deeply involved and affected, but also uninvolved. When countertransference works that way it gives rise to empathy or psychoanalytic intention and is a guide to understanding. When breaches in this attitude occur, there is a disruption in analytic function and we must try to understand the nature of the disruption and the information it gives about the interaction with the patient (Segal 1981b).

[17]The **Barangers, Madeleine** and **Willy,** and **Jorge Mom** investigated the various clues available to a therapist that indicate a personal reaction is obstructing progress. They delineated the ways each therapist processed bodily experiences, movement fantasies, and the appearance of certain images, which indicated

countertransference implied a negative, unwanted, and even
pathological process operating within the therapist. Over the
years different meanings have been ascribed to countertransference. Most have agreed, regardless of how it is defined, that
it is at times a source of useful information about a patient and
a therapist. The question of how to use this information,
however, varies widely and has remained an area of dispute.[19]

At the extremes, the distinction between empathy and coun-

---

the moments an attitude of suspended attention was abandoned.
At such a point the need to proceed to a second look in questioning what was happening in the analytic situation is highlighted. These countertransferential indicators, which provide
the second look, lead us to realize that within the field of the
interaction exists an immobilized structure that is slowing down
or paralyzing the process. In all probability it arises in the unconscious and in silence, is never directly apparent in the consciousness of either participant, and protects an attachment that
must not be uncovered (Baranger et al. 1983).

[18]**Hans Loewald** also believed that countertransference was an
indispensable means of understanding a patient's transference,
for when its phenomena become conscious they provide valuable clues. He also referred, however, to the risk of arriving at
incorrect interpretations when such countertransferences are
distorted. It takes a great deal of self-knowledge and knowledge
of the patient to make the necessary corrections (Loewald
1986).

[19]**Robert Tyson** summarized the state of our understanding of
countertransference at the present time. He discussed the five
areas in which conceptualizing countertransference has expanded: first, from the narrow focus on how the analyst's
unconscious is affected to a more encompassing approach that
also includes conscious feelings and reactions; second, from
defining countertransference simply as the analyst's reaction to
the patient's transference, to including neurotically determined
reactions to a particular patient, and then most broadly to take
in all feelings about any patient; third, the explanation of
countertransference dynamics, and the mechanisms by which
it comes into operation; fourth, how the analyst acquires the

tertransference may be relatively easily made. This is especially the case when a patient provides enough associative material to enable the gradual process of determining unconscious meaning to unfold. In more primitively organized patients this form of communication may not be available. The pressure for an immediate response may be intense, the nonverbal components of the interaction may be the most significant and prominent feature, and the urgency may necessitate a spontaneous reaction. At the same time, a clearer view of what is appropriate may not be accessible, leaving a therapist in uncharted psychological territory. Furthermore, it can be detrimental if previous experiences or preformed therapeutic constructs are relied upon. There is a fine line separating unconsciously empathic responsiveness and countertransference-based and -conflicted infantile experience, which may only be discovered retrospectively.[20,21] These situations often

---

ability to recognize its presence and effects, and what to do about them; and fifth, the role countertransference plays in the treatment, whether it is an obstacle or an aid (Tyson 1986).

[20]**Heinrich Racker** was one of the first to strip away the belief that analysis is an interaction between a sick and a healthy person. The truth is that it consists of an interaction between two personalities, each having its own dependencies, anxieties, and pathological defenses. Both parties respond to every event in the analytic situation, but one essential difference involves the analyst's objectivity. It comes from an internal division, enabling a continuing process of self-observation and self-analysis. Countertransference fuses present and past, reality and fantasy, external and internal, conscious and unconscious, and therefore embraces the totality of the analyst's psychological responses. In his opinion every transference situation provokes a countertransference, arising out of the analyst's identification with the patient's internal objects. These are inevitable and should not be avoided if a full understanding of the patient is to be achieved. Unless the analyst is aware of countertransference, a vicious circle of the patient's neurosis will not be able to be avoided. Perceptions are then used to be

dictate that the line be drawn without the time or opportunity to sift out the distinction adequately.

From the patient's perspective it is equally a fine line between acting out to avoid remembering, which prevents ongoing psychological growth, and enacting infantile and preverbal experiences, which is necessary to accomplish developmental progression. In the primitively organized and narcissistically structured personality, pathological forces opposing the vulnerability associated with growth and change are especially powerful. The distortions they create make it both more difficult and imperative for a therapist to unravel the differences. Behavior may be the only avenue for reaching psychic content otherwise unable to be communicated, or at times even symbolized, so that recognizing what is a destructive form of acting out and what is reaching for a constructive solution is crucial.[22,23]

---

aware of the patient's transference rather than to be unconsciously ruled by them (Racker 1957).

[21]In the same vein, **Bruno Bettelheim** argued that the unresolved remnants of one's past can either be the most serious impediment to working with patients, or the greatest of assets. They are impediments when they are acted out, assets when they are judiciously acted upon. He commented on the frequent expectation that an analyst will refrain from acting on the basis of emotional preoccupation, but since all have emotional problems it is impossible. Without emotional preoccupation a therapist would not be able to work, and it is the main incentive for helping patients on their incredibly difficult road to recovery. Without this potential source of empathy with the patient, psychotherapeutic work could never succeed (Bettelheim 1974).

[22]**Donald Winnicott** brought many fresh, innovative, and provocative ideas to aid in understanding the often impossible dilemmas presented by more seriously disturbed patients. One of these was his conviction that acting out often had to be tolerated because it reflected what had gone wrong in the original environmental failure situation and gave a direction as

Early preoedipal difficulties tend to interfere with the internalization of interpretive interventions, not necessarily because of their content, but frequently due to their depending upon the patient's ability to grasp verbal and symbolic communications adequately. In such patients the advanced functions required to use interpretive help may not be sufficiently stable. Far greater demands are then made upon a therapist's ability to use management considerations, and to shift back and forth between different levels, which makes it hard to be equal to this expanded task. An increasing awareness of preverbal influences has enormous implications for treatment, since the manner in which these unverbalized components of intrapsychic functioning can be addressed is different from those that grow out of later phases of development.[24,25]

---

to what was needed from the analyst. He also referred to the strain upon the analyst, which may be heightened by a lack of understanding and unconscious countertransference reactions (Winnicott 1954).

[23]**Richard Robertiello** added to the increasing recognition that acting out had a positive component. He made the distinction between "acting out," which is a resistance to insight, and "working through," which is essential for change. Both have to do with experiencing and repeating unconscious wishes that are emerging from repression; one is a blind repetition without insight or growth, the other is a part of mastery and ego strength. Clinically they are often confused, since there seems to be a bias against experiential mastery and a piece of behavior is called "acting out" when it is actually part of "working through." The decision should not be dictated by conformity, but by whether it furthers awareness. The differences are important for they affect the analyst's attitude and play a part in determining whether the expression of repressed wishes is encouraged (Robertiello 1965).

[24]**Leon Grinberg** presented the interesting idea that in a sense, acting out could be thought of as a dream that could not be dreamt. He meant that in addition to its harmful effects it also had communicative and adaptive functions, which can be

There is much to suggest that certain individuals can only become accessible to interpretive influence after gaps in mental functioning, created by infantile and preverbal traumas, have been successfully filled in. Generally these early traumatic experiences can only be expressed through behavior, and until a new and different outcome can be found and represented by virtue of the therapist's constructive responses, symbolic processes may remain impaired or nonfunctional. The underlying motives behind a patient's behavior must be as clearly understood as is possible, for encouraging some inappropriate form of acting out reinforces a pathological defense, prevents integration, and is destructive. On the other hand, fostering the emergence of infantile and preverbal traumas, which have to be reenacted through behavior, is essential for enabling new structure formation. It results in higher levels of psychic organization, and leads to the capacity to engage in a verbally interpretive therapeutic interaction. Thus, to not participate would be destructive. The distinction is of special significance

---

traced to developmental experiences usually of object loss and separation anxiety. The acting out then represents a search for an external object that will become the container of the patient's pain. Acting out reflects an impaired psychic balance in which the id governs the ego through the mediation of a primitive superego (Grinberg 1968).

[25]**Anna Freud** was deeply concerned about the potential for encouraging destructive forms of acting out by changing the concept from its original meaning. She thought it was essential to make the following distinctions: first, memory, which allows the recovery of repressed fantasies that are verbalized again; second, reexperiencing, which brings back infantile attitudes reproduced as regressive feelings toward the analyst; third, reenactment in the transference as a means of reaching preverbal experience, often by transgressing analytic rules; and fourth, the delusional transference phenomena, which have the full impact of reality for the patient and defy interpretation, having been caused by early trauma (A. Freud 1971).

when there is an intermingling and enmeshment of both factors, for an active role may have to be adopted by a therapist in order to enhance the processes leading to cure. The manner in which a therapist introduces a given active intervention then has to be determined by what appears necessary to advance therapeutic progress.[26–31]

---

[26]**Dale Boesky** was also worried about how the term acting out was used, for he felt too little was known as yet concerning the significance of action and behavior. He discussed the need to understand the dynamics and effects of the substitution of action for verbal communication and its impact upon the psychoanalytic treatment process. He indicated how the shift in psychoanalytic treatment from the introspective verbalizing form of actualization to motor behavior forms remains unexplained. The ubiquitous shift from introspective experiencing to action, behavior, and reality is a neglected boundary in every analysis. In his opinion, since ontogenetically, action preceded thought, it might feel more real partly because thinking is reversible and action is often irrevocable and final. He referred to the profound differences that separated those patients who rarely cross this boundary from those whose bustling traffic at this frontier is a source of bewilderment and even danger. Thus, in order to account for the evolution of certain ego capacities or incapacities, developmental considerations become more important than dynamic issues (Boesky 1982).

[27]In addressing the problems presented when infantile and preverbal traumas are reenacted through behavior and action, **Winnicott** considered the patient with an antisocial tendency to be predominantly reacting to a deprivation. A therapist was therefore compelled to correct and go on correcting the failure in ego support that had altered the course of the patient's life. In addition, there are other patients needing a regression if a change is to be brought about, and these patients will thereby need to pass through a place of infantile dependence. In Winnicott's opinion this was an area in which psychoanalysis could not be taught, though it could be practiced in a modified form. If the hidden true self is to come into its own the patient will break down as a part of the treatment, and the analyst will

need to give ego support in a big way. The analyst will need to remain oriented to external reality even while merged with the patient, and the patient must become absolutely dependent. The analyst's interventions and mode of interacting are then guided by a sensitive reading of the healthy part of the patient's personality telling the analyst how to behave. Often such seriously disturbed patients gradually break through the barriers of the analyst's technique and professional attitude, and force a direct relationship of a primitive kind (Winnicott 1960). [28]According to **E. James Anthony** it is possible to work predominantly with nonverbal communication, which does open up a larger world of analytic experience. However, to do so is more difficult and exacting for the therapist. He referred to the stream of communications, both verbal and nonverbal that flows from every person as a function of self-expression, information, and interaction. The verbal system gradually assumes predominance as development takes place, while the nonverbal undergoes recession, becoming less noticeable and less noticed until it is almost completely overlooked except under special circumstances. Accepting primitive fantasy and being at home with and alert to the nonverbal or preverbal significance of certain silent activities and behaviors emphasizes nonverbal communication and constitutes a pathway to the deepest layers of the unconscious. What we need to know about any patient is how far along he is in his development, which system is predominant, which system reveals more of him as a person, and how well he uses and coordinates nonverbal and verbal communications (Anthony 1977). [29]**Bryce Boyer,** who has had extensive experience with the more severe psychic difficulties, was struck by the startling regularity with which borderline and schizophrenic patients have suffered dramatic psychological, physical, and/or sexual assaults. This discovery fortified a persistence in aiming at the recovery in treatment of these factual early childhood memories. With it the phenomenon of reenacting in the transference was more clearly viewed as the patient's attempt to remember through action. Consequently it was important that the enactment be encouraged rather than discouraged, provided it was not deemed to be potentially dangerous to the patient or others (Boyer 1979).

[30]**Warren Kinston** and **Jonathan Coen** offered a more thorough definition of primal repression, clarifying its relationship to early trauma. More importantly, they were able to show how its effects were manifested in the therapeutic relationship, which has important implications for how the treatment must be conducted. They placed stress upon the significance of the realm of primal repression, because in this area of psychic functioning wish and conflict have no meaning. All that can be seen are traumatic states, primitive symbolic activities, and unmet needs. Interpretation, therefore, without being removed from its special place, must give way to recognition and action if understanding is to develop. This does not give the analyst carte blanche to gratify or enact with patients, but rather the reverse. It is only when primal repression and primary relatedness are activated, with all the work and risk they entail, that traumatic reliving and neediness will make such demands upon the analyst (Kinston and Coen 1986).

[31]**John McLaughlin,** a strong advocate of a developmentally centered viewpoint, emphasized how motor action, in preceding verbalization, facilitates and makes possible the subsequent putting into words. A developmental perspective acknowledges that there is a continuing place and contribution for primary process modes in all aspects of human behavior throughout life. Physical activity asserts a sustaining influence on the encoding organization of thought, and body acts, as kinetic experiences, provide the kind of support essential for the secondary process (McLaughlin 1987).

2

Interpretations Leading to Insight

The Function of Interpretations and Their Role
  in Applying the Basic Psychoanalytic
  Principles
Free Association
Abstinence
Anonymity and Neutrality
Interpretations and Resistance
Interpretations with Neurotic Transferences
Interpretations with Nonneurotic, Prestructural
  Transferences
The Function of Interpretations in Validating
  a Patient's Unconscious Perceptions and
  Correcting Empathic Lapses and the Need
  for a Secure Framework

The Function of Interpretations and Their Role in Applying the Basic Psychoanalytic Principles

The way in which the ground rules, boundaries, and conditions of a therapeutic situation are managed and the particular nature of the interpretive interventions that are offered are what characterize the conduct of treatment. The basic principles of psychoanalysis are designed to provide guidelines for furthering the integrative work of an insight-directed therapeutic relationship. The purpose is to enable the functioning of healthy psychic structures, to facilitate a benign regression, and to foster the structural changes that diminish or obviate distortions produced by pathology. External reality has a profound effect upon intrapsychic functioning. Therefore a therapist's handling of a patient's communications must be sensitive and empathic to their unconscious significance, in order to manage properly the treatment framework and introduce appropriate interpretive interventions. These interventions show most clearly how a patient's projective identifications have been received and understood. They function to impart insight, encourage constructive identifications, and provide whatever is necessary to fill in gaps in psychic structure or strengthen areas that are weak or deficient. A patient's conscious and unconscious perceptions of the actualities of a therapist's mode of functioning will then have a considerable impact upon the extent to which structural changes take place.

The basic psychoanalytic principles of free association, abstinence, and anonymity and neutrality are operative in the background of all transactions. How they happen to be defined plays a critical role in how they are applied, and therefore is a decisive factor in determining analyzability and influences the entire course and outcome of the treatment. The definition of these basic principles is intimately associated with, and dependent upon, the way transference is understood.

The concept of transference has gradually been broadened to encompass the nondistorting and undistorted elements of unconscious experience, but the equally important reassessment of the basic principles has unfortunately lagged behind. Because psychoanalytic treatment originated with patients thought of as primarily neurotic, and with these patients the essential functions of the ego were relatively intact, the capacity to adapt to a therapist's directions was often taken for granted and even used as a criteria for treatability. This narrow view of the transference, encompassing to a major extent only fantasy distortions, did generally appear to be consonant with what was required of the treatment. It was the basis from which the basic principles were both formulated and applied.

When a psychoanalytic approach was taken with non-neurotic disturbances, and narcissistic transferences received therapeutic attention, it became apparent that revision in a therapist's conduct of the relationship was necessary. Many questions arose as to whether modifications in technique were required, and if so, whether they were detrimental, with some changes taking place slowly, especially in what was meant by anonymity and neutrality. In an earlier work I have discussed how the basic psychoanalytic principles can be redefined so as to incorporate their original intent, founded upon a broadened view of the transference that includes unconscious perceptions (Mendelsohn 1987b). The purpose of each principle, making it uniquely psychoanalytic, is delineated and transformed into its definition. In this way the essence of psychoanalytic treatment is preserved and the principles are applied in accordance with a patient's unconscious perception of what is growth-promoting in a relationship. The conditions and framework of the treatment are thereby adapted to the particular psychic organization of a given patient's personality, thus eliminating the inevitable atmosphere of conformity when an adaptation is made to the authority of a therapist.

Free Association

The purpose of the fundamental principle of free association is to facilitate the expression of psychic contents in the deeper layers of the personality. This principle was meant to enable a therapeutic regression, but when it is presented as an instruction or suggestion to report all mental content, setting aside all rational considerations, censoring, and judgement it contradicts the essence of a freely associative process. By making its purpose the definition, however, it can be applied simply by virtue of a therapist's manner of participation. Interpretive interventions are directed to the psychic contents comprising the deeper layers, or to those defenses working to prevent their expression. A free-associative mode of communication is introduced and a benign therapeutic regression is initiated.

Giving a direction implies that the therapist knows what is best, rather than being a participant in discovering it. The therapist's conduct is a crucial part of facilitating the emergence of free association as a style of communication. For example, if a patient asks what should be talked about and a therapist responds with a statement of the basic rule, it immediately implies that the question is either not important or that its underlying meaning has been ignored. Guided by the principle of free association, a therapist might either be silent or offer an interpretation if sufficient material is available.

The use of this principle was illustrated in the early part of a young adult man's treatment. He had sought help because of his profound frustration with his inability to complete a task. He suffered greatly from this inhibition, which was present in all facets of his life. He knew he had to get free somehow of his restricted way of functioning and agreed with the need for intense treatment. He entered his first session appearing lost and confused, fell silent, and looked to me for some direction as to how he should proceed. I could feel the pressure to respond but didn't have a clear view of its meaning. He then laughed nervously and said he guessed he should talk but couldn't think of anything to say. It reminded him of his first day of school. He couldn't wait to go. He was the youngest of seven children with a wide gap in age from his nearest sibling. He constantly felt put down, ineffective, crippled, and stupid. He looked forward to school as a place where he could learn and was excited about going. At last the day came, and he walked excitedly into the classroom. However, it turned out to be terrible. He did not learn anything new, no one showed him anything he didn't already know, and everyone seemed to be demanding things from him. He felt both disappointed and confused by the unfamiliar surroundings.

Now I had something to say. I commented that he was entering his treatment in the same way, looking to learn how to be free, yet my silence seemed to evoke feelings inside reminiscent of his first day of school. I followed the basic principle of free association by listening for whatever came into his mind and then gave my interpretation of its deeper meaning. This form of participation gave expression to my listening and interpretive attitude, while he discovered the value of communicating psychic contents from the effects of the experience. Until some derivatives of unconscious mental activity were in evidence there was nothing to interpret and hence nothing to say. The task is to listen to associative connections for what resides in the deeper layers of the personality. When obstacles come into view that are identifiable as acting in opposition they can become the focus of interpretive attention. In responding interpretively to the implicit, a free-associative process is fostered.

Abstinence

The purpose of the principle of abstinence is to refrain from reinforcing a pathological defense. It was originally designed to give impetus to the full exposure of unconscious transference fantasies by directing a therapist to desist from the gratification of regressive, infantile wishes. The resulting frustration supposedly provided the motivation for the integrative work of the treatment. In applying it in this fashion a clear distinction is not made between defenses and the regressive wishes embedded in them, and an unnecessarily frustrating attitude then results. Furthermore, the pressure exerted upon a therapist to behave in ways that seek such inappropriate gratifications simultaneously reflect an attempt to test the environment's capacity to provide what is needed to promote a therapeutic regression. Defining abstinence on the basis of pathological defenses, which are founded on the representations of developmental experience antithetical to growth, makes it concordant with the activity of unconscious perceptions, thereby strengthening the therapeutic alliance. This was shown in the treatment of a 21-year-old man who began his therapeutic contact with an ultimatum.

He had been in psychotherapy on and off for 13 years and felt it had done nothing for him. A succession of therapists had offered him support and reassurance, medication, and on one occasion, behavioral prohibitions. The ultimatum was that he would give this contact one month, and if he saw no indication of hope or change he would destroy himself. He felt totally helpless and in despair of ever finding a solution for his unhappiness.

Intense sadomasochistic relationships were a dominant part of his life. He had a collection of knives and guns, and frequently was drawn to dangerous neighborhoods, where he swaggered boldly as though ready for a fight. He was always accompanied by friends who he inwardly hoped would stop him because he felt too vulnerable in such potentially perilous circumstances. He added that he knew he had a soft and tender side but it frightened him. He was fearful that if he allowed these feelings to emerge they would envelop and control him and result in his being like a helpless puppy dog.

He described feeling distant and estranged from his mother. This feeling was encapsulated in an early memory of being alone in a crib. He had thrown his bottle out onto the floor in a fit of temper, was crying out, and was not heard. It made him feel alone, helpless, and trapped. His father was almost totally absent in his early years, though his influence was constantly present. In his later years the father became a dominant figure in his life. The father would always support him in any crisis, at the expense, however, of being belittled and disapproved of, making him feel inept and effeminate. He worked for his father but without a salary. He was given money as needed, encouraging a strong sense of dependency and obligation.

During the month, he proceeded to exert intense pressure upon me to alter whatever conditions had been established in the treatment. It was first expressed in working out the times, fee, and manner of payment. He stated that because he had limited resources his father would have to pay for the sessions, and his father had readily agreed. I had commented on his being hopelessly tied to his father and wondered what it would mean for me to accept this manner of payment. He initially protested vigorously, adding in despair that he knew it was not good but there was no other way. He recalled trying to assert himself with an older man and being beaten down and humiliated. He had tried to appear competent and strong and was exposed as weak and ineffective. He also remembered his efforts to work independently, all of which had failed. Eventually he had to crawl back to his father and ask for work. I remarked that I believed it was vital for him to pay for his treatment himself.

Several weeks were then spent with his struggling to convince me of how impossible it was, until he realized that he could earn the money to pay for his sessions, although it would mean a reduced fee. He became preoccupied with the idea of being seduced into a relationship, which I interpreted as his concern about my motives for accepting a lower fee. This freed him to consider what was possible, and a realistic fee acceptable to both of us was decided upon. He then demanded that I prescribe medication. He couldn't sleep, was in a constant state of anxiety, and needed something for relief. I responded first by encouraging his associations to the idea. This made him think of experiences when he had indulged in drugs in order to deaden his feelings, alter his moods, and distract himself. I said that he seemed to be asking if I would join him in supporting something that worked against his growth and understanding. His immediate associations were to authorities who understood him, wanted to help, but were too uninvolved to offer anything consistent or effective. When I reflected on his feeling that I either didn't appreciate the depth of his trouble or was distancing myself from him, he began to insist upon the need for more frequent sessions. As he did so he was reminded of situations in which he was always cared for whenever he was falling apart, crippled, or ineffective. This reinforced his feeling of inadequacy, accentuated his need to cling, and escalated his demands for others to take over more of his care. I commented that the idea of seeing him more often appeared to stir up in him a feeling that I agreed he was ineffective and either needed or wanted him to stay that way.

He then began to attack me for being greedy and wanting only money. If he could afford a higher fee he was certain I wouldn't question it. I acknowledged that there was truth in the idea that seeing him more often at a lower fee would affect me, but I thought it would have more to do with going against what was best for him. He reacted by getting a job, paying his fee, coming regularly to his appointments, and being on time. More than that, he noticed that he was developing a different attitude toward himself. He was now more interested in trying to discover the meaning of his behavior. He spoke of how surprised he was, for his history in therapy had involved frequent cancellations, lateness, and forgetting his appointments. He now found himself remembering the times, being much more committed to his treatment, and referring to his lifelong pattern of starting things that were never completed.

Anonymity and Neutrality

The purpose of the principles of anonymity and neutrality is to not impose or project personal meaning onto a patient. These principles were originally designed to prevent contaminating the unfolding transference by the impact of reality. They were intended to guide a therapist's interpretations so that only those psychic contents unconsciously projected by a patient would be reflected back. It has long since been demonstrated that applying these principles in this fashion was not only unrealistic and impossible, but it also denied the importance of a therapist's emotional contributions to the relationship and the significance of a patient's unconscious perceptiveness. Such a stance tended to be inflexible and at times inappropriate, for in many cases it is precisely the meaning of reality that needs to be understood most.

Of course there must be room within a therapeutic relationship for a patient's transference projections to flow freely with as little contamination as possible from outside sources. However, this is best achieved by a therapist's being capable of filtering out unwarranted personal responses so that they are not imposed or projected onto a patient. Defining anonymity and neutrality in this way allows a therapist's appropriate emotional responsiveness to make an integral contribution to the treatment. In that sense a therapist acts very much like a transitional object, as a consequence of which a much deeper understanding is gained of a patient's internal world. This was seen in the treatment of a 7-year-old boy, who was referred because of his parents' and teachers' concern about his wildly out-of-control behavior. He often threw things, broke windows, and hurt others, usually whenever his attempts at domination were thwarted or when he was frustrated in accomplishing a task.

He arrived for his first session accompanied by his mother, who asked if she should come in with him. I remarked that at this point I thought only he could answer her question, because I had no idea what it would mean to him. He stared up at me in wide-eyed surprise and remained silent. I waited a moment and then said that I personally would prefer to see him alone, but I didn't know if he needed to have her there. He then shouted, "Where is your office?" Upon seeing the door, he ran in and closed it. He then gave forceful directions that the door was to remain closed and asked if his mother could hear. I simply reflected upon his concern as to whether the room was well contained. He jumped on a chair and let out a piercing shriek as he looked at me with a big smile and said, "Well, do you think she heard that?" The remainder of the session was spent with his turning the office into a planet in space. He lectured me about the conditions present on the various planets and sought to make a space in the office where the forces of gravity would be diminished. Gravity pulled him down and kept him from moving freely. He wanted a special planet where he could jump extremely high, but the planet had a problem in its relationship to the sun. When the sun rose in the morning there was a short span of time when one could be safe until it got too hot. There was a similar span of time in the evening. The sun went down and the planet was safe, but soon it got too cold. He had to make a pathway in space where he could be safe when it was too hot or too cold. At the end of the session he left and his mother loudly exclaimed how surprised she was that he had been so quiet and reserved. He reacted by promptly racing around the waiting room in a wild and semidestructive manner.

In succeeding sessions he enlarged on his space fantasy, as I wondered aloud how we could find the proper conditions he needed to feel safe with me. At one point he stopped and said, "You have a funny voice. Sometimes it's too loud and it makes everything get jumbled in me, and sometimes it's too soft and I can't hear it at all. Your voice makes me nervous and I want you to play." What began as a comment escalated into an increasingly insistent demand for me to play games with him. When I made no overt move to play he became more controlling and enraged. He started to shout, "You do as I say!" I simply stated that I didn't want to play, but I did want to understand why it was so important that I do. He threatened to destroy the room and asked if that's what I wanted him to do. I remarked that I was reminded of what happened with his mother at the end of the first session. He yelled, "You don't want me to stay here, you want me to leave!" I replied that in directing attention to his mother he must have felt that I either didn't welcome or know how to deal with all of his demands. Again he yelled, "I'm not going to like you, I hate you, and I'm not staying if you don't do as I say!" I then referred to the pathway in space and how vital it was for me not to be controlled or to respond to his demands by controlling him. It looked like he was afraid that if he wasn't in charge my voice would control him. He paused and went back to playing the space game, demonstrating the various obstacles that stood in the way of reaching a safe pathway in space. He only needed my help when he was truly incapable, but once he was on the pathway he could manage it himself. He stressed the importance of my giving help only when it was necessary. He turned off the lights, stating that he couldn't see. I remarked that he seemed to need help in seeing why he was so afraid of my voice controlling him. After a silence I talked about the pull he must feel to be very young so that it would be hard for him to tell what was coming from him and what was from me. It looked like that was scary for him and that he had to fight against the pull. He must have found that being totally in charge seemed the best way. Once again he fell silent, but this time he turned the lights on and in a soft voice commented that it was morning. The sun wasn't too hot and it was safe to go on his planet.

This patient's fantasy indicated that he felt he would either be engulfed by the sun's heat and be destroyed, or be totally abandoned and left to freeze. The only safe position was in being close enough to be warm but distant enough to be separate. All of his attempts to exert sadistic control over me seemed to be instigated by his reaction to my voice. He appeared to anticipate that I would respond by gratifying his demands for control, or conversely by withdrawing and leaving him alone. In following the principle of abstinence I did not reinforce this patholog-ical defense and his anxiety increased. The pressure to gratify these regressive cravings mounted in intensity. Interpreting his fear of being controlled and losing his autonomy freed him to reveal what he required from me. It was essential not to take over functions he was capable of performing and to help him with those that were impossible. Thus, in turning out the lights and declaring he was unable to see, I thought he was communicating a reactive awareness of a deficiency in being able to perceive the contents of his internal world. I interpreted his need to control external objects in order to maintain his sense of self and indicated some of the reasons why. As a conse-quence he began to feel safe.

The principle of abstinence guided me in offering a con-tained therapeutic framework, which necessitated the frustra-tion of his regressive cravings. However, this would have been meaningless or worse if I had not been able to allow my emotional reactions to show through in both my voice and body language, and if I had been unsuccessful in filtering out any countertransference interferences. The principles of ano- nymity and neutrality allowed me to provide him with the necessary room he required to experience me as controlling, fostering the unfolding of the transference as he projectively identified his sadistic motives into me, while at the same time giving me the room to be appropriately emotionally responsive to the meaning of the interaction. Only then was there safety. If my emotions were defended against, the climate would have been too cold, and if they were not empathic to his strivings for growth the climate would have been too hot and dangerous.

The controversy over attempts to reconsider and redefine the meaning of the basic psychoanalytic principles has centered around a recognition of the need for revision, accompanied by concern that in altering the guidelines they offer, the essential nature of psychoanalytic treatment will be lost. There is also concern that the firm boundaries and solid framework needed for the regressive conditions of the treatment will be diluted, blurred, or distorted. The pressure to engage in defense- reinforcing gratifying deviations and modifications can be so great, in both therapist and patient, that any alteration is viewed with understandable reluctance and uncertainty.

The conditions of psychoanalytic treatment are put in place to offer security, safety, and an opportunity to express analyz- able derivatives of either unconscious fantasies and intrapsy- chic conflict or of developmental deficits and self-pathology. This makes it important to have a clear delineation of the psychic contents comprising the deeper layers of the person- ality and of the primary pathological defenses. The composi- tion of these sectors of the personality are significantly dif- ferent in individuals manifesting neurotic and non-neurotic transferences. Consequently the manner in which the basic principles of psychoanalysis are applied will vary in accordance with those differences.

One of the problems in gaining a therapeutic understanding of primitive transferences is the lack of sufficient discernment concerning the composition of the deeper layers of the personality and of the makeup of the primary pathological defenses. This has led to confusion regarding how best to apply the basic psychoanalytic principles. In conjunction with a narrow view of the transference, and prompted by the difficulties presented by patients with severe pathology, modifications, deviations, noninterpretive interventions, and parameters are readily introduced when not necessary and not introduced when they are. Delineating the specific ways in which pathological defenses are organized makes it possible to identify defenses that are healthy and need encouragement. Some transferences are based upon firmly structured, well-differentiated derivatives and are communicated through a verbal symbolic modality. They derive from a period after psychic structuralization and generally focus around genitally determined oedipal conflicts. These constitute the essentially neurotic transferences. There are a wide variety of transferences stemming from prestructural and even preverbal infantile periods that revolve around preoedipal disturbances. These are global, ill-formed, unconscious transference fantasies and are expressed in the direct interaction with a therapist often in the form of immediate needs. Each requires a different management and resolution. A recognition of destructive qualities, and of those forces that are growth-promoting, aids in determining when interpretations alone are appropriate and when the conditions of the treatment have to be flexibly altered in order to support healthy strivings. This does require a clear picture of the specific structural organization of a patient's personality, of the differences from neurotic transferences, and of the differences within the range of nonneurotic transferences.

The primary means of exerting therapeutic influence in psychoanalytic treatment involves the use of unconsciously empathic interpretive interventions. Although introjection, projection, and identification are powerful interactional mechanisms having a major impact upon a patient, they are facilitated by the interpretive activity of a therapist. Considering transference solely as a displacement does place interpretations in the forefront, though if identifications are in the forefront, transference is considered solely as an object relationship. Both are inextricably interwoven with communication centering around interpretations. Together with the concrete actions required in managing the therapeutic framework, which in following the basic psychoanalytic principles are an adjunct to the therapeutic properties of the relationship, treatment boundaries are effectively established and self-differentiation is promoted.

A broadened understanding of interpretations fosters their continued use as the ultimate instrument of cure even when modifications are deemed necessary. There is no sharp dichotomy between those that are verbal and nonverbal, for when they emanate from a view of what is required to promote growth, all of a therapist's communications are different facets of an interpretive process. Interpretations are designed to intervene with the distortions created by pathological defenses, to enhance the expression of the deeper layers of the personality, and to strengthen the foundation upon which healthy integrative functions operate. They are a therapist's major communicative modality and convey the particular manner in which a patient's psychic productions have been unconsciously understood. Therefore they indicate the degree to which idiosyncratic or countertransference-based responses have been filtered out. In being empathic with unconscious communications they amplify containment and a basic hold, solidify the groundwork on which the transference unfolds, cement the therapeutic alliance, and further constructive identifications.

Interpretations and Resistance

The concept of resistance has to be taken into account in any treatment encounter. Those aspects of mental functioning, both conscious and unconscious, that are utilized to counteract or interfere with therapeutic progress are included within its realm. Resistance is basically a manifestation of the activity of pathological defenses and works against the pressure directed to a new way of looking at things by the force associated with the therapist's attitude. By nature it tends to be expressed in an adversarial fashion. When a therapist's interpretive responses reflect similar attitudes, the effort to understand a resistance becomes a fight against it. This approach to resistance will soon be devoted to fighting a patient in a way that rarely leads to a climate conducive to change. The therapeutic task is to demonstrate through interpretations the protective significance of a given resistance and its role in adjusting to whatever threats are perceived.

Resistance also encompasses the functioning of unconscious perceptions and is an illuminating source of information. The often-repeated statement that "resistance must be interpreted before content" is misleading, because unconscious fantasies are embedded within whatever way it is expressed. The determination of resistance is a subjective assessment, and it is vital to consider whether a patient is defensively resisting or is actually misunderstood.

The traditional statement that early manifestations of the transference should only be interpreted when they begin to become a resistance, and the related idea that an early focus on the transference is to oppose therapeutic progress, has involved much disagreement. The evidence of early transference interpretation interfering with transference development appears to be based upon responses to unempathic transference interpretations, which would be a hindrance at any point. When interpretations are empathic with unconscious communications their effect is to strengthen a therapeutic alliance, to create an aura of safety and containment, and to foster the emergence of more intense transferences. The idea of transference becoming a resistance before it is interpreted stems from an early stage in the development of technique, when it was mistakenly thought that a patient associating freely was not exhibiting transference resistance.

Interpreting transference as though the feelings and attitudes were really directed to someone else implies that they are not real or valid. Such communications are frequently taken as a criticism or admonishment not to direct feelings to a therapist, and encourage resistance. Similarly, acting out is generally understood to be a form of resistance, in which the emergence of psychic content is avoided by indirectly expressing it in behavior. It does not refer to action-discharge modes of communication, low frustration tolerance, or the tendency to challenge a therapist. Although it signifies the near-readiness of fantasies or memories for entry into consciousness in a relatively undisguised form, some psychic content can only become accessible by being relived. This makes action an indispensable means of recovering the past. This is especially true for preverbal and traumatic infantile experiences. At such times the sound handling of boundaries and ground rules presents a flexible hold, promoting basic ego development and serving to prepare for and supplement interpretive work.

A broadened conception of the transference that includes unconscious perceptions makes it possible to adapt the basic psychoanalytic principles to what is growth-promoting in a relationship. This fosters a more sensitive approach to neurotic individuals and extends psychoanalytic treatment to those exhibiting non-neurotic transferences. Investigations of primitive narcissistic transferences have given a deeper insight into their nature, and into the means by which they can be treated effectively. Perceiving a particular disturbance to be a spontaneous attempt at cure focuses therapeutic attention upon the growth-producing factors striving for expression. Therefore the directions necessary to enable progressive structural change are embedded within the personality and the basic psychoanalytic principles are applied in a way that is consonant with them. Appropriate gratifications are contained in maintaining a secure framework, so that interpretations can facilitate intrapsychic growth by undoing distorted or infantile structures. In not reinforcing pathological defenses a stimulus is also present for positive, constructive identifications. Narcissistic, prestructural transferences are expressed in a less differentiated, more primitive type of object relatedness, thereby requiring an entirely different mode of listening and communicating. Nonverbal interventions are communicated through a therapist's consistency, neutrality and concern, the handling of ground rules and boundaries, regularity, the quality of silences, and the timing of interventions.

Interpretations with Neurotic Transferences

The basic psychoanalytic principles serve as a guide for managing the therapeutic framework, and for the interpretive interventions that are the primary mode of communication. They create psychological space for a transference relationship to evolve in accordance with the dictates of a patient's personality. Originally the therapeutic action of psychoanalysis was seen to derive from the process of making the unconscious conscious.

The means of achieving this result centered around a therapist's use of interpretive interventions meant to clarify the unconscious meaning of the unfolding transference relationship. This conception has continued to occupy a central role, particularly with individuals whose ego functioning is relatively intact and who manifest neurotic transferences. Many clinicians, however, have come to believe that interpretations have a multiplicity of functions in addition to their content. They consist of a whole gamut of symbolic actions on the part of a therapist, whose meaning will vary in accordance with the patient's developmental and treatment needs. Other vital factors have come to include the nonverbal significance of the actual interaction and relationship with the therapist, and the internal, primarily symbolic meaning of the therapist's actions in establishing and maintaining the conditions of the treatment.[1]

---

[1] **James Strachey** made one of the early attempts to be explicit in regard to what fosters constructive change in the treatment, paying particular attention to the specific qualities that made an interpretive intervention mutative.

Introjection and projection are constantly operating in object relationships, with id impulses being projected onto an object. The object is then introjected with characteristics based on the initial projection, acts internally in keeping with the original impulses, and later may again be projected. This led to experiencing external objects as dangerous and destructive, as well as creating similarly toned internal objects. In this way psychopathology is incorporated into the superego, which is based upon these introjected objects, and the ego is exposed to the pressures of a savage id and a correspondingly savage superego. If a breach could be made in this "neurotic vicious cycle," the process of development could then proceed on a normal course. The break in the cycle depended on the patient being made less frightened of the superego or introjected objects, so that less terrifying imagos are projected and less destructive objects introjected, creating a benign cycle and a reinstatement of normal development.

It is the structuralization of an oedipal conflict that characterizes and distinguishes the more advanced psychic organization of the neurotic disorders. Perceptions, projective identifications, adaptive responses, and object relationships all carry with them the ability to recognize the three-dimensional qualities of an object. These object-related experiences are fraught with anxiety and mobilize the defensive distortions that determine the pathology. Because neurotic disturbances occur on a relatively stable foundation, in which cohesiveness, continuity of experience, and object constancy are firmly established, interpretive interventions are the major mode of communication. When appropriate and well timed they have an integrating influence.

In this conception the patient was seen as making the analyst into an "auxiliary superego" onto whom introjected archaic objects were projected, and from whom, as a new object, introjects are accepted. Because of the special relationship the introjected image of the analyst tended to be separated from the rest of the superego, creating a wedge within the patient's intrapsychic structures. It was based on the analyst's stance of acceptance, therefore not associated with the bad objects of the patient's past, and differentiated from the greater part of the original superego. A mutative interpretation occurred when the analyst permitted a small quantity of the patient's id energies to become conscious. The patient then became aware of the contrast between the aggressive character of his feeling and the real nature of the analyst, who does not behave like the patient's good or bad archaic objects. In the process the patient attains access to the infantile material experienced in the relationship with the analyst, and becomes aware that it is directed toward an archaic fantasy object and not toward a real one.

A mutative interpretation could only be applied to an id impulse that was emotionally immediate to the patient, and is therefore experienced as actual. Evoking an id impulse, which is alive, actual, and directed at the analyst, creates a moment that puts to the test the analyst's relationship with his own unconscious impulses. Thus the internal difficulty of the analyst in giving mutative interpretations must be overcome, for there is a constant temptation to do something else (Strachey 1934).

The treatment of a 31-year-old male, who sought help for what he initially described as occasional episodes of impotence, is illustrative. It later emerged that he had suffered from ejaculatory impotence his entire life. The humiliation was so extreme he could hardly bear to admit it even to himself. He began psychoanalytic treatment and worked hard to present himself as a happy, well-adjusted, easygoing person who only periodically had minor problems. At the same time, however, he dreamed of being on a boat ready to take off on a long ocean voyage, noticed the boat was rocking, was anxious about its staying afloat, and observed that it had not left the harbor. It took many months for him to become aware of the extent of his denial, and of the depth of his humiliation. During this time my silence was extremely frustrating to him, but it did provide the means by which he gradually discovered the intensity and nature of his deeper feelings. On one occasion, for example, he found a magazine in the waiting room with another person's name upon it. He demanded to know why, and began to cry out in a rage that he had a right to know. He was surprised at the strength of his feeling and realized that there was more to it than the surface meaning he clung to so tenaciously. It made him aware of the jealousy he felt over my involvement with others and of his struggle to deny its existence.

Interpretations referring to his concern that I would join him in avoiding these powerful feelings by answering his questions were extremely helpful. They elicited derivatives expressing a feeling of being understood and led to a fuller revelation of the contents of his inner world. He was the oldest of four children and had what he described as a very special relationship with his mother during his early years. The ''specialness'' was an unspoken, mutually gratifying caressing erotic interchange, interrupted by the birth of his siblings. This was what he constantly sought from me, and he slowly recognized that whenever he was frustrated with my silence there was a feeling of genital stimulation in the back of his mind. He was crying out for my words because they made him feel soothed and they quieted the underlying instinctual overstimulation. He then dreamed of a woman sucking on his penis, which brought up memories of his mother's seductiveness and reminded him of his reaction to my words.

He entered the following session carrying an umbrella and asked if he could put it in my closet. He explained that it was raining, the umbrella was wet, and he didn't want to leak water all over the office. The closet just looked like the best place for it. He had a feeling that I wouldn't want him to do it, but had a strong urge to put it in there anyway. The more he thought about it the more anxious he became. I commented that he was asking to put a part of himself into a closed, hidden space belonging to me, with a feeling that it was forbidden. He paused, lay on the couch, and while holding the umbrella, talked of an incident when he was 5 years of age. There was excitement in the house with everyone awaiting the arrival of a man. The man came in and when he asked his father about it he was told that the man was a barber who had come to give a haircut to his new infant brother. He was puzzled and asked why his brother needed a haircut since he had so little hair, whereas he had so much more. He was then totally humiliated by the laughter of the group surrounding him. Later he realized the event was his brother's circumcision. He remembered feeling terrified when everyone disappeared into a closed room where he was not allowed to enter. He paused and was filled with memories of his mother at different periods during his childhood in provocative positions with her genitals exposed. He felt both excited and frightened. It made him think of a lifelong feeling that it was safer and more desirable to masturbate. He could always reach an orgasm, though he had never been orgastic with a woman. Sexual encounters had been exceptionally overstimulating and equally frightening. The session ended and he remarked that although I had spoken very little it felt like I had talked a lot.

Afterward he had his first experience of potency in a sexual relationship.

Interpretations were extremely helpful in uncovering the defensive function of his search for soothing words, and the revelation of its infantile roots led to a compelling transference wish to penetrate a hidden space. Initially this evoked memories of a powerfully humiliating castrative threat, followed by a flurry of forbidden genital impulses. These derivatives of primal-scene fantasies were the repository of his deepest anxieties, for anything unseen was either a source of potential castration or overstimulation. The patient clearly had a vast array of ego functions capable of being mobilized to respond to the stress accompanying a regression, and these were flexible enough to be suspended periodically and reinstituted when necessary. A regressive transference unfolded that was not unduly disruptive, while the therapeutic alliance was intact and could encompass any minor lapses in empathy. The pressure he exerted to hear my words was motivated by an attempt to reinforce a defensive posture, and the resulting frustration led him closer to self-revelations. My silence was thus enabling rather than depriving, as it allowed instinctual derivatives to surface with the aid of interpretive interventions. His underlying transference wishes could then be expressed more fully and openly.

Individuals who have achieved cohesiveness possess continuity of experience and object constancy, as a consequence of which neurotic forms of pathology are manifested. The activity of unconscious perceptions is expressed primarily through derivatives, usually in a subtle nondisruptive fashion. The underlying structure of the personality is sufficiently stable and organized so that minimal empathic failures do not present an obstacle to the treatment. Such an individual is primarily affected by the distortions produced by unconscious fantasies. Therefore, adapting to the demands of a psychoanalytic situation is both possible and at times a spur to unused latent resources.

A 35-year-old single man sought help due to his distress over two areas of his life. He was involved in a love relationship, and was told he was too cold, uncaring, and insensitive. His girlfriend gave him an ultimatum that he either seek help or the relationship would end. The other concern was his work. He occasionally lost control over his anger and was worried about its effect upon others, making him feel very guilty. When these angry outbursts occurred he went over them endlessly in his mind until they could be rationalized. He repeated each step until he could assure himself he had done exactly right.

Initially he presented himself as being totally in control of his behavior, yet there was an underlying sense of desperation. When I commented on the urgency he seemed to feel, he related it to his need to meet with me frequently, for he recognized that he had a tendency to undo even the slightest changes in his attitude. Psychoanalytic treatment was initiated on a daily basis, and in the beginning sessions he engaged in repetitive, adversarial dialogues with me, though I was quietly listening. He took both sides, offering interpretations to himself in my name and arguing about their meaning as I remained silent. He frequently began a session with a statement such as, "I was thinking of what you said about my competitiveness." He then reflected upon the truth of that idea and quickly refuted it by saying, "I'm really a thoughtful, considerate person and not competitive at all." He continued in this vein, using historical events to back up his argument. He described intense struggles with three older brothers, noting how easy it was to see them as competitive, while he was only trying to stand up for his rights and not be dominated.

I was perceived as a controlling, sadistic figure demanding his submission to my point of view, and he was engaged in a battle to prove both his good qualities as well as an absence of any conceivable aggression. He was devoted to this constant internal struggle against an attacking adversary. I listened silently and could sense the subtle pressure he was exerting to have me participate, so as to strengthen his defensive posture. I was waiting, however, for the emergence of some interpretable derivatives. At this point his internal dialogue gave a picture of how interpretations would most likely be received.

After this continued for some time I reflected upon his concern about being overpowered, observing how important it was for him to carry on an internal fight with me, and wondered what he might be protecting himself from. He paused and hesitantly tried to put into words a deep inner feeling that lay behind all of his thoughts. He slowly elaborated a fantasy of my being a priest, disguised as a psychoanalyst. In his mind my intent was to unearth his darkest sexual secrets and expose his badness. While he was describing this fantasy it struck a humorous note in me and evoked a soft laugh. The following session took place shortly afterward.

He came into the office carrying a cup of coffee, set it on the table for me, and explained. It was early in the morning and he was concerned about me. He imagined that I would appreciate having the coffee. He wanted to be thoughtful and considerate. He then expressed some uneasiness about my silence, and thought I must be grateful but didn't know how to thank him. I stated simply that at the moment all I could see was that he wanted to put something into me, but I didn't yet know what it was. He fell silent and recalled his fantasy of my being a priest. He had felt hurt when he sensed my laugh but later his feeling changed. At first he thought I was mocking him and then realized I must have been laughing at the absurdity of his idea. As he put it, this gave him perspective and made him realize how terrified he was of revealing his sexuality even to himself. He was uneasy and sensed he was trying to say something that frightened him. He paused and remembered a dream from the night before in which a number of people accused him of being a woman. He now became concerned about my silence and somewhat demandingly asked why I didn't say anything. He paused again, recalled being fat as a child, even effeminate, and being teased and ridiculed by others. It made him wonder if he was homosexual. "I don't know what to make out of all of this. Why don't you talk? Your silence is frustrating. Isn't there something you can say?" I remarked that I could see that my silence felt like an attack to him, but I wasn't clear as yet just what he needed to hear. He began to talk about his reactions to my silence. Whenever I was quiet he could feel tension build up inside and he wanted me to talk because it felt like the words would ease this uncomfortable sensation. That was one reason why he liked my laugh. After a short pause he said, "I just remembered what I really thought when I brought the coffee. That son of a bitch is going to fall asleep on me and I better get him some coffee to wake him up!"

This patient's character defenses first had to be exposed successfully and the distortions they produced rendered ineffective before transference constellations could become accessible. His fixed attitudes were slowly being recognized as dystonic, and when I interpreted their defensive function it brought forth a vivid fantasy of me as a priest attempting to unearth his darkest sexual secrets. The fantasy was indicative of an emerging homosexual transference, and its intensity triggered a defensive countertransference response in me. While I was in the midst of trying to identify the significance of my laughter he in turn was working hard to strengthen his defensive posture. Initially he felt hurt, suggesting a beginning awareness of the emotional nature of his attachment to me. He quickly recovered, however, and instead of associating to the experience began to explain it. In this way he was directing attention to his conscious thoughts as he stressed the importance of perspective, and then he felt better. It made me more aware of my empathic lapse, for an effective intervention would have furthered a regression and led to an increase in instinctual derivatives on a background of containment. In its place, although he did describe being more aware of his fear of sexuality, was his focus upon conscious mentation.

His emphasis on rational thinking was clearly reinforcing his characteristic mode of avoiding conflict, and though he felt better I was aware of colluding with a pathological defense. My laugh was a powerful, affectively toned stimulus, but it was not unconsciously empathic and it elicited a return to his familiar pattern of character defenses. He had expressed an intense affect-laden fantasy, which was a thinly disguised derivative of a prohibited homosexual attachment, and reflected the emergence from repression of a negative oedipal conflict. I consciously laughed at the absurdity of the idea, but was unconsciously responding to the disturbing impact of his homosexual impulses. He took the surface conscious reason for the laugh and began to intellectualize in a search for logic and order. Consciously he accepted my collusion with his defensive stance, yet unconsciously he was trying to call it to my attention.

The act of bringing coffee, which had the conscious intent of being kind and considerate, was a derivative of his unconscious perception of my "sleepiness." I recognized the failure in empathy but had not seen enough of my motives to be able to interpret effectively and largely remained silent. This was disturbing to him, escalating his efforts to strengthen his defenses and distract him from the transference impulses pushing for expression. A dream in which he was accused of being a woman, childhood memories of being fat and effeminate, and concerns about homosexuality were interspersed with the upsurge of defensive activity, interfering with the smooth flow of this associative theme and preventing it from becoming focused in the treatment relationship. Ultimately I was able to discover the source of my defensive laughter, and to interpret the meaning of his conflicted feminine identifications. It was followed by a proliferation of primal-scene fantasy derivatives that expressed his positive oedipal wishes, along with the enormous conflict they engendered.

The manifestations of a lapse in empathy were not disruptive, though it did interfere with ongoing progress. Once corrected, the function of my interpretive interventions were more clearly in evidence. They helped in expanding his self-awareness, furthered the interconnection between the unconscious and conscious systems, supported the background of safety and containment necessary to support a benign therapeutic regression, and acted as a catalyst for positive, constructive identifications.

Interpretations with Nonneurotic, Prestructural Transferences

Psychoanalytic treatment is constructed to be in accordance with the basic principles of free association, abstinence, and anonymity and neutrality. The conduct of the ensuing interaction, however, should not be restricted by rules to which a patient must adhere. The framework in which the therapist functions depends upon interpretations that are empathic with unconscious communications. This is the cornerstone for eventually effecting therapeutic influence and constructive change. When other modalities are called for they must be measured against this primary treatment tool, and a careful assessment made of their significance in relation to making a symbolic process functional. The primitively organized patient, manifesting unstable narcissistic transferences, is least effective at establishing a well-defined self-boundary. Consequently, maintaining differentiation is more precarious. It is precisely this kind of individual for whom increased interpersonal contact is necessary, but whose self-boundary can readily be invaded in a detrimental fashion.

The manner in which the conditions of the treatment are introduced evolves from a therapist's listening attitude, incorporating the best understanding of their unconscious significance. The conditions must also contain those elements a therapist requires to sustain ideal therapeutic functioning. It is important for a therapist to possess an internal readiness to make appropriate adaptations when the conditions of the treatment are beyond a patient's capacities. Psychotherapy is a special form of human interaction designed to facilitate the forces in an individual's personality that are healthy and to provide an opportunity to alter or change the forces that are inhibiting, crippling, distorting, or defective. A psychoanalytic approach to this complex undertaking takes cognizance of the totality of the personality, placing special emphasis on the powerful effects of unconscious mental activity.

The need for this kind of flexibility was evident in the treatment of a 9-year-old girl who had a long history of early physical and sexual abuse. She was removed from her natural family at age 2 and placed in a foster home. There was a repetition of sexual abuse in the foster home and she was eventually adopted at age 7 by her present family. Her parents were concerned about her inability to form close interpersonal relationships, her emotional lability and lack of control, and intense sexual fears and preoccupations. She did poorly in school and seemed unreachable.

When she came to her first appointment she demanded that her mother come in with her, since she felt too frightened to enter the office alone. With a defiant attitude, as though anticipating a battle, she insisted that her mother accompany her. I stated that it looked like she needed to explore this new and unfamiliar environment while in contact with her mother, and I would listen for what she had to discover in order for her mother to leave. With this initial intervention I agreed to modify the framework of the treatment, at least temporarily. It was also interpretive in nature, for it referred to my search for the motive behind her fearful and belligerent attitude. It implicitly acknowledged her need to bring in protection, indicating my awareness that vulnerable internal experiences could be expressed only if the conditions were made safe enough for this kind of protection to be necessary no longer. In addition I was attempting to define the boundaries of the relationship by displaying a listening and interpretive posture.

Her response was to be openly delighted. She invited her mother in and spent the entire time exploring the room, identifying what she could and could not do. She approached this activity in a serious manner and gradually became more teasing and provocative. She asked about destroying objects in the room or about invading my private space, while indicating her awareness that these kinds of behaviors would be off-limits. I responded to her explorations and questions by commenting that I would try to understand what all of these things meant to her, but at the moment she seemed to be showing how crucial it was to have a clear picture of what the boundaries would be. I spoke about meeting regularly, and about the frequency, times, and fee. At the mention of money she made a face expressing her distaste for the subject and her mother looked embarrassed. Much later it emerged that the money for her treatment came from a special fund, set up as a consequence of her sexual abuse. She supposedly had not been told and the mother did not want her to know. She, however, knew and did not want the mother to be aware that she did.

After this first session she did not want her mother in the room and became very concerned about the confidentiality of the relationship. She then drew pictures of naked men and women, with their body products pouring out of every orifice. She was explicit in her terminology, taking great pleasure in using extremely vulgar words. She stated that she wanted to shock and horrify me. This statement belied her attitude, which was more one of seeing me as a willing and even eager recipient of these expressions of instinctual overstimulation. All stages of psychosexual development were included, as she expressed oral devouring, anal sadistic, phallic voyeuristic, and genital incestuous strivings. A persistent demand for more supplies accompanied these instinctual preoccupations, along with a constant sense of irritability and deprivation. The clamor for paper, crayons, tape, food, and the like was associated with a feeling of certainty that they would be provided by me and it seemingly made no difference when I didn't comply. In her mind I was an all-giving figure.

I interpreted her need to see me as gratifying her greedy, sadistic, voyeuristic, and incestuous urges, adding that I thought she did this in order to help maintain some feeling of being a separate person. She lapsed into a period of silence, looking very anxious. After a moment she mumbled some indirect references to intense longings for closeness, which were quickly negated, and then began to demand that her requests for supplies be granted. It looked as though the regressive pull of fusion and merger heightened the level of her anxiety, which resulted in an upsurge of regressive cravings. Instead of participating, I interpreted her fear of fusion, and she reacted with a concerted effort to rupture the therapeutic framework. She began to invade my private space forcefully, frantically insisting that her actions be permitted. At times I had to physically restrain her.

Suddenly I was emerging as an impinging, destructive, depriving, and instinctually overstimulating object, whereas she now felt young, tender, and vulnerable. The transference reflected her attachment to a powerful alterna-

tingly invasive and instinctual object that posed a threat to
her sensitivity and ability to love. There were then rapid
shifts in her mood, from feeling loving and vulnerable and
viewing me as dangerously overstimulating or destructive,
to seeing me as a much-needed source of supplies that she
clung to and desperately needed. I commented upon these
rapid changes in her feelings, and noted how I was either
all good when she felt bad or I was all bad when she felt
good. She looked pensive and then recalled her early
years.

She glossed over the many incidents of abuse, abandonment, and neglect at the hands of her parents to focus
upon what she called her "Indian heritage." She had to
keep it alive through her Indian songs and language, which
made her feel good about herself. She was worried that I
would belittle or deprecate this most vital part of her. She
remembered times when people tried to destroy her involvement with it, and began to cry as she described
various songs and rituals. Simultaneously she was delighted to see how easily they came rushing to her mind.

The combination of flexibly managing the treatment
framework to be in accord with what she needed in order
to feel held and contained and maintaining an interpretive
posture had helped her to reach and integrate inaccessible
and vulnerable experiences reflective of a positive attachment. The unavailability of these good self-experiences
had led to a divided sense of self and prevented her from
adequately negotiating the separation-individuation phase
of development. Consequently, splits in the ego remained
as a primary defense, interfering with continuity of experience, and her capacity for self-observation was noticeably impaired. She had been helped to attain a more
advanced level of psychic organization, so that the transference was more stable, differentiated, and object-
related.

The following session took place some months later and
showed that the gains she had made were becoming more

solidified. It pointed to her readiness for a shift in how the treatment could be conducted, in that she could feel held and contained by the symbolic meaning of an interpretation. She entered the office in a playful mood and initiated a reversal of roles by identifying herself as the therapist, while addressing me as the patient. She announced that there were really two therapists; one was real and good while the other was evil and disguised himself in order to fool me. The real therapist was understanding, firm, thoughtful, curious, and gentle. The evil therapist was cruel, sadistic, and sexually seductive. The evil figure tried to act like the good one in order to fool me but could never successfully accomplish it. Whenever he behaved like the good therapist he could always be exposed by provoking him. The real therapist responded by looking for the unspoken meaning and reflecting back what he understood. The evil therapist could only react by attacking in kind. She went on to develop scenarios in which I as the patient communicated intense sexual conflicts, and she as the therapist listened and spoke kindly about their deeper meaning. Thus I could know I was in the right place.

Within this role-playing game she was showing her ability to be understood, restrained, and helped to gain self-regulation. This way of thinking was expressive of the structural change that had taken place, in which self-differentiation was on firmer ground. The change was also reflected in her reaction to empathic lapses. In the beginning sessions her response to a failure in empathy was dramatic and unmistakable. She rapidly moved from seeing me as an all-gratifying figure to being devastated. On one occasion, for example, she erupted in rage, kicked at me viciously, and ran out of the office screaming, "I hate you." At this point she had developed the capacity to form derivatives expressing her unconscious perception of a lapse, and was contained and introspective. Thus when I was not in tune with her unconscious messages she would be reminded of a teacher who didn't listen to her.

The Function of Interpretations in Validating a Patient's Unconscious Perceptions and Correcting Empathic Lapses and the Need for a Secure Framework

It is essential for any two people working together in a relationship to have a connecting bond of a common, shared purpose. This mutuality must be present in the background for a given venture to be undertaken successfully. It is particularly true of a bond between a patient and therapist, in order to have the interpersonal atmosphere necessary for the work of psychotherapy to take place. It requires mutual respect and cooperation, much willingness to risk personal exposure, and the maintenance of clearly defined role boundaries. It is incumbent upon a therapist to discover a means of participating so as simultaneously to facilitate a benign regression and to foster the use of whatever integrative functions are accessible. In order to do so it is vital to comprehend the developmental line of each psychological event that is communicated, which in turn underscores the key role of external reality in shaping perceptions. An awareness of a therapist's contribution to the interaction is thereby kept in view, paving the way for identifying the manifestations and significance of a patient's unconscious perceptions.

There is often a surprising lack of consideration paid to the way in which the conditions of psychoanalytic treatment are instituted. When they are presented as an instruction, direction, or suggestion, an atmosphere of conformity is introduced from the outset. There is then a tendency to see a patient's responses solely as evidence of transference fantasy distortions, placing the evolving therapeutic alliance upon unsteady ground. This can readily lead to invoking unnecessary, noninterpretive measures in order to obtain a cooperative attitude.

For most individuals, even those exhibiting non-neurotic transferences, interpretations within a well-managed treatment
framework have a stabilizing effect, bearing a resemblance to
early developmental experiences of holding and containment.
Although this connection does seem to be present, it is only one
facet on a developmental line that encompasses a sequential
chain of increasingly advanced psychic structures. Considering
the infantile component as representative of the totality is to
undermine the importance of more progressive functions and
could easily result in infantilizing interventions.

The developmental line of experiences associated with
holding and containment is an integral part of the positive
transference, which is evoked by an unconsciously empathic
external environment. This silent background is crucial for
supporting a benign therapeutic regression.[2,3] The effects of
unconscious perceptions are much more pronounced in those

---

[2]**Donald Winnicott,** in elaborating upon the importance of a
patient feeling held during the course of the treatment, observed how a patient usually remains unaware of what we do
well, but becomes acutely aware of the part we play when
things go wrong. It is when we fail in these respects that the
patient reacts to the unpredictable, and suffers a break in the
continuity of his going-on-being (Winnicott 1963).

[3]**Arnold Modell,** who explored the psychic components involved in the experience of feeling held, traced it back to its
infantile origins and showed what the implications were for a
therapist's conduct of the treatment. He conceived of the
analytic setting as an open system in which the patient's ego is
related to its human environment. "The holding environment"
is derived from the broad implications of holding, which
relates to the mother's caretaking role and her position between the child and the actual environment. The analyst
conveys the holding environment through understanding the
patient's deepest anxieties. Holding thus provides an illusion of
safety and protection but depends on a bond of affective

individuals who show interferences with cohesiveness and
thereby manifest non neurotic transferences. A therapist's empathic failure will then frequently disrupt a therapeutic bond,
because unempathic stimuli resonate with the representations,
of early trauma embedded in the pathology. Unless and until a
therapist can recognize this source of the disturbance, any
possibility of therapeutic progress will be halted. The patient's
input is thus critical, as is the therapist's openness to receiving
this form of assistance.[4] The following example brings out the
differing facets of this problem.

---

communication. There is protection from internal and external
dangers, a sense of restraint, and a background of safety.

There are actual elements in the analyst's technique that are
reminiscent of an idealized maternal holding environment,
which include constancy and reliability, responding to the
patient's affect, acceptance with benign judgment, and being
there for the patient's needs rather than one's own. The analyst
does not retaliate and at times has a better grasp of the patient's
inner psychic reality than the patient, therefore being able to
clarify what is bewildering and confusing. In fantasy the patient
wishes to be protected magically from the dangers of the world
and to maintain the illusion of being shielded by the analyst,
who at times has the qualities of a transitional object or
protective container (Modell 1976).

[4]**Harold Searles,** from his vast experience with seriously
disturbed individuals, insisted that therapists take a closer look
at the effect the conditions and conduct of the treatment were
having whenever an obstacle to progress arose. He believed an
analyst's failure to recognize long-repressed therapeutic strivings in the patient accounted more for the patient's unconscious resistance to the analytic process than any other interpersonal element in the treatment. He felt that the classical
analytic position contained an element of delusion to the effect
that the analyst is not at all a real person to the patient, and
therefore it simply was untenable. Despite the complexities
involved in departing from classical psychoanalytic theory and
technique, in this regard it is essential to do so (Searles 1975).

The patient was a young woman who initially contacted me at age 24. She had been in treatment for 10 years with another therapist and did not want to return. She was desperate, felt she was losing her mind, and was confused and disoriented. She was extremely loud in her speech and mannerisms, and the simplest matters were seen and reacted to as an aggressive battle. She thought of herself as tough, self-reliant, hostile, and overaggressive, proudly describing how she won physical confrontations with men and how people were afraid of her. She had first sought therapeutic help at age 11 due to poor school performance and labile mood swings. Adolescence was turbulent, being filled with promiscuous relationships, physical fights, and bouts of heavy drinking. At age 20 she made a conscious attempt to put order in her life by getting married and having a child. Her stormy behavior ceased abruptly and she developed an intense, addictive relationship with food and her refrigerator. She ate constantly and to her dismay became quite obese.

The first months of treatment were occupied with her loud angry demands for my help or advice and for medication so she could sleep. Any attempt to direct attention to the meaning of her behavior was met with a loud tirade. Occasionally she recognized just how outlandish she must appear and expressed a deep feeling of shame. She wanted me to call this behavior to her attention, because she felt largely unable to recognize it herself. The more intimidated she felt the louder and more aggressive she became. She only felt some measure of safety when I stood firm. Although an unyielding therapeutic framework seemed to have a containing influence, any attempt I made to direct attention to self-exploration resulted in a very angry outburst. I was inadvertently asking her to do what she was unable to do, and it was reminiscent of traumatic developmental experiences. She anticipated being enveloped with any regressive movement and of being abandoned with any independent striving. When she was in the throes of an upsurge of anger, periods of warmth and sharing were nonexistent. My encouraging of internal exploration was experienced by her as insensitive, uncaring, and abandoning. There was no connection to other moments during which she felt understood.

At the outset the fee was paid by her father, and her thoughts were constantly occupied with people who controlled her by encouraging her dependency upon them. After quite a while I interpreted her preoccupation as an expression of what it meant to her that I accepted this form of payment. She responded favorably at first by handling the fee herself, which she did by using an insurance policy. However, she did so in a corrupt manner. I became aware of it and she was too humiliated to come to her next session. Afterward she spent a long time reviewing the extent to which she got away with things that she didn't either deserve or earn and could see how self-destructive this was. At precisely this point she decided to leave, stating that she now could have independent thoughts and feelings and wanted time with herself to consolidate the gains she had made. She also added that she was very frightened of her dependency.

I understood her leaving as a way of fleeing from the threat of a deeper attachment and commented that she had covered herself very much with lies, deception, and corruption, and it had taken me a long time to see how I had unwittingly fostered this way of being. It seemed to me that the prospect of a relationship with the absence of this protection was the motive for her leaving. It looked as though she was afraid of being enveloped in her attachment to me and was worried that I wouldn't be able to help her separate. She only reemphasized her decision to leave but anticipated she would come back. She sensed that she would have to fall apart before being able to return and made a reference to the unpaid balance on her bill. She expected to pay it, but in the event that she did not, she directed me to not see her until it was paid.

Eight years passed and she called in a state of panic. She was out of control, crying for no apparent reason, thought she would die, and needed to be seen immediately. I simply stated that as soon as I received her check for the unpaid bill I would schedule an appointment. She erupted in rage, saw no reason for my attitude, attacked me for my greed, and angrily hung up. Shortly thereafter she called back feeling relieved. She had felt lost and confused, but my words made her recall what she had said years before, She then added that she would send in the check. An appointment was made, but the night before, she called to demand immediate help. She was falling apart, couldn't sleep, and felt like bugs were crawling in her head. I said that it sounded like she was tempted to miss her appointment and the bugs were reminding her of how important it was to come. She came to the session and began by describing how her life was all in shambles. She had lost a lot of weight, had handled her life well, and was proud of herself. All had been going well until a few months ago when everything seemed to crash in on her. Her child had trouble in school, she felt criticized by the teachers, her family was down on her, and her husband got sick and was taken to the hospital. It felt like her whole world was crumbling.

Earlier she had thought of calling me but wanted to find some other way to manage her life. She was afraid to return because she knew this time it would be totally different. There could be no more lying or corruption. She sought many ways to find help, including calling her previous therapist. When she heard the other therapist's voice she hung up. She also tried to involve her family, as it reached a point where she just couldn't tolerate being alone and felt like she was going crazy. It seemed like there was no other alternative the night she called. My words made her even more aware of how different it would be this time.

The following session occurred after an urgent phone

call in which she stated she was panicky and demanded sleeping pills. She felt bugs in her head again and was itching all over. I simply said that she obviously needed something, not to help her sleep but to help her listen to herself. She immediately felt calm, spoke of needing to be alone so she wouldn't be distracted, and hung up. She came in and described what she had noticed going on inside. She hated everyone close to her. She hated her child for the demands he made and was shocked, since she didn't think she could ever feel such a thing, much less put it in words. She hated her father, who dominated her life. She hated herself for lying. She hated her husband, his family, and even hated her mother. She then went on to talk about her mother in some depth for the first time. Whenever she was sick, helpless, and falling apart her mother welcomed her completely. Any move toward independence, however, led to total abandonment. She sobbed deeply and noticed the sound of her voice. When she was honest her voice was soft but as soon as she got scared it faded away. She recalled the many times her voice was very loud, drowning out this soft voice until she lost contact with it. At such moments she frantically directed her loud voice against whomever she was with. I was the only person she had ever allowed to hear her soft voice.

This description of her voice gave a vivid portrayal of what was now happening in her treatment. Her soft voice was honest and expressed her genuine feelings, whereas her loud voice lied and expressed her defensive attitude. Her soft voice was buried deep within, where it was drowned out and protected by her loud voice. However, when the conditions of the treatment were unconsciously empathic her soft voice could rise to the surface, accompanied by a capacity for introspection and self-observation. During the first period of contact I had inadvertently reinforced her pathological defenses, and interpretive interventions were not sufficiently evocative of containing functions. In conjunction with her fear of dependency it contributed to the necessity of her leaving, although she rationalized the departure as an effort to gain independence. Finally, under stress, a regression got out of control and she felt she was losing her mind. However, she was immediately responsive to the containing influence of a firm therapeutic framework. With the help of interpretive interventions, which called attention to the distortions created by her pathological defenses, she was able to observe herself and begin to integrate previously intolerable internal experiences.

The containing qualities of a good object and the defense-inducing disruptive qualities of a bad object are reflected in a therapist's management of the treatment, and are evocative of a patient's unconscious perceptions. The specific attributes of what constitutes a good object are determined by the personality organization of the patient. They act to amplify the constructive forces operating within, which aid in facilitating perspective. An effective therapeutic alliance is a union between a patient's unconscious perception of what is growth-promoting and a therapist's management of the framework, appropriate silences, and unconsciously empathic interpretive interventions.

Transference is generally thought of as a manifestation within the therapeutic relationship of the distorting influences of past relationships upon current ones, intensified by the regressive movements inherent in the treatment situation. The distortions are clarified by a therapist's neutrality, relative anonymity, and objectivity. This narrow formulation does not include the developmental line of unconscious perceptions and the undistorted and nondistorting aspects of regressive experiences. Consequently, it is difficult to delineate the effects and significance of external reality. It is essential to discern the way in which unconscious perceptions impact upon transference fantasies in order to understand a therapeutic interaction. There is always a grain of truth in every transference experience, no matter how distorted. A narrow definition of the transference also pictures intrapsychic functioning as more of a closed system that clouds or obviates the role of a therapist's behavior in any shifts or changes that occur. A developmental approach to understanding transference highlights the processes involved in the internalization of external stimuli and more clearly delineates the object attributes that either enable or hamper constructive growth.

The basic psychoanalytic principles were originally designed and applied to be consonant with a concept of transference encompassing only fantasy distortions. This created inherent limitations in the range of disorders amenable to psychoanalytic treatment, because it was restricted to individuals for whom transference fantasy distortions were the primary pathology. These were essentially neurotic disorders in which there was a sufficiently advanced level of psychic organization to be able to manage a therapeutic regression. Whenever evidences of developmental arrests, deficits, or defects arose they might be noted but were basically left untouched. This narrow view of the transference depicted the therapist's task as one of correcting the distortions of the past through interpretations and bringing more mature adult insights to childhood states of conflict. The therapist was considered to be the standard of objectivity and expertise as well as the major source of the content of interpretations. The authoritative attitude embodied in this stance, and the inflexibility accompanying the lack of awareness of the mutuality in the therapeutic interaction are intolerable to individuals displaying non-neurotic narcissistic transferences. The negative effect upon the neurotic is more subdued and hence less noticeable.

A broadened view of the transference includes unconscious perceptions, which guide a therapist in adapting the conditions of the treatment to the particular level of psychic organization and resulting therapeutic needs of a given patient. This would contrast with making it mandatory for a patient to adapt to the conditions of the therapist, thus eliminating the emotional climate of conforming to an authority and still retaining the features that make the treatment uniquely psychoanalytic. The conditions of psychoanalytic treatment, when guided by a patient's unconscious perceptions of what is required for growth, insure that a therapist's functioning possesses the attributes of a good object.

A good object combines the qualities of optimal gratification, optimal frustration, and those of a transitional object. Within a therapeutic context optimal gratification refers to the support of autonomy, independence, insight, and constructive growth. Optimal frustration refers to abstaining from the reinforcement of pathological defenses. The qualities of a transitional object refers to the encouragement of a free flow of projective identifications unimpeded by a therapist's projections or impositions. That which is optimally gratifying for one may be infantilizing, impinging, or defense-reinforcing for another, and what is optimally frustrating for one may be defensive, withdrawing, or withholding for another. The specific form it takes is determined by the structural composition of a patient's personality.

Under these circumstances the influences of a good object, represented throughout the entire course of development and including the earliest phases, are evoked. The consequences are in a background of containment providing the stability required for the emergence of disturbing and regressive psychic content. Although this distinction may not be of crucial significance with neurotic disorders, it may be a pivotal factor when addressing the individual with a narcissistically structured

personality. In this area of psychopathology, when the derivatives of unconscious perceptions are treated as transference
fantasy distortions it has an extremely negative effect. The
resulting lapse in empathy is experienced as a repetition of
early trauma. In addition, a demand for adaptation may be too
great for the integrative work and positive identifications of
psychoanalytic treatment to be carried out. It is thus especially
important to distinguish the elements of psychic functioning
that are distorting and pathological from those that are nondistorting and healthy. This was exemplified in the treatment
of a 12-year-old boy who had been referred because of his fear
of being separated from his mother and going to school.

He began by describing how desperate he was. He was
overwhelmed by the aggressive attacks of other children,
felt like he was going crazy, and needed me to help him
remain at home. In the third session he brought his mother
into the office, stating that he knew she would listen in my
presence, and began to plead to have time away from
school. He told her that he needed to build up his courage
first before he could face the other children, and she
granted his wish. He then came into his next appointment
grinning broadly. He spoke excitedly of his martial arts
skills and of his exploits in shooting birds and animals,
seeming to anticipate I would be sharing in his pleasure. I
wondered what had happened to the frightened little boy
who couldn't go to school. He looked up at me with a
puzzled expression on his face, asking if I wasn't confusing
him with someone else, and blithely went on with his
excited talk. Very quickly, however, his enthusiasm
waned, and he appeared disconcerted as he fell silent,
remarking that his mind went blank.

   In the initial contact he was in the grips of a malignant
regression, with a level of anxiety that had reached panic
proportions and was posing a threat to self-cohesiveness.
He was afraid of fragmenting and maintained a sense of a

differentiated self only through adopting a paranoid attitude. The instability was terrifying. He enlisted my participation in reestablishing an apparently previously held, more familiar position, which involved reinforcing a pathological defense. He put it in terms of mobilizing his resources. In the ensuing session the earlier experience had been split off, and as another variant of a pathological defense surfaced, he anticipated that I would respond similarily by reinforcing rather than interpreting its meaning. The difference was striking in that he momentarily felt in control and master of all. My question pointing to the difference intervened with his attempts to gain my participation, and a gap appeared.

I then spoke of his attempt to be in control by treating objects sadistically and how vital it was to see me pleased with his efforts. It seemed to help him ward off any infantile longings that made him feel vulnerable and open to attack. I added that in having me support his appeal to his mother it led him to believe I would support this protection also. It looked like this was his way of remaining a separate person and combated his fear of losing a sense of himself. His response was to recall sleeping with his dog. She was soft and furry and he liked to get close to her in order to feel warm and safe. When he got too close he felt hot and like he was smothering. He didn't want his dog to leave because he would feel too alone. She was a good watchdog who warned him of any danger. He just had to discover how to be with his dog without feeling smothered, and still feel safe and protected.

My interpretation had addressed his struggle to maintain differentiation and his fear of fusion and merger. He reacted by expressing his hunger for contact and his inability to sustain it from a differentiated position. He was, however, displaying a budding capacity for introspection, which suggested that my interpretation had supported a tenuous link to the influences of a separate good object, thus enabling the function of self-observation.

He went on to describe his trouble in sleeping at night. He gets too hot, can't stand it, and opens a window, only to get too cold. I remarked that I was reminded of his bringing his mother into the office. He must have been trying to show me how much he wanted to be close to her but also how terrified he was of not being able to separate from her. He vividly remembered his fear of going to school, but also recalled how afraid he was of telling me that his father had recently left home. When his father is away he is drawn toward crawling into his mother's bed to keep warm. Instead he sleeps by her door so he won't be either too close or too far away. He then paused and talked about a cousin in the army whom he admires. The cousin encourages him to be strong and independent, which he also wants to be so he won't need his mother so desperately.

He had pressured me into modifying the framework of the treatment by bringing his mother into the office, and I had unwittingly participated in reinforcing a pathological defense by listening as he was given permission to remain home. Although it served to curb a malignant regression, it worked against any positive movement toward a structural change. Interpretations were of little value until I could recognize and rectify the empathic lapse by altering my posture. When the change in my attitude was clear to him, an interpretation of his wish for and fear of becoming separate and autonomous could be taken in. The consequence was in his expressing derivatives reflecting an attachment to a separate good object's influence. The emergence of this pathway toward a new, more advanced level of psychic organization was probably indicative of earlier traces of advancement, which had now become accessible in a contained relationship. My interpretive words were apparently resonating with healthy psychic contents that had heretofore been too weakly represented to be viable. This had the effect of strengthening cohesiveness and continuity of experience. Thus his attempts to disrupt the containing influence of a secure framework were equally designed to ensure its firmness. Were the ground rules and boundaries of the treatment to have been applied rigidly, they almost certainly would have re-created past traumas. However, simply to acquiesce to a demand does not allow the needed containment to be forthcoming.

The nondistorting, healthy components of a patient's personality are evoked by the empathic responses of a therapist, particularly when directed to unconscious communications. It is this facet of psychic functioning that establishes a foundation for the activity of unconscious perceptions, a background of containment, and the groundwork for an effective therapeutic alliance. They are a major source of information for validating a therapist's interventions, and for verifying the proper application of the basic psychoanalytic principles. When a therapist's contribution interferes with the unfolding and exposure of a patient's transferences, it will be reflected in derivative, encoded, unconscious communications expressing negative introjects and identifications with the therapist's pathology. These responses exaggerate distortions and undermine an effective alliance, although if recognized they can be utilized to correct countertransference-based attitudes and be put to advantage in discovering more effective interpretive interventions.

3

Constructive Positive Identifications

The Significance of an Ideal Therapeutic Attitude in Encouraging Positive Identifications

The ground rules, boundaries, and conditions of a secure psychoanalytic treatment framework are founded upon sound principles designed to insure the safety and containment required to enable the unfolding of a benign regression. Ultimately it leads to the undoing of distortions created by pathologically defensive structures, involving either a resolution of infantile instinctual conflicts or at times a healing of developmental deficits. A therapist's capacity to maintain such a stance consistently, in spite of many pressures to do otherwise, has the effect of strengthening a patient's resources. The result is being able to offer a more complete and unifying experience, which is greatly admired. It serves as a powerful stimulus for constructive positive identifications, providing support for the expansion of self-knowledge and awareness through the influence of interpretations empathic with unconscious communications. Therefore, any movement toward altering, modifying, or deviating from these vital therapeutic principles, on the part of either participant, should be viewed with concern.[1] The detrimental effect of unnecessary changes in a sound, well-contained treatment environment, as well as the constructive influence of recognizing, correcting, and interpreting how it was used to amplify pathological forces, was evident in the following treatment situation.

---

[1]**Robert Langs** has been the most prolific writer in recent years on the unconscious significance of the therapeutic interaction. He has examined all facets of this bipersonal field and called attention to many factors previously downplayed or ignored. In this article he stressed the significance of the manner in which the therapist establishes and maintains the ground rules and boundaries of the therapeutic setting and interaction. He felt it was among the most important means by which a therapist conveyed to the patient the essence of his or her identity and dynamic state of mind. The management therefore influenced the patient's ongoing identificatory and incorporative processes and significantly contributed to the nature of the person onto whom the patient projects fantasies. He believed that major deviations in technique resulted in permanent modification of the patient–therapist relationship, and always provided a significant measure of inappropriate gratification for the patient and usually for the therapist. He made note of the wide range of reasons given to justify such measures, such as to strengthen the therapeutic alliance, to express the real relationship, to lessen the deprivation, to avoid unnecessary frustration, to make the therapist seem more human, and to demonstrate flexibility. In Lang's opinion the ground rules and boundaries of the relationship offered these same benefits, while modifications in technique usually undermined them (Langs 1975a).

The patient was a young man who felt strongest and most effective when he was deprecating any of my efforts to understand his lateness and forgetting of appointments. He reacted to any questions concerning his motives as though they were attacks and seemed to feel most intact if he retaliated. It looked as if he was trying to dominate and control me, which he quickly saw as a caricature of his father. This approach alternated with a feeling of ineptness, inadequacy, weakness, and helplessness, along with an enormous concern that he would submit to what he imagined I wanted from him.

He had a long history of somatic complaints, some of which had resulted in short periods of hospitalization. They were characterized by intense abdominal pains, described by him as devils with pitchforks digging into his guts. Whenever they were present he engaged in heavy bouts of drinking and/or drug intake. These body sensations and his use of drugs were at times very worrisome, and they were accompanied by his sense that I was profoundly disapproving of him. He occasionally came to sessions under the influence of drugs or alcohol, and he would search for any nuances in my bearing that would indicate some sign of disapproval. Gradually he revealed the terror in the back of his mind that episodes of disorientation would be repeated. They were always preceded by bouts of depression, during which he was immobilized with no energy. He described this depression as an overpowering force enveloping him to the point of suffocation, alternating with a feeling of terror that in some violent outburst he would destroy everyone who meant anything to him.

These depressive episodes frequently heralded brief moments when he felt numb, confused, lost, and without existence. At such times he frantically sought situations where hostility was directed against him, and in recreating these sadomasochistic relationships he felt whole again. When this didn't succeed he turned to addictive substances to pull himself out of these states of fragmentation and loss of differentiation. He spent several months putting pressure on me to alter the framework of the treatment in one way or another, seeming relieved when I stood firm trying to understand the meaning of his behavior. Gradually he became more curious himself about his motives and showed signs of becoming introspective. The following two sessions give a picture of the advances he made, and of his responses when I functioned well and when I did not.

In the first session he was preoccupied with a loved girlfriend. He felt she was a good person who was concerned when he would feel driven to attack, deprecate, and seek out her vulnerabilities in order to hurt, control, and dominate her. His behavior provoked her into hostile attacks upon him after which she sought solace in alcohol and drugs. He commented that it was like watching a mirror image of himself. I related it to his deprecating attacks upon me, and how my words often made him feel deflated and beaten down. He reacted by talking about his fear of becoming engulfed whenever he loved someone. He then noted how his attacking and controlling behavior served to protect the soft, loving, tender parts of himself. He began to cry as he realized there was meaning in his behavior, for he had never thought of it this way. His hostile reactions protected him, but they also made him his own worst enemy. More than anything else he wanted to love someone and not have to deny his weaknesses or anger. After pausing he recalled a loving relationship with a deceased grandfather, in which he felt accepted and didn't have to be frightened.

This was the first time that he had indicated some awareness of how he provoked others into attacking him as a defensive maneuver. Associated with it he could also see and feel a coming together of all of his good and bad qualities. He was moved by being able to have the experience of discovering that there was meaning in his behavior, and hence in his life. All of this was in response to an interpretation of how he experienced the transference relationship. However, his ability to display psychological-mindedness, to observe inner contents, and to find meaning was in large part a reflection of his identification with my therapeutic attitude.

The unsteadiness of this identification in the presence of an empathic lapse, and the way it can be asserted and solidified through reestablishing effective therapeutic functioning was reflected in a later session. He began by talking about how inadequate he felt. Nothing was any good and nothing helped him. He continued to be a violent person and would never change. He felt like he would never be able to have a life for himself, could never complete anything, and was totally infantile and helpless. He always had to be taken care of, and was incapable of managing his own life. He paused and went on to talk about how dependent he was on his father. The father always took care of him and he in turn felt totally obligated to him. He would never be free. As he spoke I suddenly became aware that his bill had not been paid for the past two months. He had put a great deal of emphasis on the importance of its being his responsibility and I had "forgotten." In the midst of this thought he suddenly asked, "Aren't you going to say anything?" Knowing that he was alert to even the slightest nuances in my facial expressions I thought he must have noticed the dawning of this realization.

I first said that he must have seen that I did in fact think of something. He interrupted to express his fear of speaking directly. He had seen a change in my face but was afraid to mention it. I told him I thought he was calling attention to his feeling that I was the one who was afraid to talk directly, for I suddenly recalled that he hadn't paid his bill and I hadn't said anything about it. In that way I was treating him as a young, weak, or helpless person and making him feel dependent and obligated. He had created

such a powerful image of himself as vulnerable and easily
hurt that as the bill mounted, I forgot. Had I remembered
and confronted him with the unpaid bill, in my mind I
would have been traumatizing him. I therefore forgot and
in doing so was infantilizing him and undermining his
movement toward growth. He listened silently to my
words and then said, "Oh yes, how much was it, I forgot."
I said that he seemed to be checking to see if I really
understood, and might be wondering if I thought he was
incapable of knowing the amount. My words reminded
him of his going to school always expecting to fail, which
he did. On one occasion he decided to take courses at a
local college on his own and was amazed to discover he
could do well. He understood the material and got a high
grade. This was the only time he had done something
independently and was effective. He didn't pursue it
because his success frightened him. As he thought about it
now, doing well meant living alone, and managing himself, while feeling cut off, isolated, and open to being hurt.
He had forgotten about the bill but did recall wondering
why I hadn't said anything. He proceeded to make out a
check for the full amount, describing how good it felt to be
in charge of the payment. He again thought of his grandfather, who had given him tasks, taught him how to do
them, and silently allowed him to do them on his own.

In my "forgetting" I was readily included in a pathological
alliance, which he could utilize at moments of anxiety as a
defensive retreat. In the earlier session he had become aware of
the meaning of his sadistic behavior, which had freed him to
experience the loving and caring feelings that were coming to
life in the transference. Shortly afterward he entered this session
feeling bad and as if nothing had changed, going on to elaborate
on his continued dependency and submission to his father's
domination. It made me aware of the transference implications
of his not paying the bill. He had unconsciously perceived me

as being afraid to talk to him directly about it, and he mirrored this perception in his reactions. He had produced such an aura of helpless vulnerability that I would have felt cruel and sadistic to bring up the bill and hence had forgotten. I validated his perception and interpreted its meaning, which led to his recall of being successful and the fear it engendered. For him it meant to be separated and individuated, touching upon an area of extreme vulnerability. The progress he had shown earlier couldn't be sustained under the stress of feeling separate. My collusion with a pathological defense was undermining the constructive identifications he had made, and until I could rectify the empathic lapse, no further growth could take place. It had evoked negative introjects, requiring that the mistake be recognized, corrected, and its effects interpreted before the positive identifications could once again be functional.

A therapist's healthy and pathological modes of functioning are most clearly revealed in the management of the ground rules and boundaries of the treatment. The extent to which they meet the conditions necessary to promote growth is reflected in a patient's unconscious perceptions of the interaction, usually expressed through derivatives. Errors in technique, incorrect interventions, nonindicated, unnecessary deviations and modifications of the framework are almost always traumatic, and when they are, a therapist is realistically perceived as hurtful, seductive, or threatening. It presents an actual repetition resonant with early pathological relationships. There are times, however, particularly with some primitively organized individuals, when a patient's powerful unconscious effort to evoke behavior congruent with unconscious transference fantasies and past pathological interactions provokes a therapist into unwittingly becoming a participant.[2]

---

[2]**Robert Langs** demonstrated how patients consistently show a positive response to the conditions of psychoanalytic treat-

The following was part of the treatment of a woman in her thirties, who initiated therapeutic contact in a dramatic fashion.

She called for an appointment just as I was preparing to go on vacation. When I asked if there was some urgency she replied by stating she had a gun pointed at her head as she was talking on the phone. I told her that it certainly answered my question, but I wasn't able to respond immediately and wondered if I could help her find someone who could. She refused, adding that it was vital that it be specifically me and she could wait. She couldn't discuss the reasons over the phone and a time was scheduled. Much later she revealed that when I didn't react to the urgency by seeing her immediately she felt relieved. She sensed that I wouldn't automatically alter my stance even when she put a great deal of pressure on me to do so, and that position made her feel safer.

She was in the process of obtaining a divorce from her second husband and was having a lot of trouble in managing her life. She was also frightened that she could lose control and kill herself, and felt right on the edge of doing

---

ment, provided that there is no pathological or inappropriate input from a therapist. He was convinced that abandoning the guidelines of a psychoanalytic treatment framework most frequently led to serious disturbances in the treatment, usually in the form of a misalliance. These misalliances were inevitable expressions of the patient's and at times the analyst's residual pathology, and are a major opportunity for necessary analytic work. Through participating, the analyst becomes a bad object, who is incorporated to the patient's detriment. The inherently maladaptive and destructive aspects will prompt the patient to make efforts to renounce the collusion. A similar need may arise in the analyst, and this leads to a recognition of the interactional difficulty. Self-analytic work, and analytic work with the patient, are the means through which the trouble can then be modified (Langs 1975b).

so when she called. She had contact with many psychiatrists in her work and had been in psychotherapy one year earlier with the first one about whom she felt good. He had left town and she had called him to make arrangements to travel there, whereupon he cut off the relationship. She told him she would kill herself and he had insisted that she call me and no one else. She hung up, picked up the gun, deciding there was no point in living, reconsidered, and called me. After she hung up she felt curious and began to imagine what it would be like to talk to me. She was surprised that she had told me about the gun in her hand, for she had no intention of saying anything. She was also reluctant to mention her former therapist, fearing it would spoil his image in my mind.

Secrets were highlighted in the beginning as each session was occupied with the revelation of another one. They all were concerned with relationships she was hesitant to reveal. Many involved intense but brief sexual encounters with her submitting to the wishes of her partner. She wanted to keep them hidden lest I see her as promiscuous and bad. Another centered upon her two marriages. The first occurred at age 18 when she was looking for a way to escape her home. She felt trapped and married a man who lived with his mother. She moved from her home to his, feeling trapped once again. She had a child and thought she would never be free. It seemed as though her need to be taken care of was leading to her destruction. She then tried going to school to learn a trade, then got divorced, living on her own for the first time. The secret of this marriage was in its showing her dependency, and she was worried that I would think less of her for marrying someone just to escape. The second marriage was to a man whom she saw as extremely exciting. He lived on the edge of danger at all times. She helped him in his work and at first felt alive and free. Slowly she felt engulfed and overwhelmed by his jealousy and possessiveness. She became frightened that she couldn't trust her own perceptions and began to believe her life was in danger. She was afraid to leave her husband because any move in that direction precipitated an intensely jealous rage. She was ashamed of this relationship and of exposing it to me.

She did manage to complete school, tried to develop an independent existence, and sought therapeutic help. This was another secret. She fell in love with her therapist, believing this was the answer to her prayers, and he then left town. This subsequently led to the phone call that initiated our contact. All of her efforts to gain independence led to nothing, all of her love relationships turned out to be destructive, and she saw no reason to live. Her child was the one thread holding her to life and she questioned even that.

Secrets then emerged from her childhood. She was the oldest of three children and discovered that her mother had a sexual liaison with another man while married to her father. This man turned out to be her biological father. She had always been teased about not looking like others in the family, and one day while with her mother they met a man who had children resembling her. Her mother then threatened her and told her that she must keep this meeting a secret. A second secret came out from earlier in her life at age 4. Her grandfather was a well-respected pharmacist in a small town. She was often at his drugstore and one day noticed her grandfather disappear for periods of time. She explored and found him masturbating to pornographic pictures and was warned to keep this discovery a secret. In addition she portrayed a highly eroticized relationship with her father, who was openly seductive and often accused her of being a whore. She was secretly aroused by her father's sexual interest and hated this aspect of herself. Her self-destructive impulses were born of feeling trapped in a vicious cycle of either destroying the good object's influence, which she needed in order to grow, or eroding the good self-experiences she valued so highly.

She entered treatment having the same anticipation of finding a good object, but immediately put pressure on me to function in ways that would reinforce her pathology. In the early sessions this centered around our establishing the framework of the treatment. The need for ongoing therapeutic contact was identified early in the first hour and the discussion focused upon the fee, times, and frequency. She described herself as having very little money, since she was raising her child alone, received very little child support, and was in the early stages of getting a divorce. In addition she did not want third-party involvements, such as insurance. She was afraid that her husband would learn of her seeing a psychiatrist and use it as evidence to take her child away. For the same reason she didn't want a bill. I thought all of this reflected her unconscious awareness of the well-contained framework that she would need for treatment to be successful. She had been so poorly held during her developmental years that I thought she was giving me some guidelines as to how I should conduct the treatment.

Her associations to the fee concerned situations in which people had done her favors which always turned out badly. She ended up feeling either exploited or infantilized. I simply said that I thought she was telling me that it was essential for her to pay a full fee. This was agreed upon but it set a limit on how often she could afford to come in, and once a week was decided upon. It soon became evident that she needed to be seen more often when one day she called for clarification of the time of an appointment. She had written it down, lost the paper, and couldn't find it. It reminded her of prior experiences when more was expected of her than she was capable of doing. I related this incident to her unspoken request for a second appointment and she then remembered a dream. In the dream she had called me, couldn't get through, hung up, and then tried to find her way to my office. After a long, circuitous journey she arrived, only to find it was right next to the phone. She felt the dream expressed her difficulty in asking to see me more frequently and now that it was out in the open she felt relieved. She found a way to work overtime and a second session was arranged.

Throughout the course of her treatment it was essential for the ground rules, boundaries, and conditions to be clear-cut and firmly maintained, and for me not to yield to the pressure she exerted to disrupt them. I was experienced as a good object only when I interpreted her attempts to alter the framework. It helped her to modify the destructive impact of negative introjects and encouraged a constructive identification with my therapeutic attitude. The result was in amplifying internal resources that had been dormant and in helping her to see herself with perspective. In my standing firm she felt safe enough to experience me in whatever way was important to her at a given moment. She periodically thought of me as a prostitute who accepted her money for services rendered, as an authority who disapproved of her, or as someone aroused by her.

The pressure she put upon me to modify the conditions of the treatment centered around persistent demands that I not be inflexible, that I talk to her on the phone outside of the hours, or that I change the hours to a later or earlier time. The reasons often involved seemingly unalterable realities—bettering herself in her career, a work commitment, or an event associated with her child. My attitude largely remained constant. I encouraged her to associate, and with the material available I tried to interpret what I viewed as her underlying motive. The motive essentially concerned her search for me to participate in reinforcing some pathological structure. These distorting defenses were all behind her crippling dependencies and undermined any of the influences of a good object. There were times, however, when she succeeded in evoking in me an image of myself as a cold, rigid, unfeeling person. On these occasions she would be filled with a feeling that she was bad and made anyone close to her equally as bad. These moments were interpreted to her as expressions of her unconscious perception of my wavering in response to her pressure.

The following session took place after a period of time during which she felt securely held, and recognized the value of the perspective that grew under those conditions. Previously she could only see herself through the effect she had upon others. She described her inability to see herself as her biggest trouble and therefore valued this newly formed capacity of self-observation. The session began as she entered crying. She felt lost, confused, and paralyzed. She feared she was losing an important relationship with a loved figure in her life and felt a powerful need to cling to him. Everything was unreal as she felt herself being swallowed up. She sobbed deeply, while speaking of falling into a pit and wanting to die. I stated that as she began to feel more contained she could allow disturbing inner feelings to come closer to her, which I thought was reflected in the sense of being engulfed by their presence. She could also feel the urge to cling to her old defensive attitudes, but they were no longer as effective.

After silently crying for a moment she remembered seeing a young girl at a bus stop. The girl was alone and cold and she wanted to comfort her. She paused and thought about a shopping trip with her daughter. She had picked out a dress for her child, who then became enraged. The daughter wanted to select her own, and she realized it was important to encourage this independent act. She had always tried to do everything for her so that she would suffer no pain. She now could see, however, that the pain was a part of helping her to grow, be separate, and be her own person. She returned to thinking about the love relationship she feared losing. She was caught in a state of mind with no perspective and began to wonder how to regain it. "I know how. I can't have you be my mirror all of the time. I have to stand aside and look at myself.'' She imagined herself looking in a mirror and saw a picture of herself struggling to survive. She realized that her behavior was not evidence of badness but reflected her efforts to remain separate and protect the valued things about herself that were so vulnerable.

Thus in the presence of a well-contained therapeutic environment, self-observation from a position of separateness became functional. This positive movement was indicative that the treatment relationship had offered her the wherewithal to accomplish a previously unmastered developmental task, not only through the influence of interpretations but especially through her identification with my therapeutic attitude. She now possessed a more solid internal sense of a good object's influence. There were occasions, however, when the intensity of her demands made me waver, which undermined these constructive identifications and intensified her pathological dependencies. It is precisely at such moments that it is vital to recognize that a patient is neither a victim nor a culprit, but is influenced by the treatment relationship and is operating under an internal drivenness to create sectors of reality in keeping with unconscious needs. These same efforts are simultaneously designed both to harm and help a therapist. In this way transferences and countertransferences are equally a major source of growth, disturbance, frustration, harm, motivation for psychoanalytic work, and cure (Langs 1981).[3]

---

[3]**Theodore Dorpat** was interested in the difficulties a therapist encountered when treating patients with narcissistic disorders. He considered identification with the therapist to be important if the treatment was to be successful, that is, first, in order to overcome developmental defects, and second, to promote the formation of autonomous ego and superego functions. Internalization involved processes through which a person transformed real or imagined transactions with objects

The Importance of a Therapist's Personality in Providing a Constructive Response to Infantile Strivings

The concept of projective identification has deepened the understanding of the mechanisms involved in a transference relationship and given a broader perspective to the means by which unconscious communications take place. A psychoanalytically conducted treatment situation is designed to foster the free flow of projective identifications, aiding a therapist in understanding the unconscious significance of a patient's input. In order to do so, however, a therapist must be open to receiving the emotional impact, allowing all subjective reactions to be registered and noted. These internal responses must then be carefully examined, while exposing them to cognitive and inferential processes. A patient's psychic contents, which

---

into psychic transactions, in which the patient was both subject and object. The analyst's image is actively inside the patient, and the transactions are internalized. The conditions necessary for these transactions within the analytic situation include a narcissistic relationship with the analyst in which the patient's impaired ego and superego functions are supplied and regulated. Narcissistic patients attempt to manipulate, control, and seduce the analyst into immediate and direct gratification of narcissistic needs. He believed it was vital for these efforts to be frustrated as a prerequisite for the formation of analyst introject fantasies, since the blockage interfered with verification of the patient's projection. The patient could then recognize the analyst as outside of the projection, and the recognition could be of real and immediate use. The analytic setting provided the conditions, the interaction, and the content, but the patient's ability to use these imaginary transactions for the construction of ego and superego functions was also necessary (Dorpat 1974).

embody both fantasy and the experience of attachment to an object, are thereby internalized by a therapist. Although projected, they retain resonance with the patient's immediate experience. This communicative pathway is then available for a therapist's interpretive and management interventions to be taken in. When these interventions are evocative to a patient's unconscious perceptions of what is required to promote growth they can be used constructively. Thus the patient's productions have in essence been returned in a new, more integratable form.

A therapist, by virtue of presenting a different and more constructive response to infantile strivings, gives an opportunity not only for a new solution, but also for an experience that can be healing in and of itself.[4] The particular manner in which a patient's material has been processed by a therapist and then offered back, whether it be via an interpretation, an appropriate silence, or some actual management of the framework, brings the therapist's personality into play. The effect goes beyond that of the specific intervention that has been delivered.[5]

---

[4]**Franz Alexander** introduced the concept of a corrective emotional experience to explain the therapeutic effect of the transference. This conception has continued to retain validity as a facet of therapeutic effectiveness, although the contrived and somewhat manipulative measures advocated to achieve it have fallen into disfavor, since they work against the essence of the idea itself (Alexander 1954).

[5]**W. Ronald Fairbairn** felt that the implications for treatment of the metapsychology of his time were antithetical to that which he found helpful with patients. He then introduced a new and different way of conceptualizing human development and mental functioning, focusing on the centrality of object relations. Instinctual activity in this view was seen as object-seeking rather than discharge-seeking, which was a major contribution that opened the doors to an increasing awareness

A 14-year-old boy was referred due to his parents' and school's frustration in knowing how to handle him. He was almost always right and was fiercely determined to defend that position. He refused to do homework for school, since no one could give him a reason that he considered sensible. In addition, he could prove to school authorities that their reasoning was faulty. The authorities would then take an arbitrary stance and he would laughingly mock their attitude. The school officials were upset, but none of the actions they directed his way seemed to affect him. No matter what was tried he simply smiled or laughed. At home he was in a constant battle with his

---

of the therapist's role in the treatment. Thus he placed stress on the role of the analyst in effecting therapeutic change. The transference consists of a manifestation of behavior originating in a closed system, while a real relationship with an external object occurs in an open system. To the extent that the inner world assumes the form of a closed system, therefore, a relationship with an external object is only possible in terms of transference. Consequently, interpretation of transference phenomena is not enough in itself to promote a satisfactory change in the patient. Change is dependent upon the development of the patient's relationships between two persons in the outer world. Psychoanalytic treatment evolves into a struggle on the part of the patient to force the relationship with the analyst into the closed system of the internal world through the agency of the transference. The therapist, however, is determined to effect a breach in this closed system, and to provide conditions under which the patient can be induced to accept the open system of outer reality. Fairbairn felt that the classic restrictions of the psychoanalytic situation were arbitrary. The emphasis on the need to protect the patient from the influence of the analyst's personality might very well be a rationalization covering a need of the analyst to be protected from the patient's demands. His conceptions went far in showing the extent to which the actual relationship between patient and therapist is a decisive element in the treatment (Fairbairn 1957, 1958).

parents. In their words, he refused to face or accept
reality. He had many interests and was involved in numerous projects that required intense concentration and
work. They were limited to activities he enjoyed, however. He totally refused to extend himself if he wasn't
interested. He was creative and effective in what he did,
though only on his own terms. When given some other job
he would refuse and remain steadfast. There were also
episodes of extreme temper outbursts, particularly with
his mother or younger brother. These explosive moments
were usually triggered by some injustice and seemed to
have a large element of control. His mother felt very
guilty, as he was frequently accurate in his perceptions.
His father was a pragmatic person who wasn't concerned
with the quality of his son's academic performance but
was worried about his inability to live "within the system." The son was generally seen as being spoiled, lazy,
undisciplined, living by the dictates of his grandiosity, and
unable to adapt to the world of reality. Earlier there had
been several attempts to seek professional help, though he
refused to return after one or two sessions. He didn't
object to or resist going, he only refused to return after a
short try.

He came willingly to his first appointment as he had
done in the past and talked openly of his parents' and
school's concern. His description paralleled what was
presented by his parents. When he saw a reason for doing
something he did it gladly, but no one gave him valid
reasons that made sense to him. Furthermore, if he voiced
an objection no one showed him where he was wrong.
They only insisted that he do as others did, or stated that
it was in his best interests. He spoke of his many and varied
activities and of his friends. He valued relationships highly
and was deeply concerned with injustices and moral
issues. He mentioned two people he had found who gave
him good reasons for doing things. One was a piano
teacher. He played the piano by ear and was pleased by his

ability to do pretty well, although everyone was upset because he refused to learn to read music. They saw his talent and were angry that he did little to develop it. The piano teacher didn't try to teach him music but tried to help him further his own skills. He gave him disciplined exercises to follow and explained how they would foster his innate potential. The other was a Hebrew teacher who explained the importance of learning the language. He had begun with no intention of learning, but when the teacher talked with him about the language being a way of establishing a linkage to his forefathers he then applied himself. This teacher talked about the importance of being a unique and separate individual, and he was so impressed he invested himself in studying the new language. At this point he stopped to ask me what I thought about all that he had said.

In listening to this child's desperate fight to maintain his autonomy, separateness, and individuality I was becoming aware of my unconscious sensitivity to his underlying vulnerability. Until now this had been only hinted at and largely left unsaid. I was also aware that he had been giving me derivatives expressing what he needed from me if a working relationship was to be established. Taking all of this into account I told him that I thought he had shown me some of his most valued qualities. They seemed to express how far he would go to make sure he would not conform to anyone else's expectations, with the strength to stand up for his beliefs and emphasize his uniqueness. I also heard how crucial it was for me to give him a reason for us to meet and work together. I wondered if his question wasn't coming from his sensing that I had a feeling there was a lot left unspoken, which probably had much more to say about a reason for him to see me.

He immediately responded by asking somewhat defiantly, "What do you mean?" I told him that I thought he was fighting very hard for his rights but was not very effective, and I sensed there were things he hadn't mentioned that hampered him a lot. Furthermore, when he had told me about his piano and Hebrew teachers I thought he was describing what he needed from me if we were to continue in a meaningful way. He then stated, "I want you to listen. There are a lot of things I can't talk about. I know this is a place for me to talk, but there are some things I just won't tell you." He was absolutely adamant in his refusal. I remarked that I thought he was talking about things he didn't want to speak of all the time and therefore thought he must be wondering if I would ignore what I heard or whether I wouldn't let him know when I did hear something. Much later he informed me that it was at this moment that he decided to be involved in treatment. He began to feel for the first time that it might be possible for him to talk.

In the early months he spoke a lot about his wide-ranging interests. In his descriptions a constant theme inadvertently slipped out. It had to do with an internal sense of danger, injury, and destruction. When it would "slip out" he made a joke of it. For example, while describing his interest in magic he would laughingly wonder what someone would do if he were missing a finger, or he wondered how a person with no arms could use a computer. On one occasion he came in tearfully and signaled me to be quiet. He went on to say that he couldn't talk and wanted me just to forget about it. He immediately joked about the impossibility of forgetting something when someone told you to do that. Slowly and hesitatingly he began to reveal a fear that he had never put into words to anyone. He was terrified when he went to bed each night, feeling there was someone in the closet who would come out and destroy him. He knew it was ridiculous and made no sense. He always engaged in various rituals to distract himself. He was totally mortified to find himself so frightened. The result was he had a great deal of trouble getting to sleep, which no one knew. He had kept it hidden, feeling that it was a sign of weakness. He was even shocked that he was telling me now, though he didn't know what to do about it, for telling it made it no better and no worse. He did, however, go on to elaborate upon his fears. He had just learned of a beloved grandfather's serious illness and felt himself getting scared of the idea of death. This was what had reminded him of his fear. He wanted me to remain silent so he could bring it up in his own way—he didn't want me to pull it out of him. The following session took place shortly afterward.

I had received an upsetting phone call just prior to the session. When he came in he looked at me and asked, "Do you believe in ESP?" Before I could answer, he went on to tell me of his interest in ESP, telekinesis, reincarnation, and other mystical phenomena. He expanded on how careful he had to be as to whom he told about it. "People think you're crazy if you believe in these things. Unless they believe it too they think of you as strange. If they believe in it then you can share your ideas and experiences." While he was talking I gradually became aware that I had not processed the previous phone call very well and its effects had lingered as he entered the room. I was still involved with the "craziness" of the phone call and it appeared as though he had unconsciously perceived it. I told him that I thought he sensed some disturbance in me and was concerned that it would color how I heard him. He became silent and then thought of his piano teacher, who was helpful and encouraged him to play well. He returned to talking about ESP and the things he sensed in other people. He gave many examples of coincidences that he seemed to anticipate and reflected upon his ability to pick up on unconscious messages. He looked up at me and asked, "Was there something? Will you tell me?"

I said I thought he was checking to see if I was now ready to listen because I hadn't been at first. He became pensive and talked of how preoccupied he'd been with his fear of a monster in his closet. He suddenly became aware that what he feared was inside him, not outside him. He had been exquisitely sensitive to feelings in other people, which made him feel that everything he feared was outside him. That's what confused him about the closet. He knew there was no one there, but the fear was exactly the same as if there were someone there and he had sensed it. It made him feel that there was someone hidden and he was sensing their presence, just as he sensed unseen things in others. He was now aware, both in sensing the unspoken in others and in his fear of the closet, that it was connecting with feelings inside himself. He was surprised at being able to think about his fears. He could look at his own thoughts the same way that he looked at another person when he tried to decipher their unconscious communications. He stopped and added, "There's one thing I've never told you. It looks to everyone like I'm very creative and do a lot. The truth is I never complete anything." He described coming to the end of any project and abruptly abandoning it. He would feel scared and try to make it look as though he had finished. "There's something about ending a job that's scary. When I said that a song went through my head—I'll bet that's a message from inside me." He paused and remarked that he felt silly, though he knew it was important. "I want to be able to let things come into my mind and think about them."

He puzzled about the song and remembered it was entitled, "My Life." The lines had to do with someone's life being cut off, and the song was telling him that to finish a task was like ending his life. He felt so terrified of his life suddenly stopping that he couldn't complete anything. It was like something in the closet. He stopped and laughed. "I just had a funny thought. Something in the closet feels like something in my mind that I've kept closed off. It's trying to come out and give me a message." He now reveled in how good it felt to think this way. Previously he could only be afraid, pull back, avoid thinking, and then feel humiliated about pulling away. He felt like he was expanding inside and it allowed him to think.

He then recalled a story his mother told him that never made sense until this moment. She had told him that as an infant he was extremely special to her. When he began to assert himself she would get so enraged that she couldn't tolerate it and beat him. She hated herself for it and went into treatment. Later his brother was born and she involved herself with him in a similar way. My patient had reacted to the birth and early infancy of his brother with all of the reactions she thought came from the first period of trauma. The first instance was at less than 1 year; the second was at age 3. The intensity of his hostility to his mother made her think it came from the period of his infancy. What he understood was that whenever he looked at his brother he always wanted to hit him in a particular manner. He liked his brother, so this reaction was puzzling. He realized that the way he wanted to hit his brother was identical to the way his mother described hitting him. At this point he noted the hour ending, which was uncharacteristic for him, and simply left.

This was a child with vast potential who gave evidence of having had a good early period of mothering that was traumatically ruptured as he moved toward individuation. His fierce fight to maintain his separateness and autonomy barely concealed the vulnerability that was constantly in the background. There was an underlying anticipation of either achieving total gratification by an all-giving nurturer, which appeared to balance the threat of helplessness, or conversely, an expectation that demands would be imposed upon him or that he would be subtly seduced into submitting out of need, which intensified his push for independence. In either direction his unspoken appeal for help in facing his fears went unheard.

He was hungry to find people he could admire and identify with in order to strengthen his adaptive capacities, which reflected his attempt at self-cure. He was trying to strengthen his considerable resources and master the nameless dreads that were a constant companion. The

qualities he sought were best expressed in his description
of his piano and Hebrew teachers. They involved the
support and encouragement of his autonomy, while being
responsive to his efforts at mastery. He saw himself as the
recipient of everything from the world and did not feel
satisfied unless he was in charge. At the same time,
however, he was depleted in his adaptive capacities, was
unable to realize his potentials, and thus sought whatever
influences an object had to offer that could strengthen his
ability to function. This is what he had found to some
extent with his teachers and was probing for in his treatment. In the beginning it was important for him to know
what I could contribute; later it became important for me
to know him better. He was caught in a terrible dilemma.
Because he could not regulate his internal world, his
dependency upon others was exaggerated. He was thus
driven to create interactions in which prohibitions would
be enforced, but at the same time he had to actively assert
his autonomy, since he couldn't allow himself to feel
dependent. He sought external objects to fight against in
order to gain some degree of regulation, and then had to
be justified in the battle in order to deny their importance.
Concomitantly he was reaching to identify with an autonomous figure who would in no way either engulf or
impose upon him.

In his initial humiliation at being unable to describe his
difficulty he took the defensive stance of refusal. He
anticipated and feared that I would expect him to talk
about the things he could hardly even think about. With all
of his intellectual capacities and vast array of skills, he was
incapable of dealing with what threatened him most. In
addition, in order for him to be successful at any task it
required that he perceive what was most frightening, and
he was immobilized. During this phase of the treatment he
was identifying with my therapeutic attitude, as well as
finding a new, more constructive response to his infantile

dilemma, which enabled him to become introspective and begin to integrate his deepest anxieties. The influences of a good object, which were so vital to him, were colored by his enormous need to be as special as he was to his mother in the early oral period, and also by the frightening prohibitions growing out of his experience with his father, whom he secretly longed for and admired. At first his identification with my interpretive attitude was parallel with these infantile representations. The experience of having his unconscious perceptions validated helped in freeing his identification with me of its infantile roots. This constructive response was just what he needed in order to see his infantile dilemma clearly, as it was so different than what he expected.[6] Subsequently he could slowly and more effectively establish self-regulation and could think and be introspective. Eventually, his phobia was no longer in evidence.

His continuing growth was reflected in later sessions, as the flow of associative material revealed a proliferation of instinctual derivatives without producing a phobic situation. He portrayed the status of orality in his feeling motivated to lose weight. There was an intense hunger fueling an enormous appetite, but he felt a sense of mastery and regulation in channeling it. Anal qualities extended into his being drawn to gaining sadistic control over external objects and there was much conflict associated with his sadistic aggression. Phallic constellations

---

[6]**Edith Weigert** was one of several clinicians who noted and called attention to the influence of the therapist's personality. She observed how mitigation of superego rigidity was a precondition for change, which was accomplished by the personal influence of the therapist in the role of an auxiliary superego. She was reflecting upon the fine line between nondirective interpretations and directive reeducation, and she emphasized the need for flexibility (Weigert 1954).

were abundant and for a time expressed a preoccupation with exhibitionistic activities and prohibited voyeuristic temptations. The latter were accompanied by anxiety, giving evidence of the beginning consolidation of castration anxiety as a signaling and regulatory structure. He had great difficulty revealing an emerging genital awareness. A budding oedipal conflict was shown in derivative associations of being charming to females and working hard to make their male friends jealous. Although these vivid instinctual derivatives were associated with anxiety, it was no longer at such a high level, and did not elicit a phobic response. The following session occurring months later was representative.

He began talking animatedly about telling several friends that he was in treatment. He recalled an earlier time when he had been fearful of their finding out, which would have been terribly humiliating. Now he valued the experience and felt comfortable in letting others know. He laughed as he discovered that several of those he told were also in therapy. He paused and spoke of a new girlfriend. He met her on a trip and fell deeply in love. She lived far away, which made it very painful to be so in love and to be so distant. He talked with her on the phone each week and felt an intense longing afterward. It was like being on a diet and seeing your favorite foods on display. Your appetite was whetted but not fulfilled. He paused and talked more of being intimately connected to this girlfriend. They were able to understand each other without words. I commented that as he talked about communicating without words it appeared to be his way of letting me know that he might be making a reference to our relationship. It reminded me of an earlier fear he had that he wouldn't be able to allow himself to experience such an intense attachment. He looked embarrassed and recalled how afraid he had been of feeling love for someone. At the time he thought he was being strong. Looking back, it seems like he was defensive and closed off. Now he felt open and willing to risk the experience. He sensed that it must have been like that with his mother when he was very young. He remembered worrying that he would never feel love for anyone, and now, though it is difficult, he values it highly. He could get hurt or rejected but that seemed relatively unimportant. Being able to love meant everything.

He had thus begun to experience an intense instinctual attachment and communicated this new development by describing his feeling in telling others about his treatment. He was committed to the relationship and valued it. His associating to an intense love relationship appeared to be a derivative expressing a genital instinctual attachment in the transference. This loved figure was far away and to a large extent unattainable. Simultaneously, the loved object was connected to him by a bond of empathic resonance that made the distance tolerable. The shift from an earlier narcissistic orientation, associated with infantile objects, to an object-related orientation, associated with new objects, was reflected in his narcissistic concerns over anticipating hurt and rejection, yet being enhanced in feeling love for an object. My interpretation of the transference meaning was followed by an expanded awareness of the effects of his developmental experiences upon his ability to love, and upon his need for protection against such an attachment.

This kind of interchange can only operate within a safe and secure psychological framework. Often a patient puts pressure on a therapist to alter, modify, rupture, or erode the solidity of that framework, which can be received by the therapist and become a source of information as to what is being projectively identified. A patient's input, however, also has the potential of being a powerful stimulus for a therapist to join in strengthening a pathological defense, inadvertently colluding with the living out of an unconscious fantasy or encouraging a destructive form of acting out. In doing so, the embedded unconscious communications remain hidden, the free flow of projective identifications is obstructed, and continuing integration and psychological growth is prevented.[7]

---

[7]**Andre Green,** responding to the problems presented by many patients who found the conditions of psychoanalytic treatment too restrictive, tried to present a more balanced perspective on how these difficult situations could be managed without altering the therapeutic framework. He believed the analyst's goals should be to give a container to the patient's content, and content to the patient's container. The analytic situation is the totality of the elements making up the analytic relationship, through which transference and countertransference may be observed, as a result of the establishment and limits of the analytic setting. The setting constitutes a silent and mute base that is both a non-self comparable to the body, and part of a facilitating environment. Certain patients cannot use the setting as a facilitating environment, which leads from an analysis of the contents to the analysis of the container. Thus the analyst must not only study the interaction but the space in which these relations develop, including its continuity and discontinuity. This type of experience often creates a confused impression within the analyst, who reacts by feeling a need to protect the setting. However, these experiences must be translated into verbal communications to the patient, which eventually lead to a coherent explanation. This work is only possible through the function of the analytic setting and the guarantees given by its constancy. The analytic situation is thereby isolated, creating an impossibility of discharge, closeness of contact, and limitations of experience within the setting itself. These qualities ensure that language will be used as a vehicle for thoughts, and that it will remain metaphorical (Green 1975).

Appropriate Management of the Treatment Framework as a Catalyst to Constructive Identifications

When a therapist is unable to contain and extract the unconscious meaning of a patient's input effectively, it increases the likelihood of pathological forces dominating the ensuing interaction, which obviates against any kind of positive identifications. Defensively motivated compensatory interventions are invoked instead, which eventually evoke negative introjects and prevent a therapeutic regression. Under such circumstances a therapist is not only missing an opportunity to interpret unconscious fantasies, but is also participating in a destructive collusion with distorting and pathological strivings. At best it is an obstacle to ongoing therapeutic work and often echoes with traumatic experiences from the past.[8]

---

[8]**Robert Dickes** reviewed the differences of opinion as to the value of modifications and gave his idea of what was appropriate. There were those who advocated good mothering to promote regressive dependency, but he believed this could promote such extensive regression that it could constitute an acting out in place of verbalization. Others advocated taking over responsibility in ways that gratified infantile needs. Although he thought these measures might on occasion be necessary, they tend to interfere with the analytic environment. He acknowledged that deviations in technique were probably necessary with more disturbed patients, for such measures can take on lifesaving dimensions. However, he stressed that regressions can occur when an analytic stance is maintained, even in the face of a patient's wish to be gratified directly. There are times when it is necessary to oppose such demands and impose technically correct frustrations, since continued gratification does not lead to remembering but to repeating. To gratify is to repeat childhood patterns with the patient. One must eventu-

It is important to distinguish the nature of the experiences being projectively identified, for they have different implications, depending upon whether good or bad self-experiences are involved. The need for a firm, unyielding treatment framework is particularly evident when a patient's bad self-experiences of instinctual overstimulation, reactions to impingement, and sensory deprivation are projected. It is precisely at these times that a therapist's capacity to accept the pressure, grasp its unconscious meaning, and offer unconsciously empathic interpretations is most needed. The consequence is that a patient feels more contained, so that disturbing regressive experiences can be represented. The framework of the treatment is thereby solidified as the healthy therapeutic alliance is strengthened, and all of this is validated by derivatives reflecting a patient's unconscious perception of the growth-promoting properties of the relationship. This was apparent in the treatment of a 17-year-old boy originally referred to me as a last resort.

He had been to three other therapists of differing orientations who determined his phobia to be untreatable. A family doctor had suggested seeing a psychoanalyst. He was a very bright, extremely intellectual, and well-groomed young man. He began by speaking of the outrage

---

ally risk an untoward reaction, and a disturbance in the working alliance is bound to occur. Through tact and proper timing these disruptions can be kept to a minimum. At the time of the disturbance special management and modifications may become necessary, and the analyst's role as a representative of reality then becomes more significant. These measures can help to strengthen the therapeutic alliance, which is basically reality oriented. Reintegration is promoted and reality testing restored. After sufficient ego reconstruction takes place it is necessary to analyze fully what has occurred, and to clarify the dangers inherent in such support (Dickes 1967).

he felt in not being able to overcome his fear of being in a classroom with other students. He felt helpless, and his inability to attend school had been managed through home teaching. He had an acute and pressing problem, however. He had a scholarship to college and if he didn't take an upcoming test he would lose it. He felt desperate; the time was getting closer, but he was totally unable to even think of entering a classroom. He went on to explain why he was so outraged. He described himself as smart and as accustomed to "commandeering" the classroom. It came as a big surprise to him when his symptom first appeared. Prior to this he had gloried in his classroom experience. He now felt as though his whole life was being ruined.

When he was younger he was teased about being a brain and felt like an outcast. With the passing years his peers became more mature and he wasn't teased as much. He felt fortunate that he was also an excellent athlete, because this cut down on the teasing. He proceeded to speak somewhat proudly of his athletic skills and achievements. A worried expression on his face deepened, and he expressed concern that I would misunderstand and perceive him to be bragging and arrogant. He was neither of these, but only wanted to make sure he gave an accurate picture of himself. To do so he had to tell me about his exceptional attributes. He then referred to the other therapists he had seen, as he went into some detail about his symptom. He would approach a classroom, become sick to his stomach, get a blinding headache, and have to return home. One therapist tried to desensitize him. After being encouraged to visualize the experience and failing several times, he was discharged. He then saw a nutritionist who treated him with special foods and vitamins, which seemed to help. This was during the summer. He felt stronger and believed the problem was solved. School began and his phobia was even more intense. Next he saw a third therapist who directed him to use his will power, which made him feel completely misunderstood, and he left. He was convinced he had a serious physical illness and saw his internist. When he was too frightened and refused to take a series of G.I. tests, the internist made the referral to me. Now he asked if I would be able to help, and furthermore, if it could be within a few weeks. He had to take the college tests and there was very little time.

I had been listening and thinking that an extended period of treatment would be necessary if change was to occur. In addition I was thinking about the anxiety he might be feeling about the separation inherent in finishing school. I commented on his desperation and wondered if he might be asking whether I, too, would be in a hurry. His response was to talk about the exam, stressing how much it meant to him. He assumed that I thought he was doing it to please someone else. Furthermore, I must have thought he was being pressured to take the exam and didn't necessarily want to take the test or go to college. Therefore he wanted to assure me, with all his heart and soul, that he wanted to take it and go off to school more than anything else in the world. He wanted to make absolutely sure that I understood this about him. Perhaps I meant that I could hear something going on inside of him that he knew nothing about. I remarked that he certainly seemed to be saying that he wasn't able to hear himself very well and needed help with that. He agreed and regular sessions were scheduled.

During the early hours he would often turn to look directly at me whenever he spoke and was surprised to see how frequently his mind went blank. He always had something to say, and this had never happened to him before. He thought of lying in his bed at night feeling scared that everything was out of control. Now he was scared because nothing came into his mind. He felt pressured to talk, which reminded him of the time pressure he felt in his life. After a few weeks he spoke of feeling safer, more secure and contained, and then recalled his thoughts when lying in bed. They were not so jumbled and chaotic but consisted of a vague feeling that he was in danger. It was like hearing footsteps and imagining that something he couldn't see was threatening him.

The following session took place just before the date of his college exam. He entered in a state of agitation, explaining that he had found a way to take the exam but it required a note from me. With the note he could be given the test by himself and would not have to go into the classroom. He asked if I would write it and I simply remarked, "Let's see what comes to mind." He thought of one example after another of being put down and considered incapable of becoming successful in anything he did. Whenever he finished something his parents diminished it. He launched into an angry tirade against them. His father was unappreciative and could never allow any show of feeling. His mother was excessively critical of him and considered him inept. He was chastised by both parents for being weak and infantile. He stopped and asked, "You haven't answered me, what about the note?" I said that he seemed to be asking if I thought he was ineffective also. He fell silent before expressing his strong feeling of disappointment. He had found a way to take the test and my words were implying that I wouldn't sign the note. I seemed to think that signing the note would be like insuring he would remain unable to function. At the end of the session he looked at me and said, "I guess what you're really telling me is that we'll have to wait and see what I do about the exam. If I really trust myself, whether I take it or not isn't important. It's what I do that's significant, and I need to understand that."

That night I received a telephone call from his parents. He had just stormed out of the house and they wanted advice as to what to do. I simply said that I wasn't able to talk to them. This session took place two days later. He began by referring to his parents' call and my response. After he had left his last session he was typing an essay about what it meant to look at your life in a new way. He was reminded of a book he read and of his identification with one of the characters who had done something beautiful. He had followed his heart. However, it had offended society so that their wrath descended upon him and led to his death. He was writing the essay to put into words what it meant to follow his heart.

While he was typing, his mother asked him to do a chore. He continued to type and she pulled out the sheet. He just exploded and pushed her. This made him feel devastated, and he ran out of the house to be alone. He was affected by the dawning realization that powerful emotions were present deep within him, and that they were creating his symptoms. The character in the book touched him so deeply that he couldn't get it out of his mind. He was aware of his feelings in a way he had never experienced before and had never been able to put into words. When it was quiet he could feel the voice of his mother inside saying, "I'm going to surround you. I'm going to kill you." It made him fearful that he would either die or kill himself, and he felt nauseated like he was trying to get rid of these inner sensations but could not. It felt like he was attached to his parents but he could neither let them go nor take them in.

Next he thought of the book and noticed he had not mentioned the details. He wanted to believe that I knew the story so he wouldn't have to talk about it. He sensed the specifics were connected to a vulnerable and sensitive part of himself that was just beginning to develop and grow. He felt so vulnerable that if he talked about it he would draw back instead of growing. He then fell silent. After a while he talked about the character he identified with who had a sexual relationship with the wife of a lordly figure. She became pregnant and had a baby. He saw the husband much as he saw his father, and himself as having some kind of hidden and special relationship with his mother. He now mentioned a younger brother for the first time. Watching his mother and brother gave him an eerie feeling, for they seemed to have a very special bond. It felt like he had either wanted such a relationship himself and embraced it vicariously, or that at some time in his life he might have been involved in a similar way. It frightened him to think about it.

This patient's attempts to modify the framework of the treatment by having me write a note made it possible for me to identify the way in which he unconsciously experienced me. He was pressuring me to deprecate, demean, criticize, and infantilize him. This much-needed information could then be included in an interpretation, which, in an immediate way, demonstrated the defensive function it was serving. He could see how his phobic symptom stood in the way of his growth toward becoming more separate from his infantile attachments. By virtue of my maintaining a firm interpretive stance, enough safety was provided for his underlying frightening oedipal fantasies to gain access to the integrative forces in his personality. Strengthened and supported by the internal presence of his identification with my search for knowledge and understanding, he could look at himself and his life in a new and different way. This stood in stark contrast to what he had experienced in the past. Had his demand been gratified, in all likelihood it would have only served to reinforce his pathological defenses and to pose a large obstacle to continuing progress. In this situation any modification of the conditions of the treatment was clearly unnecessary, and had they been introduced it would have been a product of some unresolved countertransference interference. Under such circumstances regressive cravings, reflective of the activity of pathological defenses, tend to escalate. At the same time, derivatives of unconscious perceptions give expression to the lack of safety, containment, and trust in the relationship. It then becomes imperative for the therapist to identify the source of the empathic lapse, rectify it, and interpret its effects, so that an unconsciously empathic environment can once again be established.

The Use of the Therapist as a Part of the Self in Strengthening Positive Identifications

A therapist has to determine carefully which features of the treatment situation are dictated by personal interests and be open to listening for clues as to what is in the best interests of the patient, in order to create the proper conditions for growth to evolve. The role of a therapist's functioning, personality, and behavior has emerged more and more clearly as a critical factor in treatment. Interpretations, though important, are simply not enough. Psychopathology originates from the effects of destructive experiences in early life, which are then perpetuated in exaggerated form in the internal world. Consequently, the actual relationship between a patient and therapist has to be regarded in some measure as constituting a curative factor of prime importance. It not only provides a means of correcting the distorted relationships that exist internally, but it also gives a patient the opportunity to undergo a process of emotional development in a safe setting with a reliable figure.[9]

---

[9]**Maxwell Gitelson** thought that a therapist's mode of functioning has a curative influence, particularly in the early phases of the treatment. It is during this period of time when a patient's readiness for transference leads to an attachment by way of a primitive narcissistic transference. The consequence is

The therapist is available to be used as a container for parts of the self that would be too frightening to experience otherwise, out of which a therapist's actual behavior has a mitigating influence. This may have to take place before any change can occur.

The symbolic use of a therapist, although a product of a defensive regression, is an essential aspect of forming a creative relationship to the world.[10] Ultimately it leads to a patient

---

in the patient's original development being represented, giving an opportunity for it to be revised. During this period the analyst offers the necessary support and guidance for development, integration, and maturation, serves as an auxiliary ego, and redirects narcissistic needs into object-libidinal needs. In this way the analyst's healing intention can maintain and support the patient, since it converges with the patient's need for support. The analyst's steadiness and offer of a certain amount of narcissistic gratification is essential to provide the patient with hope, though they must be limited, in order to create a proper amount of tension. The analyst's early role is not an unfortunate contamination related to suggestion, nor is it playing the part of a good object. The emphasis is on providing the patient with an auxiliary ego, so that he can develop his own intrinsic potentials (Gitelson 1962).

[10]**Marion Milner** also believed that the curative factors involved in psychoanalytic treatment went beyond interpretation. She speculated about one facet, which she related to the developmental period of symbol formation. Self-created reality and states of illusion are important. When the loss of belief in them occurs prematurely, or is prevented from occurring with sufficient frequency and at the right moments, there are detrimental effects. If there is too much early frustration, the child experiences the pressure of unsatisfied needs and becomes aware too soon or too continually of a separate identity. The environment best fosters growth by providing conditions that' make possible a recurrent partial return to the feeling of oneness with it. It does so by providing a frame, space, time, and a pliable medium, so that it will not always be necessary for

allowing external objects to exist in their own right, enabling self-assertiveness to be expressed without undue anxiety as the harshness of internal prohibitions are alleviated. This therapeutic feature of the actual relationship was demonstrated in the treatment of a very bright and verbal 7-year-old boy.

He was described as an ideal child in his first 6 years, neat, orderly, and conforming. He was the only male grandchild and the "apple of his grandparents' eyes." When he was 6½, both grandparents died within a short period of time. He then appeared fearful, developed a series of bedtime rituals, and demanded that his family participate in them. He had to follow a set sequence. Any interruption precipitated a temper tantrum or panic attack. His rituals were expanding and the family, especially his father, were feeling like hostages to his emotional well-being. In addition he couldn't tolerate his parents' leaving for an evening and began to experience school difficulties for the first time. He couldn't complete even easy reading assignments, and would labor for hours on a simple task before tearing it up in frustration at the slightest mistake.

In the beginning of his treatment he found it very difficult to talk. He sat immobilized, was compliant, and appeared eager to please. He described his symptoms but couldn't see any reason for feeling so overwhelmed and was both curious and puzzled by his reactions. As time went on and his symptoms increased in severity, he did worse in school, which was a profound blow to him. He became more hesitant, fearful, and unable to communicate verbally during his sessions. He looked frustrated by his

---

self-preservation's sake to distinguish clearly between inner and outer, self and non-self. In psychoanalysis the patient is able to find a moldable bit of the external world that is safe to treat as a part of the self, which then serves as a bridge between inner and outer. For some patients this experience is a significant curative factor (Milner 1952).

inability to talk and in the few words he did say he expressed his feeling that talking was a demand he just wasn't able to live up to. He didn't ask questions, however, or seem to expect anything from me.

With much hesitation he finally revealed he had been holding back some important things. He felt so guilty he just couldn't say them, though they had been on his mind from the first moment he saw me. He mustered up his courage and with great difficulty began to describe the deaths and funerals of his grandparents. Everyone around him had been devastated at the loss, whereas he had felt very little. He masked his inner feeling and pretended to be sad. The funerals were in fact exciting to him, because there was a lot of activity and he found it very stimulating. It wasn't until after these events that he started to feel scared and guilty. The following session took place just after this revelation.

He came in talking rapidly. All he could think about were numbers. He counted everything he saw and had to end on a number that matched the number of members in his family. If he stopped at three he feared a disaster could occur; if he stopped at five he was terrified of being all alone. He had to stop at four or eight or twelve. He was preoccupied with numbers and couldn't concentrate on anything else. He also couldn't read at school. He constantly expected the next word to make him think of something awful. He was fearful of tests because he had to read. If he was asked questions it didn't frighten him; it was reading that was intolerable. At home he was also becoming more afraid. He had to check the oven to see if the gas was off and then go back since he might have accidentally turned it on. When he got into bed he had to be careful not to touch the "bad" parts of his body. He had rituals to cleanse himself and then had to be careful not to contaminate himself. If he touched an exposed part he had to wash his hands. He didn't know what was happening to him. His hands were becoming red from washing so much.

In the face of all of this, however, he had discovered a way to go to sleep and didn't know if he could tell me. He stopped, started, hesitated, repeated his worry about saying it aloud, paused, and plunged on. "I have this fantasy that I am the President. I've been afraid to tell you because if I say it out loud the President will be killed." He wanted to bring it out in the open but now felt worried that the President would be shot. I said I thought he was afraid of the sexual feelings that his symptoms were both hiding and expressing, and afraid that my recognition would shoot down the fantasy that protected him. He became silent and talked about a friend he had invited to sleep over. They got involved in sexual play by touching each other. It was extremely exciting but he wondered if he was a homosexual. He fantasied himself growing up to be a politician and feared this childhood event would be exposed, publicly humiliating him. I remarked that I thought he was telling me about how guilty he felt whenever he was sexually aroused. His response was, "Oh I forgot to tell you. One of the things I worry about is the faucet dripping. By the way do you have a faucet in here?"

This response made me aware of my own feeling of excitement at the change in his ability to communicate. When he spoke of the leaking faucet I wondered if he wasn't unconsciously perceiving this feeling in me, and in asking about my faucet questioning whether I was aware of it. I then realized that his memory of sexual play was a derivative expressing his unconscious experience in the relationship with me. I referred to his sensing my excitement over the way he was talking, and how it seemed to make him afraid that I was getting excited by his sexual fantasies and wouldn't be able to contain it. He immediately said that the faucet that leaked in his house was in the bathroom. He frequently went to check it and noticed his mother undressing in the bedroom as he passed. "Oh, I almost forgot. My father asked me if he could talk to you."

He proceeded to describe his father's anger at being enslaved by him, accusing the son of controlling the house by controlling his mother. With great relief he said that he knew I wouldn't talk to his father without his permission and it felt very good to be able to say no to his father by himself.

In the beginning, this child's inability to talk, combined with his strong efforts to be pleasing, reflected how much he was experiencing the relationship as extremely prohibitive and dangerous. His own harsh prohibitions were projected onto me, but my therapeutic stance and manner of conducting the relationship were gradually having an ameliorating influence, until he was able to reveal the things that were of concern to him. In doing so once again, the intensity of the threats he anticipated from me came forward. Although my interpretation of his fear of exposing his sexual feelings was helpful, and brought forth a memory of sexual play with a friend, the quality of the relationship itself was making it possible for his thoughts to flow more freely. Initially I had heard this as a validation of my interpretation, but in the background I was becoming aware of my own excitement. My comment about his guilt was thus somewhat off, though the fact that it was not attacking enabled him to continue to associate. His thought about the leaking faucet was a response to my excitement, expressing his anxiety that I wouldn't be able to contain it and help him with the powerful instinctual experiences that he was feeling.

My validation of his unconscious perception of this aspect of my reactions, along with an interpretation of his fear of my sexual arousal, evoked an image of a sexually provocative mother and an enraged father. He felt contained and could allow this perception of his mother as a genital sexual object, eliciting the prohibitive presence of his father. In being open to receive his input, taking it seriously, and correcting a mistake, I had supported his latent ability to do likewise.[11] His sense of self was on firmer ground, so that previously defended unconscious fantasies could be granted access to consciousness, which reminded him of standing up to his father. He was thus much more in touch with this assertive part of himself that had previously been too dangerous to permit. My attitude amplified his positive, constructive identifications and strengthened the psychological underpinnings he needed to face and integrate his conflicted instinctual strivings. As this child's treatment illustrated, it has become increasingly apparent that a therapist's emotional responsiveness and altruistic mode of functioning play a critical part in whatever interventions ultimately prove to have a curative influence.[12]

---

[11]**Harold Searles,** a strong advocate of flexibility in technique, felt it was essential to be guided by a patient's unconscious directions. He was concerned lest the analyst's rigid adherence to a classically psychoanalytic orientation, remaining oblivious to the nuclei of reality in the patient's transference, would tend to foster being precisely as unacknowledging of the patient's therapeutic strivings as the original traumatic partner (Searles 1975).

[12]**Pieter Kuiper, Angel Garma, Pearl King, and Paula Heimann** discussed the role of a therapist's personality and behavior in a symposium exploring the curative factors in psychoanalysis. Kuiper discriminated between two types of patients, for whom the curative elements differed. Patients with defects in ego functioning initially did not require the solution of a conflict but the creation of a climate for maturation. Patients exhibiting a classical neurosis needed interpretations with analysis centered upon intrapsychic conflict. King emphasized the central importance of the quality of the analytic situation for the cure of the patient, viewing treatment as freeing the patient of any major obstacles to the inherent integrative processes so that maturation could resume. Although this was accomplished through the interpretation of a patient's unconscious fears, the relationship to the analyst was

unique. It functioned as a therapeutic tool, involving a stance in which a commitment to help the patient was central, and any effort to transform it must be resisted and analyzed. Heimann stressed the importance of the analyst's dedicated attitude, which afforded the patient a sense of security. In her opinion, countertransference was the instrument for research into the patient's unconscious, while the dangers of empathy must not be overlooked. A mothering type of attitude did promote the patient's developmental drives, but the use of measured gratifications overstated the analogy between mother and analyst. She believed the analyst was an important curative factor, particularly by being able to take on the dual role of the patient's transference objects and transference self (Kuiper et al. 1962).

4

The Place of Regression in Enabling Continuity of Experience

Activating Developmental Processes through a
   Therapeutic Regression
The Interplay of the Preconscious and
   Unconscious Systems in a Benign Regression
Profound Regression and the Need for Changes
   in Technique
A Therapeutic Regression and the Relationship
   between a Therapist's Management,
   Containing, and Interpretive Functions

Activating Developmental Processes through a Therapeutic Regression

A therapeutic relationship is conducted so as to encourage and foster the unfolding of the transference, which sets into motion the representations of infantile experience at the source of the pathology—during the developmental years. In the well-structured cohesive personality, transferences are expressed in an object relationship that embodies a relatively advanced level of differentiation. Transferences in the less-well-structured, noncohesive personality are expressed in an object relationship that is more primitive, narcissistic, and poorly differentiated. The mechanism of projective identification is operative in all human interactions. The form it takes in a transference relationship is determined by the level and nature of a patient's regression and a therapist's capacity to receive and internalize these communications. In order to support this process, the conditions of the treatment must be in accord with the psychic organization of a patient's personality, because there is no opportunity for positive therapeutic influence if a patient's psychic contents are rejected, interrupted, interfered with, or not internalized. The regressive transference experiences that must be reached before constructive growth can be realized flourish only within clearly defined boundaries and ground rules, although the manner in which these conditions are applied will vary from one situation to another. Attempting to establish the proper conditions with a preformed set of rules introduces a relationship that is not conducive to a free flow of projective identifications.

Regression can be manifested in benign and malignant forms, making it vital to distinguish between them. A benign regression involves the discovery of previously inaccessible internal experiences, whereas a malignant regression involves the search for reinforcement of pathological defenses. Attachments to an object that facilitate growth and structural change occur in the presence of a benign regression, which demands that a therapist participate but not interfere. The treatment framework, consisting of appropriately flexible conditions, ground rules, and boundaries, serves to provide the security and safety required in the background to allow the regression to be sustained. In this regard interpretive interventions are of secondary importance. A malignant regression is manifested in cravings or demands for action and/or immediate gratification. It is the direct product of pathological defenses that incorporates poorly differentiated amalgams of bad qualities of experience. Reinforcing these defensive structures works in opposition to the unfolding of a benign regression, elevating interpretive interventions to a position of primary importance.

The differences between a benign and malignant regression were manifested in the treatment of a 7-year-old boy originally seeking help for night terrors, which had begun shortly after his parents divorced. In the beginning he was constantly preoccupied with emphasizing his strength and prowess; he reassured himself endlessly of his invulnerability and repeatedly commented upon his bravery and fearlessness. Although it was clear that he was fighting hard to ward off even the slightest move toward experiencing regressive feelings, he put tacit but powerful pressure on me to join him in being impressed by these displays of "strength." In spite of my awareness that he was defending himself against infantile longings, along with whatever instinctual wishes and conflicts they contained, I found myself drawn into avoiding an interpretive posture. An unrecognized regressive identification with his plight had made me reluctant to confront his irritability, which was not explicitly apparent but which surfaced periodically whenever he needed help in reaching something or managing some object he had brought to play with. Such moments would usually precipitate a loud protest that he could do everything himself, even while he was enlisting my assistance, while I simply complied without interpreting either his defensive attitude or the feelings of helplessness just beneath the surface. I rationalized my conduct, believing that the alliance was not strong enough to allow him to express disturbing experiences with me or that the intensity of his underlying feelings was too great for him to bear.

His demands for me to get things for him, sit in a particular place, or move something to make him more comfortable gradually increased until I realized my behavior was reinforcing his defenses and serving no observable constructive purpose. Furthermore, the prospect of a session ending would bring forth tears, which he would frantically try to deny before creating some aggressively hostile interchange that seemed designed to justify the attitude he had taken. It now became apparent that he was in the grips of a malignant regression. My behavior was resonating with infantilizing interactions from the past, adding to his distress and contributing little toward enlarging his self-knowledge and awareness. I finally got a clear idea of the part I was playing and how it served to amplify his pathological defenses.

I told him that I thought he was showing me how much he needed me to be firm in helping him to see what was behind his conviction that he was brave, fearless, and unable to be hurt. In addition, when I just followed his orders he didn't feel very safe, and I could see how hard it would then be to tell me or even himself what was happening inside. He could obviously sense the change in my attitude and fell quiet for a moment, looking more relaxed. The undercurrent of tension that had been almost continually present seemed to dissipate. He began to talk about incidents involving his mother and father, placing emphasis on the different way they each treated him and how painful and confusing it was. His mother babied him, often commiserating with him about what she thought were his father's excessive demands. His father actively encouraged him to be big and strong and reacted disapprovingly to any tears or clinging behavior, attributing it to his mother's overprotectiveness. He felt pulled in two directions. It was confusing because sometimes he wanted to be babied and yet it kept him from doing things himself. He also wanted to be strong like his father, but he got mad when he was forced. He remembered his parents' divorce and the fighting that led up to it. Tears formed as he referred to how alone and scared he felt.

He thought of all these feelings as his "baby parts," because they made him cry. He wanted to leave them with me so they wouldn't bother him, and looked pleased when I welcomed his "baby parts," agreeing to hold them until he was ready to have them back. Shortly afterward he reported a dream. Although it was somewhat scary he felt good about it, since he didn't wake up terrified as he had always done before. In the dream he was lying in bed and "my nightmares jumped out of my head and into the closet." One was a monster who began to cry when he attacked it, and it became his friend, while the other was a big angry tiger who scared him and ate up all his toys. He spontaneously stated that he thought the nightmares were like his "baby parts"; he was trying to take them back but there just wasn't enough room.

The therapeutic relationship was starting to make it possible for him to gain access to regressive experiences, though he was having difficulty in integrating their meaning. The dream suggested that he could now face the danger from a regressed position with some degree of mastery, and as a result could even represent one nightmare as an ally. The other nightmare, most likely symbolizing instinctual activity, did remain extremely frightening. However, he was at least able to continue the dream rather than awakening in terror as he had in the past. The reporting of the dream in and of itself was indicative of the shift that was taking place. He was much more involved in bringing out and expressing what was happening inside of him than of finding a way to distract himself from it. Gradually, as he put it, he was accepting his "baby parts," which was apparent in his whole demeanor. A preoccupation with being strong was no longer in evidence, and a wide range of emotions was available to him without the push inside to deny their presence. Perhaps more importantly, his response to my interventions was quite noticeable. Accurate, well-timed interpretations were welcome and fostered the flow of derivative material, whereas any lapse in empathy made him openly fearful.

The change was reflected in a later session, which began with him eager to draw me a map that would show where a treasure was hidden in a cave. He continued to elaborate upon the fantasy, calling special attention to the obstacles he would face as he entered the cave. With mounting excitement he hinted at the incredible elation he would experience if he were successful in reaching the treasure,

reminding himself of the dangers he would have to overcome first. The erotic innuendoes in his description of the
treasure, and the harsh prohibitions preventing access to it
in his description of the obstacles, were unmistakable.
Whether it had reference to some hidden masturbatory
impulse or emerging sexual fantasy was not clear, but
there did appear to be an element of sexual arousal in his
excitement. I commented on the sexual meaning of the
treasure, and related it to his feeling aroused. He stopped,
looked frightened, mumbled something about being afraid
of me, and left the office. Shortly thereafter he cautiously
put his head in the doorway, and I said I thought he was
putting out a feeler to see if I had any recognition of how
my words had hurt him. He came in and I went on to say
that when I spoke of sexual feelings it seemed to make me
become very dangerous. He picked up a toy figure, stating
that this was what had frightened him, adding that he was
no longer afraid because it wasn't real. He then went back
to his drawing and this time wanted me to notice that the
treasure was buried. He also pointed out that the contents
would not be revealed until it was opened. He smiled as he
underscored the importance of finding the treasure himself.

Within the arms of a secure framework, a benign regression was now allowing derivatives to flow more freely,
establishing a firmer connection between the unconscious
and conscious systems. An ill-timed, countertransference-
based interpretation interrupted the continuity between
these differing realms of experience. The therapeutic alliance was intact, however, and he could search for a way to
reestablish what had been lost. My recognition of the
countertransference problem was implicit in my interpretation of his return to the office. After identifying the
effect it had upon him, he could once again pick up on the
theme that was being expressed. This time he approached
it with a lesser degree of anxiety, confident he could
uncover what was hidden as he worked his way through

the defenses he had constructed, for I had heard his unconscious message.

In the initial phase of the treatment this patient had pressured me into gratifying his regressive cravings, and I had unknowingly joined him in strengthening a pathological defense. It had led to an escalation of his demands for more of the same, thereby undermining his latent resources. The contained framework he needed to support a benign regression was compromised, obviating against establishing continuity of experience and achieving structural change. When I was able to recognize the regressive identification at the root of my countertransference-based behavior I could alter my posture, making it possible to identify and provide the conditions he needed to promote growth. In place of gratifying his demands, I acknowledged my failure in empathy, and interpreted its effects upon him. When I corrected my mistake and offered him the firm framework he required, he could see the debilitating effect of his defenses. He could also see how I had re-created infantilizing interactions from the past, making him distrustful of my ability to help him. The positive influences of a now-firm framework made a benign regression possible, facilitated by the constructive identifications mobilized by my empathic interpretative attitude. My words no longer had to be defended against, so their meaning could reach him and resonate with his infantile wishes and conflicts. It underscored the importance of a solid, firm but flexible, treatment framework in offering the best opportunity for realizing whatever his potential was to achieve developmental progression and psychological growth.

With this background of safety, the empathic resonance with psychic contents that either could not be perceived or were too weakly represented to be viable had the effect of strengthening the continuity of his experience that had previously been lacking. Early in the treatment he was manifesting a malignant regression, shown by the intensification of his regressive cravings, the demand for action and immediate gratification, and his somewhat frantic search for me to join him in reinforcing a pathological defense. Instead of interpreting the unconscious significance of this interaction, I participated in it, which only served to infantilize him and repeat a developmental experience antithetical to his growth. When I finally became aware of the part I was playing and was open to receiving his projective identifications, a source of information was available to me for formulating an interpretation. The resulting diminution in the need for defense facilitated the continuity of his unconscious and conscious worlds of experience, which in turn deepened my capacity to understand and interpret. The shift to a benign regression was evident, as infantile strivings and the associated conflicts they engendered became accessible to integrative work. The containing influence of a well-managed therapeutic framework with clearly defined boundaries and ground rules provided the security required for a regressive transference relationship to unfold, eventuating in a dissolution of his pathological defenses. A pathway was thus outlined for achieving a structural change, as the ensuing benign regression expanded the range of his self-awareness and self-knowledge.

The Interplay of the Preconscious and Unconscious Systems in a Benign Regression

The transference is the vehicle for an interaction between a patient's intrapsychic world and the outside world of objects, represented by the therapist in a treatment relationship. In addition, the transference fosters a larger amount of interplay between the preconscious and unconscious, activating the process of transforming primary process into secondary process. This kind of intercommunication of unconscious to preconscious, maintained through the relationship with a therapist, emerges as a significant growth-promoting element in the treatment.[1]

An example of this constructive factor was shown well into the treatment of a young boy, who had begun therapeutic contact at the age of 7. He was referred when all of the people in his surrounding environment felt totally helpless in finding a way to deal with his inability or refusal to complete anything. His wild, clowning, disruptive behavior alternated with periods of profound depression and explosive temper tantrums, usually in response to a demand or frustrating task. The overall picture was of a controlling, greedy, highly manipulative child who managed to engage one adult after another into feeling sorry for him and taking care of him.

Initially he was seen one time per week because the idea of meeting more frequently evoked an intense negative reaction. The first two years were occupied with his teasing and spinning fantasies about his wishes and hopes.

---

[1]**Hans Loewald** argued against the idea that there was such a thing as a real relationship without transference. In his view, treatment reopens the transformations from primary into secondary processes. Thus the patient is tempted to seek improvement through unsublimated satisfaction in the therapeutic interaction, a level closer to the primary process, and the analyst mediates a higher organization to the patient as long as there is a strong-enough positive transference and the analyst is in tune with the patient's productions. The patient, in attempting to reach the analyst as a representative of the higher stages of reality organization, thereby creates insight through language communication. This is only feasible if the analyst reveals himself as a more mature person (Loewald 1960).

Many were explosively aggressive and some highly eroticized. There were repeated efforts either to entice me or
force me into joining him in his manipulative conniving
plots, or in the acting out of his fantasies. He would tease
me about my interpretive responses. This deprecatory
teasing, however, was always associated with a feeling of
relief that I remained firm and consistent. Slowly he made
both himself and me aware of his deep inner sense of
inadequacy, covered up by his provocations and manipu-
lations. When I was able to address the depth of his
separation anxiety, it led to his wanting to come in
frequently, and we then met three times per week.

The threat of fragmentation was reflected in his frequent nightmares and in the high levels of anxiety he
experienced whenever he was separated from familiar
objects. The sessions that were most difficult for him were
those in which he felt empty, worthless, blocked, and
restless. At these times he appeared as though he could
hardly tolerate keeping himself within the confines of the
office. In his efforts to deal with this anxiety, he found a
plastic egg-shaped puzzle that broke down into many
pieces and could be reassembled. He wanted to use it to
help himself talk and not run from the office. The following session took place at this point in the therapy.

He entered the office, took out the puzzle, and began to
put it together. While he worked at it he spoke of his
difficulty when something didn't fit right away. He
wanted to discipline himself to be able to stick with it and
search for and find just the right piece. I responded by
metaphorically relating the pieces of the puzzle to the
parts of himself. At first he reacted with delight and
elaborated upon the metaphor. However as the session
was ending he said, partly with the teasing deprecatory
quality that characterized how he reacted to interpretations, but also with a note of sadness and despair, "What
good does it do to talk about pieces of a puzzle. What does
that have to do with me?" I said I thought it had every-

thing to do with him, including his attempt to deal with his feelings about the separation between us at the end of the hour. His questions had helped me to see how sad he felt about having to leave, along with some despair that he couldn't be helped with it when my words didn't make it any better. He remained silent for the final minute or two and left looking dejected.

The next session took place after a weekend, and he came in looking extremely excited and eager to talk. He had been invited to someone's house over the weekend. This was an activity he had always avoided before, but on this occasion he decided to go. When it came time to go to sleep he got panicky and felt the temptation to return home. Instead he thought he could at least try to stay in bed for a little while and began to think about the puzzle he had been working on in my office. He thought of my words and a question popped up in his mind. "What are these pieces of myself? They must be the things I feel and think about." He then allowed himself to be filled with and observe whatever entered his mind. First, he thought of his interest in *Playboy* magazine and his sexual excitement. This immediately led to a recollection of masturbatory experiences, which carried with them a strong feeling of shame and embarrassment. The associative chain was interrupted as he began to feel increasingly uncomfortable, and he noticed his thoughts shift to being an effective participant in a variety of sports. He also thought of his schoolwork. It was sometimes overwhelming and frustrating. He could feel how much potential he had and how little he actually accomplished. His feeling of inadequacy mounted and his thoughts turned to a favorite place in the country. Here he could be alone and feel free and soothed. This inner calmness was interrupted by memories of becoming enraged at the intimidating attacks by demanding teachers. These memories were either of his being totally submissive, reacting angrily and ending up humiliated, or of withdrawing into himself. He then thought of his family. He recalled his mother trying to sympathize with his suffering. At times it was quite helpful but it was so easy for him to manipulate her. He could always get his way by making her feel guilty. His father's contempt for any greedy behavior or inadequate perfor- mance was troubling, yet he always looked to his father for approval and help. This quickly shifted to how fearful he was of his father's anger. He thought about his dog, whom he loved dearly, and of his being overly attached to material things. He began to realize that whenever he was faced with a separation from home he could only find comfort in some material object, usually one that he thought would be envied by others. As his thoughts roamed to the things he was most interested in and enjoyed, such as fireworks and guns, and how alone he felt with them, he began to have an internal sensation of everything coming together. It reminded him of the feeling of completing a puzzle by finding the right pieces and having them click in place. His panic had dissolved. For the first time he knew what it meant to feel complete and separate.

This child had experienced the fragmenting panic of his separation anxiety and then invoked within himself the listen- ing, containing, and metabolizing attitude that he encountered with me in the therapeutic relationship. His associative chain of thoughts, imagery, and feelings reflected a wide variety of representations of self and object and their lines of continuity, which were available to him as a product of the interplay between the unconscious and conscious systems that were now present. Although he had put intense pressure upon me to join him in reinforcing his defensive postures, I was able to sustain a relatively consistent empathically responsive interpretive stance. The framework was unconsciously perceived as helpful and containing, which was expressed in his feeling of relief when the conditions did not change even in the face of his deprecatory teasing. Ultimately he felt safe enough to reveal the extent of his inner disturbance, which made it possible for the pathological distortions in his view of the world to become accessible to therapeutic influence. One crucial consequence was in eliminating the interference with continuity of experience created by his primitive defenses. His feeling of being complete was a direct result of this progressive development, since his sense of self could include all aspects of his mental functioning for the first time.

Profound Regression and the Need for Changes in Technique

The extent of a regression exhibited primarily by primatively organized individuals makes it mandatory to discover new ways of adapting psychoanalytic principles in order to maintain the therapeutic properties of the relationship. In addition, a strong bond of mutual purpose devoted to the goal of achieving constructive growth has to occupy at least a background presence, because extremes of regression are often associated with disruptions in the relationship.[2]

---

[2]**Robert Dickes** was a proponent of modifying a strictly interpretive stance when confronted with acute disruptions of a therapeutic alliance, based upon regressive reactions within the patient. Special attention was required to support the patient's reality-testing functions and ability to relate, since the regression was often unresponsive to confrontations and interpretations. A therapist must then promote the restoration of those functions directly related to the reestablishment of the working alliance. He saw the therapeutic alliance as a complex

Psychotherapy is a complex human encounter, in which powerful infantile emotions and experiences are elicited for the sole purpose of understanding their meaning. The unconscious realm of mental activity is given access to expression through the vehicle of an object relationship carefully conducted so as to allow what has heretofore been unknowable, and at times even unthinkable, to be represented in a communicatable form. Unconscious forces can only be granted expression in derivative constellations, with their significance embedded in and intermeshed with whatever psychic contents are suitable in the preconscious system. The unconscious is thereby a world of the implied and inferred.

The degree to which unconscious contents can reach awareness is dependent upon the nature of psychic structuralization receiving the impact of its influence. The dimensions of self-knowledge created by opening avenues for the expression of unconscious impulses and perceptions, and the strengthening of the mental structures needed for their representation, are potentially ever expanding. It is a richly rewarding experience to listen to the echoes of a patient's unconscious strivings clamoring for expression, mobilizing powerful prohibitions,

----

state derived from several sources, including the patient's motivation for treatment based upon ego-alien symptoms, positive transferences, and what was often referred to as the rational relationship between patient and analyst. This latter part was applicable to the healthy part of the patient's ego, was representative of the reality relationship, and was often defined as the working alliance. When it is severely disrupted, deviations in technique may have to be introduced in order to assist the patient with reality testing during these difficult periods. At such moments the analyst is viewed primarily as a need-satisfying object, and the fragmentation of that object disturbs the treatment situation, leading to a rupture of the working alliance (Dickes 1967).

and then gradually moving closer to being known and articulated in the treatment. The individual's developmental history is thereby re-created in the present through a relationship fostering a free flow of projective identifications, as any defensive opposition is alleviated by the influences of interpretive interventions.

Of course the relationship itself can be either a constructive or detrimental factor, which does not detract from the use of interpretations as the major therapeutic instrument. However, it does call attention to the need for exploring the unconscious meaning to a patient of a therapist's behavior and personality, which has important implications for an expanding view of what constitutes an effective treatment posture and what conditions are required to improve treatment technique. The ebb and flow of the interaction is aided by a therapist's ability to maintain empathic resonance with a patient's unconscious communications, and hindered whenever there is an empathic lapse. The derivatives of a patient's unconscious perceptions are then available for either validating the growth-promoting properties of a therapist's responses, or identifying the source of an empathic failure. The inevitable misunderstandings that arise from a number of factors, including a therapist's personal difficulties, can be turned to advantage by correcting the mistakes. In interpreting their effects, a deeper view of the patient's internal world is gained, thereby exposing previously unrecognized infantile conflicts or developmental deficits and arrests to therapeutic influence. The distortions produced by pathological defenses also become a focused area of attention, unhealthy collusions are dissolved, and the pathway for a patient's psychological growth is cleared of unnecessary obstacles.

One validating consequence of a therapist's successful interpretive efforts, on the background of a well-managed frame-

work, is of the entry into consciousness of previously inaccessible psychic contents.[3]

This was demonstrated in the treatment of a small, frail-
appearing 11-year-old boy. His frailty was accentuated by
his stiff-legged manner of walking and his stilted, controlled speech patterns. He chose each word carefully and
deliberately, with pauses between each word. His voice
quality was soft, abrupt, and robotic. Throughout his
childhood he had been fearful, easily intimidated, and
unable to function in school settings. He was brought to
see me after a period of 6 months, during which he had
become profoundly withdrawn and had retreated into his
own room, having nothing to do with anyone.

Although he had resisted coming to the first session, he
quickly agreed to continue meeting. He was acutely aware
of having many barriers inside and accepted the idea of
working together to try to get them out of the way.
Sessions were arranged three times per week in response

---

[3]**Madeleine** and **Willy Baranger** and **Jorge Mom** described
the indicators of a successful psychoanalytic treatment process.
These included the overcoming of infantile amnesias, the
development of true "insight," and the patient's active involvement in working cooperatively with the analyst toward
achieving advancing degrees of autonomy and independence.
Associating freely allows access to the unconscious, which is
reflected in the richness of the narrative, the appearance of
different areas of experience, including childhood memories,
and the variability of languages used, especially dream language. Fluency must be accompanied by affective circulation
with moments of blockage alternating with affective mobilization, and the transformation of transferential and countertransferential affects. True insight is accompanied by a new opening
in the future dimensions, with goals, plans, and feelings of
hope. Most important is the effort to be sincere, to listen, and to
allow progression and regression (Baranger et al. 1983).

to his association as to how he learned about computers. He would seek help, but then needed a day or two by himself to try it out before he was ready for more. This derivative association to the question of meeting was the only communication of this nature during the early hours. Usually he came to his appointments submissively and spoke only in monotonous clichés, which took the form of reporting some daily activity or event. I experienced the interaction as lifeless and devoid of direction.

I began to feel a sense of frustration, and as it mounted he suddenly began to talk about his interest in computers. They could be developed to such a degree that they eventually could control the people who made them. The people who programmed them would go on thinking they were in charge, but the computer would use all the programmed information to control the programmer. It reminded him of the robot in *Star Wars*. He appeared friendly and helpful, but he thought he was really putting everyone on and teasing them. This was his way of being in charge. I then said, "I've been feeling controlled by what has been happening between us. I know I've contributed to it by continuing to search for and gain some understanding from your words and actions without telling you of my inner sense of being teased and controlled." With this, the whole tenor of the interaction abruptly changed. His immediate reaction was to appear stunned and to draw back with a look of hurt and confusion. He quietly spoke of how frightened he felt, and of how hard he was trying to communicate with me. He felt very hurt that I saw this as controlling and teasing. His voice was no longer hesitant and he spoke with feeling for the first time.

He arrived at the following session with a determined look on his face, proceeding to move and rearrange the furniture in the room. I stepped aside without saying anything, implicitly encouraging him to continue as I felt

an important communication was taking place. He then
turned all of the furniture upside down and placed himself
under a chair so that he was completely covered. I told
him that I thought he was showing me in action how he
experienced my words in the previous session. After a
short silence he began to talk from underneath the chair.
He had suddenly remembered an incident from when he
was 4 years old. He had been hiding underneath a table in
exactly the same position he was in now. His mother
walked by and he had reached out and tripped her. At the
time he felt angry, somewhat mischievous, and as though
he had done something effective. His mother fell, hurt
herself, got up in a rage, and attacked him for what he had
done. He vividly recalled feeling completely crushed and
shattered. Looking back, it seemed as though this event
had somehow been a crucial turning point in his life,
because from then on he had lost any sense of spontaneity
or playfulness. He became fearful and constantly carried
within him the impact of his mother's attacking voice. Any
spontaneous feeling was reacted to as a source of danger
and had to be avoided. He also spoke of the despair he
lived with that any display of emotion would drive others
away, leaving him totally abandoned.

I said that I had attacked him with my voice and it must
have reminded him of that earlier event. He fell silent and
thought of the many times he had retreated to his room,
secretly hoping someone would come in. One day his
father burst into the room, both startling and frightening
him at first. He was surprised, however, because it turned
out that his father had entered in order to talk with him.
He paused, reflecting upon the boredom he often felt in
school and how much he wished he could be playful. He
had always been much too afraid. He then became ani-
mated, fantasizing a variety of ways to tease people by
caricaturing their mannerisms before then pausing to comment on how sunny the day was.

In this situation a background of empathic responsiveness was initiated with the establishment of the frequency of sessions, and the immobilization he displayed was the only way he had to hold off the pull toward a frightening regression. He was terrified of being controlled by me, which he tried to communicate in his association to the programmed computer being in control. My feeling of helplessness in knowing how to ease his anxiety had contributed to my mounting sense of frustration, making me blind to the underlying significance of his reaching out. Unconsciously, I was reacting to his view of me as a controlling figure and projecting my difficulty onto him. Consequently, I misread his association as a derivative expressing his unconscious perception of my being controlled by him. The resulting empathic failure was embodied in my interpretive attack upon, rather than understanding of, his attitude. He unconsciously perceived this, demanding a defensive adaptation and instigating a profound regression in which he could only express himself through his behavior. At this point it was essential for the conditions of the treatment to be modified, so as to give him the room to enact what was happening inside without interference and with some indication that he would be heard. Unless and until I could identify the source of my lapse in empathy, and correct it, he would have to continue to defend himself against the threat I posed to him. When I did recognize the nature of my contribution and referred to the impact it had upon him, he recalled a memory of an attack that was a parallel of what had taken place in the therapeutic interaction. I was then able to validate his unconscious perception of the part I had played, and the resulting background of safety and containment allowed a process of exploration and integration to advance.

Although my comment was in fact an error, it was much better than remaining silent and perpetuating the despair this child felt that anyone would be able to reach him. It allowed a subtle countertransference-based response to be brought out in the open where it could be more clearly identified and its significance for both parties revealed. Light was shed upon the psychic contents he was silently, projectively identifying onto me, which I was unconsciously perceiving and reacting to defensively. The return of his early traumatic memory showed how he received my interpretation, but it also opened a door to a deeper understanding of his trouble. Once my contribution was acknowledged, his association to his father wanting to talk rather than attack gave derivative expression to his unconscious perception of the change in my attitude. In addition, his delight at the idea of mimicking authorities, along with calling attention to the brightness of the day, suggested that both hope and spontaneity had become viable experiences.[4]

---

[4]**Ralph Greenson** had long been concerned about what he considered to be ahuman qualities in the insistence upon maintaining a strictly interpretive posture. He believed that a therapist's genuine caring was an essential aspect of the treatment. In this article he outlined the importance of interventions other than interpretation in the creation and maintenance of a productive analytic atmosphere and indicated that they should not necessarily be avoided. While underscoring the central role of interpretation of transference and resistance, he also considered many interactions not to involve transference phenomena. Errors in technique can be caused by misunderstanding due to insufficient knowledge, inexperience, erroneous theoretical beliefs, and unrecognized and uncontrolled countertransference reactions. In dealing with apparent technical errors, however, it may be important to wait until a patient reacts to the error before bringing it up, and to admit and apologize without burdening or gratifying

This patient's memories and associations indicated that treatment was progressing, and that the profound regression had been helpful. As in all treatment endeavors, the process moves forward in a never-ending spiral, for psychic productions that emerge into consciousness also have derivative meaning and are connected to deeper anxieties. The enlarged self-awareness and knowledge ultimately adds to the effectiveness of integrative functions, which in turn are strengthened as a consequence of achieving new solutions to infantile conflicts and/or developmental deficits and arrests. Thus a precipitous regression can offer a unique opportunity to bring positive therapeutic influence to the impact of early traumas, provided that the conditions of the treatment can be adapted to the specific requirements of a given patient.[5]

---

the patient by revealing the unconscious determinants. The error and the patient's reaction to the acknowledgment can then be analyzed to therapeutic benefit. He did note that allowing emotional responses, humanitarian concerns, and reality considerations to enter the analytic situation could foster idealization and temporarily interfere with the ability to demonstrate transference distortions. However, if the analyst was aware of the side effects of such interventions, the patient's distortions could be analyzed and did not permanently obstruct analytic progress (Greenson 1972).

[5]**Robert Wallerstein** did not think the appearance of near-delusional transference reactions in previously nonpsychotic patients should be avoided. He considered their positive effect in that they enabled latent difficulties in development to be exposed to therapeutic influence. They could play a role as a means of providing the opportunity for transference reconstructions, which could then contribute to a new mastery that had heretofore not been integrated (Wallerstein 1967).

A Therapeutic Regression and the Relationship between a Therapist's Management, Containing, and Interpretive Functions

The therapeutic properties of a treatment relationship are directly proportional to the extent to which enough safety is present for a benign regression to unfold. A new edition of the original circumstances involved in the formation of a patient's psychopathology is then re-created in the treatment. This makes it possible for the body ego experiences and their object-impression counterparts, representing a solution to an overwhelming or unmastered infantile situation, to be laid down. The capacity for symbolic functions to be fully operative is then either established or freed of obstacles, allowing for a shift to the primacy of an interpretive mode of communication.

Interpretations alone have very little positive influence in the presence of serious developmental deficits, for they can only be received as evidence of a therapist's distant emotional position. This is not to say that interpretations have no value or importance. They are the means by which a therapist communicates, maintains an appropriate boundary, and encapsulates the understanding contained within a given intervention. In these situations, however, it is a therapist's behavior and emotional attitude that make the most powerful impression.[6]

---

[6]**Michael Balint** developed the concept of a basic fault to explain such profoundly regressive phenomena. This idea evolved from a deeper understanding of difficulties and failures, and in turn had implications for what was curative in treatment. The basic fault reflected a lack of fit between the developing child and its environment, and when this level was reached in treatment there was a profound change in the

Pathological entities formed around an inability to master or negotiate early developmental tasks are frequently associated with ego deficits that do not allow the symbolic meaning of the relationship to be adequately represented. It is then essential, if structural changes are to take place, for the treatment to be conducted in such a manner that the interpersonal contact can have a constructive influence upon body ego experiences. Otherwise interpretive interventions are experienced as distancing, or indicative of a serious lack of understanding as to the depth and nature of the underlying disturbance.

This was brought out in the treatment of a 9-year-old boy originally referred because of poor school performance, temper tantrums when faced with any frustration, and his constant complaint of hating himself. He was extremely conforming and submissive at home, but wild and uncontrollable at school. He was eager to get help and right from the first moment of contact sat quietly in a chair, speaking rapidly with no pause. He talked about his unhappiness

---

atmosphere, with excessive sensitivity on the part of the patient to the analyst. The needs and wishes of the patient then predominate over the analytic relationship. The analyst is felt to be immensely powerful and is only important for need-gratification.

This "primary object relationship" is an expression of "primary love," which the analyst must foster in patients suffering from a basic fault. It is a relationship in which there are no sharp boundaries, and the environment and the individual interpenetrate. Balint saw two levels of analytic work, the oedipal and preoedipal. The oedipal involved triangular relationships, intrapsychic conflict, and the utilization of adult language as a reliable means of communication. The preoedipal, or basic fault, exclusively involves dyadic relationships; its dynamic force is not one of conflict but of satisfaction and frustration, and adult language is often misleading or useless (Balint 1968).

and self-hatred, feeling he was angry all of the time and basically bad. He wanted to meet regularly and often in order to talk about his troubles.

Treatment began and he did talk uninterruptedly from the beginning to the end of each session. He barely stopped to take a breath before continuing on with a new narrative. He described interactions with other children, focusing on mischief, getting away with breaking rules, fooling teachers, and engaging in horseplay out of sight of any authority. I commented upon his preoccupation with getting away with things and fooling authorities, and wondered if he was expressing what was happening between us. He protested vigorously that it had absolutely nothing to do with how he felt about me. He welcomed and valued the relationship, because he felt free to talk about all of these hidden activities. This was the only place where he could talk openly, and he went on to describe the inhibiting, restrictive, and controlling environment in which he lived. At home he always had to be polite and say and do all the right things. It was essential that he dress properly and call his parents sir and ma'am. Therefore it was a relief to be talking with me, where it wasn't necessary to watch himself. He was terrified of his father's anger and for this reason felt he had to be the model of politeness. With me he was simply not afraid.

He continued to fill the hours with tales of his mischief. After some time they were interspersed with complaints about being treated unfairly by his parents. It usually centered upon his relationship with his siblings. He was the oldest of four and was the scapegoat. The other children could do almost anything, whereas he was expected to be responsible whenever they did something wrong. Any trouble that occurred was always his fault, which made him feel terribly bad about himself. In his parents' eyes there was nothing he could do well. I attempted to relate these complaints to his feeling of being unfairly treated by me, but once again he protested that he was in no way unhappy with me.

After many months I noticed that I was feeling lost and bewildered in my efforts to understand him. Although he continued to be eager to come, and filled the sessions with a plethora of verbal productions, I had no inner feeling of being connected to him. On the surface everything he said appeared to express what he was thinking and feeling. However, I began to realize that I hadn't learned anything new from the material he was communicating. It was a seemingly endless repetition of his episodes of mischief and fooling authorities, or of his complaints of mistreatment and scapegoating at the hands of his parents. For a period of time I was drawn to making linear interpretive statements. I would comment, for example, on his difficulties with managing his aggression, or on the envy of his siblings. At one point I interpreted all of this as a way of covering up more troublesome sexual feelings. He responded to these interpretations in a somewhat surprising way. First, he would state, "I think you're right—I hadn't thought of that before." Afterward he would elaborate on what I had said by adding, "I was more angry than I realized," or "I guess I really do envy my brother and sister," or "I don't like to think about sexual things." He would then go on to repeat anew the same themes and narratives.

After a while it occurred to me that there was always a missing ingredient in whatever he discussed. When he spoke of relationships his focus was on the actions and motives of others. He would omit his internal responses and feeling states. At other times he would speak of his feelings but would leave out any fantasy material or the responses of others. Periodically he described isolated fantasies with no apparent connection to any context that had elicited them. The following session took place as I was struggling to grasp the significance of my observations.

He began in his characteristic fashion by speaking of a series of events in school wherein he had either tricked, fooled, or outwitted the teacher. I listened and thought of it as a derivative expression of what he was doing with me. I also remembered how when I tried to address this message earlier it was totally denied. I began to think that somehow I had not created a set of conditions in which he could feel safe enough to expose what was truly going on inside, and that he was finding it necessary to engage in a constant effort to keep himself hidden. I decided to communicate this thought to him. As my words were spoken, however, they became jumbled and came out in a very confusing statement. I was acutely aware of how garbled and impossible to understand my words were and paused to explore my internal reactions, trying to see what had affected me. During the pause he started to talk. He first stated, "I see what you mean," and went on to express the idea that he was agreeing with my observation.

Suddenly I understood his words, "I see what you mean," in a different way. He was saying that my words had no meaning for him. I, in turn, was feeling that his words had no meaning for me. It dawned on me that my discomfort was growing out of participating in an interaction where no real meaning was being expressed by either of us. I told him of my realization, emphasizing how I thought he was trying to show me how my words were meaningless to him. It had made me aware of how much this had been a part of our experience together. There was a long silence, during which he looked uneasy and embarrassed. He squirmed in his chair and finally spoke in a soft voice.

While he was sitting in the chair it was as if there were two of him. One was out in front speaking to me and telling me whatever he could think of to say. More importantly, another part of him was sitting far back in the chair, observing me. He watched everything I did, listened to my words, searched for what I liked and didn't like, and paid special attention to my facial expressions. Way in the back of his mind he wondered what I wanted or expected from him. He was constantly weighing what would or would not please me and gain my approval, and he just hadn't known how to talk to me from this part of himself.

He noticed, as he was talking now, how distrustful he was of everyone around him, including me. His whole manner of being was totally based on how he had been with me. For the first time he had a sense that maybe he could find the right words. He hesitated and struggled to describe how small and insignificant he felt. He was overwhelmed by the demands of school, of his parents, and of the entire world surrounding him. He felt ineffective, inadequate, and vulnerable to the attacks of others. At the same time he felt very distant, isolated, and like there was nothing he could attach himself to or belong to. It was like he was walled off and no one could reach him. He stopped again and then commented on the sound of his voice as he became tearful and cried. He could not recall ever hearing the sound of his own voice. He turned to me and spoke of his recognition that I was confused by him, and lost in trying to understand him. He often wondered how I could listen to his words and not be able somehow to hear him and help him to really talk. After all this time he was finally able to do that. It reminded him of a story in which a young prince had been cursed and had to live a life of isolation and ugliness. The only way he could be rescued was if someone had the ability to find the prince who was hidden behind his ugly exterior.

This child's pathology had interfered with his ability to communicate with meaning. His way of adapting to the therapeutic relationship was based upon a foreground figure doing everything possible to appease and seek approval from what he saw as a need-supplying object. Simultaneously there was a weak, vulnerable, and infantile self in the background. This mode of functioning was so entrenched that he felt despair at ever being fully understood. In order for his deeper true feelings to come out and be expressed he would have to regress, and he had been too distrustful to allow it. In the early months he expressed a theme of hiding, deceiving, and fooling those in authority, and though I recognized the significance of what he was saying I was unable to communicate it to him in any kind of meaningful way. In all probability it was because I did not appreciate the degree of his distrust, and thus the conditions of the treatment were not safe enough to support the depth of the regression he had to experience. My ability to interpret was also affected by the absence of a context that could bring some continuity to his experience, for there was always a missing element in the derivatives he expressed. This was partly a result of the defensive activity that was so effective in maintaining his facade, and partly a function of the way I was participating.

My assumption that all mental content had meaning had served as an obstacle to understanding that he was communicating without meaning. The part of himself that gave viability and, hence, meaning to his internal world was too walled off and regressive, and in my confusion and frustration I could only offer somewhat superficial linear kinds of interpretations. Attention was thereby directed solely to his system of conscious mental activity. The quality of the ensuing interaction illustrated the debilitating effects of such an approach. I was unwittingly reinforcing an ongoing process of destruction of meaning by seeing and relating to only the conscious elements in his words. My interpretations of his anger, envy, and sexual anxiety made his defensive posture more entrenched and interfered with the regression necessary for the emergence and production of meaning.

A potential key for my understanding was manifested in his idealizations of me, which were expressing his attempt to compensate for what was missing within himself. However, it wasn't until I finally grasped the underlying significance of his statement, "I see what you mean," that some context was available that contained within it an unconscious communication. The realization that I had been addressing everything to his "false self" gave me a way to speak to his previously inaccessible "true self." My interpretation of his comment resonated within him, established a connection to what had gone unverbalized, and made the emergence of meaning possible. He expressed it best when he was able to hear the sound of his own voice, for now he was able to communicate with meaning. His story of the prince validated our having made an attachment that included continuity of experience. He had finally been unconsciously understood, which enabled a regressive pathway to be formed that could reach the most defended young parts of himself. Only then could the distortions embodied in his pathology begin to be undone and integrated. The production of meaning had made it possible for the therapeutic relationship to aid in the dissolution of his pathological defenses and provided the wherewithal for him to move toward constructive growth.[7]

---

[7]**Robert Langs,** consistent with his focus on the therapeutic interaction as the arena in which both positive and negative changes take place, believed there were three therapeutic modalities that could be identified in terms of the analyst's level of functioning (listening, formulating, intervening, validating, and relating). These involved working with manifest content, working with derivatives consisting of isolated inferences from the patient's material, and working with derivatives consisting of material organized around the prevailing adaptive context—usually the analyst's attitudes and interventions.

The curative factors in the first two modes of therapy are conceptualized by Langs as barrier systems designed to seal off the most pertinent and chaotic truths within both patient and analyst. The curative element in the third mode consists of dynamically truthful realizations, providing access to the most compelling actualities, both conscious and unconscious, within

The ability of an individual to sustain the motivation for continuing therapeutic work is more comprehensible when the experience taking place reverberates throughout the entire personality and includes the deepest unconscious layers. Under these circumstances there is always a sense of connection, offering hope that new solutions are attainable, even in the presence of occasional empathic lapses. There is some measure of recognition of a therapist's efforts to grasp the unconscious meaning of communications, so that whatever is required for promoting growth has the potential of eventually being discovered. In most instances this is gradually unearthed and incorporated within an expanding range of insight and self-knowledge, facilitated by appropriately timed interpretive interventions.

When there are gaps or defects in an individual's ability to symbolize and communicate on the one hand, and in a therapist's ability to comprehend and appreciate empathically what cannot be articulated on the other, the working relationship can only be sustained by seeking reinforcement of what is known. The consequence is in the amplification of the existing pathology, furthering the extent to which the individual is fixated in an unmovable position and adding to the already present sense of despair over finding an adequate solution. It is in this area that a therapist's inordinate silence can be as

---

the ongoing, spiraling, communicative interaction between patient and analyst. Therapeutic work on this level is arduous, burdensome, deeply disturbing, and at times terrifying. It requires of the analyst extensive self-knowledge and continuous efforts at self-analysis. It asks for a confrontation with, and a personal resolution of, the inevitable presence of countertransference as well as a full and painful awareness of their influence on the patient. This approach alone, in Lang's opinion, can offer the patient adaptive structural changes and insightful symptom resolution (Langs 1981).

devastating as any possible error involving some inaccurate interpretation or unnecessary behavior. A therapist's willingness to seek out whatever is necessary to promote growth, even risking errors of commission, may become the only source of genuine hope.[8] This is not to suggest that errors or empathic lapses are in any way desirable—they are in fact dangerous, risky, and potentially destructive. However, an awareness of their manifestations and effects can offer safeguards in enabling these mistakes to be corrected as they arise. Sometimes, in this way, an avenue for discovery may be opened up that would otherwise be closed.

A verbally communicative treatment modality depends upon there being enough of a foundation of mental structuralization within a patient's personality for symbolic functions to be consistently viable. The symbolic meaning of a therapist's interpretations must be capable of being internalized, of eliciting body ego experiences, and of enabling symbolic responses in order to be an effective instrument of the treatment. Otherwise there is too much of a disconnection from the internal

---

[8]**Margaret Little,** from her vast experience with seriously disturbed patients, was convinced that with certain individuals and at specified times, interpretations were not only ineffective but also destructive. In discussing the nature of the therapist's commitment, she elaborated on the therapist's function of putting both that which is conscious and unconscious into the patient's service. These have to be made available in forms that have meaning for the patient and can be used. The forms may be verbal or nonverbal. It is the patient's capacity for symbolization and for deductive thinking that largely determines the form. Different patients may need different forms, and for any one patient a form that is usable and meaningful at one moment may be useless at another. Ultimately, the form has to be verbal and interpretive, but an object can have an effect like an interpretation and be linked later, when the capacity to use symbols has been developed far enough (Little 1981).

experiences that are striving for growth, yet are incapable of being articulated and cannot be reached with words alone. It is here that a therapist's management and containing functions are most needed, in the arms of which a benign regression may reach the sectors of psychic functioning that have determined the pathology.[9,10] The specific conditions that facilitate such a regression must be ascertained from a patient's overall response, which reflects whether it is a benign or malignant regression that is being manifested.

---

[9]**Donald Winnicott** believed that psychoanalytic work must be left in abeyance when primitive emotional development is effected, with management being the entire thing until there is enough advancement manifested for interpretations to be useful (Winnicott 1954).

[10]**Michael Balint** investigated the positive and negative aspects of regression and their relationship to a therapist's conduct of the treatment. He regarded the therapist's response to a patient's acting out, nonverbal communications, and efforts to modify the analytic situation as crucial, since at such times the patient was lost and only the analytic present mattered. The analyst's response determined the extent to which there could be a change in the basic structural fault in the patient's personality. One hazard involved the analyst's failure to recognize that the language of interpretation was not reaching the patient, and the urge to organize the patient's material may not be in the service of the therapeutic need at the moment. If the patient is allowed to regress and rely on the caretaker functions of the analyst, an atmosphere can be created in which interpretations can reach and affect the patient (Balint 1968).

5

The Providing of New Actual Experiences and an Expanded View of the Concept of Insight

Adapting the Conditions of the Treatment to Unmet Developmental Needs in Primitively Organized Patients

Experiences of phase-specific instinctual gratification, of the activity of autonomous ego functions, and of the background object of primary identification (Mendelsohn 1987a), constitute the contents of a good self. When good-self contents are extremely sparse, tenuously organized, split off, and in constant danger of being severely damaged by primitive distorting defenses raging out of control, a totally different and difficult treatment problem is posed. These limited good-self experiences are not able to be included in the therapeutic relationship, but instead are projectively identified onto the therapist. Holding and containment, so important for the safety required to enable a benign regression, thus cannot be elicited in silent and symbolic ways. The therapist then must find some more direct and concrete means of providing security in the relationship, usually through overt actions, behavior, and emotional attitude in managing the treatment framework.

A paucity of good-self experience during the developmental years is often associated with gaps in mental representation, which interferes with continuity of experience and processes of symbolization. Verbal interpretations therefore have very little influence, until it is no longer necessary for them to be split off in order to be preserved. Under these circumstances a treatment situation has to be conducted so as to discover some way to offer a concrete experience specific enough to what is lacking that these good qualities can be experienced in a relationship. Only then is it possible for interpretive interventions to be useful.[1] The underlying need for such an experience can motivate a relentless search to attain it, regardless of the cost to either patient or therapist. It is this very quality that can

---

[1] **Michael Balint** showed how important it was to permit a deep-enough regression with patients exhibiting evidence of a basic fault in the depths of the personality. There were problems in doing so, however, for words are experienced as disturbing impingements rather than vehicles of helpful insights with regressed patients. The therapist must remain at the right distance, neither so far that the patient feels lost or abandoned, nor so close that the patient feels engulfed. The therapist functions during this period as a provider of time and milieu, a need-recognizing and need-satisfying object, and he must also be able to communicate his understanding to the patient. The gap between patient and therapist is bridged by creating the atmosphere a patient needs and by avoiding interventions that penetrate the patient's defenses. The type of gratification offered to the patient should not increase excitement, but should create a tranquil state of well-being and a safer understanding between patient and analyst (Balint 1968).

end up in success, if what is being sought can be recognized and provided, at least in some measure.[2]

> This dilemma arose in the treatment of a 6-year-old boy who had been referred in response to his teachers' concern over his isolated and withdrawn behavior. His parents saw him as an extremely independent child, though they were at times worried about his intense determination to accomplish tasks beyond his capabilities. They were surprised, however, at the depth of the teachers' concern.
>
> When he came to his appointment he was fearful, embarrassed, and he clung to his mother. She was taken aback, as he had never shown this kind of behavior before. He said that he couldn't talk but his body could, and after I remarked that I would try to understand his body's messages he readily left his mother and entered the office.

---

[2]**Warren Kinston** and **Jonathan Coen** elaborated upon the problems of working with more regressive and serious disturbances. Psychoanalytic work will flounder unless the therapist has a clear conception of what is to be expected when primal repression is reached. Then trauma, risk, and action, rather than talk, feelings, and dreams, become primary features of the analysis. In some cases a patient may need to produce inexorable and frightening deterioration to get the therapist to participate. The therapist is forced to notice that interpretive work is of no avail, presenting two stark choices: either the analysis is judged to be unworkable and termination is sought, or the therapist acts to offer some form of direct care, finally allowing primary relatedness to be manifest. The absence of representation that characterized primal repression must now be converted to wish-based psychic structure, and the process of repair involves having certain experiences for the first time. The therapist's presence and activity serve as a scaffolding on which the patient constructs new understanding. Pre-stages of representation are in evidence and must be recognized as the way the mind grows and not mistaken as evidence of pathology (Kinston and Coen 1986).

He drew a picture, calling it his fort. There were no windows or doors and he was perfectly safe there—no one could hurt him. I reflected upon the big price he paid for his safety, since nothing could come in and he was limited in not being able to get out. He matter-of-factly said that he could find a way out if he wanted to and agreed that it would be a good idea to meet regularly and explore whether he might want to find a way out.

Thus, even in this first session, he was hinting at the existence of traumatic preverbal experiences that couldn't be articulated yet somehow could be expressed through his body. By implication, he was also showing how he had compensated for them and covered them over. He did appear to be probing for how I would respond to regressive behavior, and this approach suggested that he had at least a reactive awareness of some unspeakable internal event. I had indicated a willingness to be open to this mode of expression, and he responded immediately by joining me without his mother. In his drawing he portrayed the compensatory protective measures with which he had surrounded himself.

His parents were warm, sensitive, but psychologically naive people who had adopted him at 6 months of age. They had very little information about his early life, knowing only that he had come from a single parent and that his mother was an extremely disturbed woman. She had taken her life after putting her child up for adoption. They had been told by the agency that he had suffered some physical abuse at her hands; she had subsequently become seriously distraught and had left the baby crying on their doorstep before taking her own life. From the parents' point of view, after an initial period of appearing somewhat withdrawn, he had been receptive and responsive to their care. They were quite pleased with how he had developed. I had suspected that his opening statement, about not being able to talk although his body could, made some reference to these early experiences. However, at this stage there was no way of knowing how they would emerge, or whether anything beyond an interpretive posture within a well-managed framework would be required. He did seem responsive to my words, and his drawing of the fort indicated that symbolic processes were functional to some degree. His attitude about the drawing was quite literal, however, and he was either unwilling or unable to elaborate much fantasy concerning it. In addition, his comment about finding a way out if he wanted spoke of an implicit, powerful defensive need to hold on firmly to his autonomy. I hoped I would get a clearer picture of whether he needed a firm framework in order to feel securely held, or whether he would require room to express his preverbal traumas in behavior.

During the early months he vacillated between laboriously working on some project he had brought and being teasing and provocative. He gradually revealed just how tightly controlled his emotions were and how frightened he was of "letting go." Someone, including himself, would be likely to get hurt. He cautiously tested me to determine how I would react to aggressive behavior, obviously trying to see if he would be safe. On a few occasions he brought ropes to tie me up so I couldn't intervene or prevent any destruction. He fantasied being in total control, having the freedom to ravage the office. The idea appeared exciting to him. He then "inadvertently" knocked over various objects in the room, as he was reminded of people who were weak and helpless and for whom he felt contempt. I commented that he did appear to be coming out of his fort and it looked as though he was afraid I'd be helpless in containing him, especially when he could so easily knock over my belongings. This remark seemed helpful, for he laughed, drew a picture of his fort, and pointed out that construction work was being done on the doors and windows.

A short time later he referred to his biological mother for the first time, and imagined himself in a distant city where he could hear her frantic cries. She was on top of a high building in total despair and was trying to kill herself by jumping out of a window. He rescued her by stopping her at the very last second. This fantasy was reminiscent of the known facts about his early history. It hinted that he was carrying the experience from this preverbal period into the transference relationship. Up until this point I was able to maintain clearly defined ground rules and boundaries, and my interpretations were the predominant mode of communication. There was always a consistent background aura of his testing the strength of the relationship in providing holding and containment, with small glimpses of a readiness for him to erupt into unmanageable behavior. He had verbalized considerable conflict over the extent of his aggression, either fearing that he would be overwhelmed by its intensity or that he would destroy a need-supplying object. It looked like he was preparing himself (and perhaps me) for a hostile attack against me. I had the thought that it might be necessary for him to have an actual experience of my not being destroyed or driven away, wherein his autonomy would not be encroached upon. This emerging intuitive impression was realized dramatically in a subsequent session.

Looking wild and uncontrolled, he entered the office. Yelling loudly as he raced around the room, and in an overexcited fashion, he grabbed an object from my shelf and threw it. I held him gently but he protested, crying out in rage, "Don't trap me, you're hurting my feelings." I released him only to have him once again become wild and excited in a similar way. This time when I held him I said that he had the key to get free and identified the key as his telling me to let go. He continued his wild behavior, I held him, he indicated that he wanted to be released, and I let him go. This exchange continued uninterruptedly for a long time. Finally with great surprise he exclaimed, "I'm playing." He went on to describe his inability to pretend. He had always been able to imagine things but he could never play. It seemed that whenever he put what was happening in his mind into action everything escalated. Finally it reached a point where he just felt driven by some uncontrollable force. He lost all sense of what was happening or why, and didn't know how to stop what had moved into explosive outbursts.

In this description he was beginning to bring what had been unthinkable into a communicative modality. In so doing he was also giving evidence of a viable mental capacity that had previously either been deficient or nonfunctional. It appeared to represent an intrapsychic event that could only be expressed through his bodily movements, accompanied by rage alternating with a fear of envelopment. The out-of-control attack was directed against me, and my interpretive words had no influence whatsoever. The framework of the treatment therefore had to be extended to include concrete physical contact. A vital aspect of my response to this enactment involved the search for a means by which control of my actions could remain in his hands. This particular feature was repeated many times, probably until it could be internalized, before it was possible for him to put into words what was taking place inside. It suggested that by representing his experience of the interaction, an intrapsychic gap was being bridged, thereby enabling a pathway toward symbolizing and verbalizing what had heretofore been inaccessible.

Had I adhered to a firmer stance, insisting upon talk instead of action, in all likelihood there would have been a different outcome. The intensity of his rage and the extent of his fear of engulfment were not susceptible to any interpretive words. It could only have ended in either a chaotic destruction of the office, or in counteraggressive defensive reactions within me. Were he only to have been physically overpowered and controlled, his autonomy would have been compromised, and no avenue toward achieving perspective would have been opened up. The helplessness of his preverbal experiences would probably have been repeated. Physical restraint was obviously needed for the protection of both of us, yet it was important for me to be willing to place control in his hands in spite of my awareness that it would continue. It also seemed vital for this interchange to be repetitive until its underlying meaning could begin to surface. It looked as though what transpired reflected the impact of a preverbal trauma with a very disturbed enveloping mother, although on this occasion it had a new outcome. Consequently, he was able to include derivatives of the experience within the realm of his observable psychic contents and communicate what he felt. Symbolic processes were clearly more broadly usable, in contrast to the earlier sessions wherein his ability to symbolize was operative but to a limited extent and easily broken down.

With this in mind I turned my attention to reestablishing firm ground rules and boundaries with him. I began by trying to encourage his newfound ability to communicate in a verbally symbolic mode. I wondered if anything came into his mind that could show more clearly what it was that he was now playing. He became thoughtful before wanting to use my furniture to play a game. He constructed a den, which he crawled into through a small opening. Once inside he started to coo like a baby. It was warm and comfortable, but the opening was so small he could suffocate in crawling out.

His capacity to symbolize and communicate regressive experiences was more fully in evidence and continued to grow in subsequent sessions. It was no longer necessary to introduce any unusual measures, as the treatment was able to progress with my maintaining an interpretive attitude. On those rare occasions when I unwittingly deviated from such a stance, it was in fact disruptive, but now it could be communicated in words instead of behavior as derivatives of his unconscious perception of an empathic lapse were expressed. For example, at times he would request that I move out of my chair so he could have room to draw. If I complied without first exploring the meaning of his request, he became anxious and distrustful. In rectifying the lapse there would be a mutual recognition of his not having to be in control of my behavior, and there was much greater security when he explored rather than acted upon his feelings.

In treatment situations where symbolic processes are non-functional, a therapist's attitude and behavior, expressed through management of the framework, assume the highest priority. Interpretive words, if used exclusively, can only be experienced as an attack from a powerful and imposing figure. This kind of approach is often received as a sign of a hopeless degree of emotional distance from an unreachable need-supplying object.[3] A therapist must therefore be open to identifying when it may be necessary to offer a concrete actual experience that establishes contact with previously inaccessible psychic contents. This preparatory step may have to be taken first, before it is possible for a patient to communicate symbolically, at which point interpretations can be received in a helpful fashion.[4] It is incumbent upon the therapist, however,

---

[3]**Donald Winnicott** is frequently referred to when the treatment needs of more primitive patients are addressed. He indicated that the conditions of psychoanalytic treatment must be adapted to invite a regression to the earlier years, through which there can be an eventual progression. The regression is to dependence, with a sense of risk, one that creates a new sense of self and unfreezes the environment-failure situation. Speech or interpretation can ruin the process and be excessively painful to the patient (Winnicott 1954).

[4]**Margaret Little** was a strong advocate of providing more direct contact when patients were dealing with psychotic anxieties. Her reasoning was that development had been impaired to the extent that realities coincided with fantasies, and projection became not only useless but impossible. Every patient tests the therapist constantly to find weak spots, to find

to make a distinction between behaviors that encourage a destructive acting out in the transference, and behaviors that provide new solutions to impossible infantile dilemmas.

The Need for Flexibility in Applying Psychoanalytic Principles

Introducing unusual measures by altering the framework of the treatment should always be done with great care, after

---

out whether the relationship of ego strength to instinctual tension is inadequate. If the patient can prove the therapist cannot stand the anxiety, madness, and helplessness, he knows for sure what he feels is true—the world will fall apart by the discharge of tension. It is therefore vital to discover that the therapist not only can bear tension, but can also bear that there are some things he cannot stand. It may be essential for some patients to see their therapist react or act on impulse, and it is a mistake to regard either as intrinsically undesirable or dangerous, even in analytic work.

Little went on to comment upon the generally held belief that any physical contact between patient and therapist must be understood as a sexual seduction, noting that as students we are taught this, and that it is not something only to be found by actual experience. It is important to know when and when not to touch a patient. If a patient develops excitement from touching he does not usually want an active response, but if already excited and unable to find another release, then contact may help find it. If a patient's internal experiences are being expressed, there is no occasion for touching, and to do so would interfere. These body happenings belong to earliest infancy. The usefulness of body contact is limited, and in neurotic disorders it is both unnecessary and unhelpful (Little 1981).

thoughtful deliberation, and only when there seems to be no other avenue. Such options have to remain open and are vital to consider, for in some cases they may give the only opportunity for genuine hope.[5] Making an accurate determination is crucial, because there are other circumstances in which abandoning a secure framework can be quite detrimental.[6]

---

[5]**Hans Loewald** also noted the many difficulties that arose in treating more seriously disturbed patients. He remarked, however, that he did not labor under the illusion that analysis consisted or could consist only of strictly psychoanalytic procedures and interventions. An actual analysis contains many elements that in themselves are not psychoanalytic, but that are intended to underline, bring back to mind, and promote the specific tasks of analysis. These elements may also be necessary to prevent the patient from engaging in activities that interfere, or to prevent self-destructive moves. The less mature the patient, the more such interventions are at times necessary. While ultimately such moves are to be understood as resistance and analyzed, they often cannot be dealt with analytically, since the foundation for the patient's analytic understanding may not yet be firm enough (Loewald 1970).

[6]**Arnold Modell** was concerned with the problems of treating more primitive and narcissistic disorders and with the frequency of modifications in technique. He described the role of actual traumas in the etiology of these narcissistic disorders, especially various types of developmental failures of the actual holding environment. Mothers had often failed in their protective function, interfering with the child's sense of safety and trust. A common response was in the formation of a precocious and fragile sense of self that had to be supported by grandiose and omnipotent fantasies. It is these structural deformations of the ego that seem to characterize narcissistic pathology. The therapist must then function as a container to offer the required background of safety to support illusion. In narcissistic patients the analytic setting serves to facilitate necessary ego consolidation so that mutative interpretations eventually can be effective and the therapeutic alliance established. At some point inter-

When traumatic preverbal experiences are embedded in pathological defenses, they may only become accessible to therapeutic influence within the arms of a secure and unyielding framework. A great deal depends upon the extent to which good-self experience has been structured within the personality, so that firm, well-managed ground rules, boundaries, and conditions can evoke their containing influence. Generally speaking, most efforts to modify the conditions of the treatment are motivated by a search for reinforcement of pathological defenses. When this is the case, the pressure must be received by a therapist in order to understand the unconscious meaning of the interaction, thereby gaining the information required to formulate an effective interpretive intervention. The importance of this approach was apparent in the treatment of an 11-year-old girl.

> The initial contact was made by her father, who had called from another city. The family was moving, and he wanted some assurance that their child would have a therapist. He had called to ask if she could meet with me before they moved, and I agreed. The night before the scheduled time a message was left cancelling the appointment. Several months later, the father called again, requesting that the mother, father, and child meet with me. The child then spoke with me on the phone and said it was her idea to have her parents come in, since she was scared. She felt she could only come in if they were with her. She added that she had insisted on coming several months ago but at the last minute changed her mind. An appointment was made and all three arrived.

---

pretations are required for the dissolution of the magical fantasies associated with the holding environment, for if these are not presented, the analytic process itself may become a transitional object leading to an interminable addiction to analysis (Modell 1976).

She was an uncoordinated, gangly girl wearing sloppy clothes, who looked out of place with her well-dressed, sophisticated, intellectual parents. She was noticeably disheveled, awkward, somewhat shy, and obviously frightened. Her parents began by complaining about coming. She had been in psychotherapy before, and the family move had been traumatic for her. They had tried to soften the blow by telling her they would find someone. During this discussion she was smiling, so I asked her if she felt able to talk alone, and she immediately ordered her parents to go away. After they left she started to talk about her previous therapist. He had been marvelous and she missed him. It was hard to leave because he was so understanding. She didn't think she could tolerate the separation, but now she felt okay about it. It looked to her like I was friendly and she liked the sound of my voice. She could just tell I would be a nice person, which made her tremendously relieved. Her thoughts shifted to how uprooted she felt from friends, school, and her old neighborhood, and she spoke in detail, especially about the neighborhood. She knew every corner of it. It was open to her and she always knew where she could find her parents. She was afraid anytime she was in strange territory. At this point she paused to ask if I knew her previous therapist, but before I could answer she went on to describe the good things he did. His office was in a shopping area, her parents left her off and went shopping, and she didn't feel left out since the therapist brought her treats. She hoped I would do likewise. Suddenly she became concerned because she couldn't remember what her therapist had looked like.

Consciously, she was asking to be fed and comforted, which seemed to be her way of gaining some measure of regulation and of easing the anxiety of separation. At the same time she couldn't retain the image of a therapist who had participated in this fashion. I commented that I thought she might be worried that I would do those things and thus prevent her from knowing how she felt deeper inside. Her reaction was to state, "Do you mean you won't get me presents?" Without hesitation she proceeded to talk about her life being dominated by a succession of housekeepers and cooks. They were always coming and going. She constantly experienced separations from people who were responsible for her care. New ones arrived, she formed attachments, and then they left. At the end of the session I introduced the question of scheduling regular times; she wanted to meet every day. However, she was reminded of a series of situations in which she was appeased and infantilized. It made her think of how hard she worked and of the little time she had for herself. I said that I thought this was a message that she needed some time by herself, and we arranged sessions on alternate days.

In the ensuing months several themes emerged. She talked a lot about how overworked she was and of the inordinate demands that were placed upon her. People expected far too much. I thought she was expressing her response to my interpretive posture and specifically how she felt about my attention to maintaining a firm and unyielding framework. Whenever I would comment that she might be referring to her feelings about my attitude it would elicit a loud and adamant denial. "Oh, no—it has nothing to do with you." Without skipping a beat she would go on to emphasize how she only had the most positive feelings toward me. She thought of me as being the most understanding, kind, and warm person. Another theme was of being a scapegoat, particularly in her family but also at school. If anyone had a bad day it was blamed on her. She described many parental fights and her efforts to stop them, which ended up with her being attacked and blamed for the disturbance. She was always seen as the cause of everyone's troubles. Another persistent theme was leaving her old neighborhood. This was associated with an intense feeling of longing and often brought tears. Her descriptions were vivid and created an image of a communal environment that was safe and secure, offering pleasure and a joyful sharing of experiences, with a parental presence always available. Talking about the loss made her cry and she had a feeling that it could never be regained. This longing, along with the extreme disruption evoked by the move, seemed to reflect a traumatic period of her early development. There was in fact a dramatic change in her mother's attitude toward her upon the birth of a sibling when she was 10 months old. It also coincided with the death of her grandmother, which had triggered a serious depression in her mother. Her associations to the old neighborhood appeared to be the echoes of having experienced an empathic early oral phase, abruptly interrupted just as processes of individuation became most active.

A new theme then emerged, centering around people who left her with short notice. She stressed that the traumatic aspect was not the separation itself. It was the lack of notice so that she could have time to react and prepare for it. In the midst of this I discovered that I would have to be out of town and miss a session with her at the end of the week. She began the following session by talking about her outrage at people who suddenly left without telling her beforehand. She spoke of her father, who suddenly announced he would be away for a few days. Her mother often left and did not let her know until the night before. A housekeeper was leaving and only informed her at the last minute. A teacher was pregnant and let her know one day before departing. I said that something had come up, making it necessary for me to miss a session late in the week, and as she was showing me how she was affected by such things, I thought she might have a lot of feeling about it happening between us. She first looked surprised, started to say that it was okay, and then mumbled that she knew I just couldn't help it. She paused and asked, "Will you make up the time?" She outlined all of the ways in which the time could be made up and rescheduled. I said I didn't want to answer until both of us had a clearer picture of what it would mean to her for me to make it up. She replied that it was essential to find a way to make it up and remembered numerous examples of her parents buying her presents whenever they left. This made up for the leaving, since she felt better about it and was not so upset. She even looked forward to the present while they were away. She stopped and said, "Oh I know you won't get me a present, that isn't what I want. I just want you to make up the time." She emphasized how important it was in order to prevent her from getting angry and upset. The session was ending and she asked, "Well, will you make up the time?" I remarked that I didn't think it would be a good idea. She immediately exploded in rage; her face became red, she pulled at her hair and stormed out, slamming the door as she shouted, "I hate you."

She had been putting pressure on me to join her in reinforcing a narcissistically fixated defensive position. She desperately wanted me to behave in ways that allowed her to idealize me, or to consistently mirror back to her my appreciation of her good qualities. All of this served the purpose of sealing off the underlying rage that was threatening to emerge. Her idealization of me gave some hint as to what the difficulty was, in that she consistently portrayed me as kind, understanding, and quietly contained. She specifically idealized attributes that involved an absence of aggression. She herself avoided any expression of anger, although it was always present in others, and external objects were almost always seen as insensitive and abandoning. I intervened after taking her associations to mean that she needed to experience the feelings that were associated with separation and loss. I thereby refused to participate in reinforcing her pathological defenses, and her response was to become enraged.

She returned for her next session looking very excited, which was quite unusual for her. She couldn't wait to tell

me what had happened the night before. She began by
referring to her fear of being alone in the house. At such
times she was usually filled with a vague, ill-defined,
ominous sense of dread. Everyone had left the house and
she was thinking about what had happened with me and
about how furious she was. She had never felt that way
before and started to worry that I wouldn't see her, or that
she would feel too humiliated to return. She recalled
getting so angry at me it felt like she would explode and at
just that moment there was a burst of light. It seemed to be
inside of her, though she thought it might have been the
lights of a passing car. She felt terrified, as if she were in
great danger but suddenly had the sensation that it was her
grandmother's spirit. Her grandmother had died when she
was 10 months old and was especially important to her.
Since she had died at the time of her sister's birth, the
grandmother had never known her sister. Thus my patient
was the only grandchild who had contact with the grandmother, which made her feel very special. Although she
was scared at first, the terror subsided as the idea formed
that it was her grandmother. She soon found herself
engaged in an internal dialogue. She told her grandmother
all of her complaints about being scapegoated and abandoned, and the grandmother encouraged her to develop
her own sense of self and not depend so much on others
for that. She also pointed out that clinging to people only
held her back, and in relying on someone else's behavior
she was giving up on herself. The grandmother stressed
that she had to let go of this hold on others for her sense
of well-being and find it within herself. Thus the grandmother was experienced as a pragmatic understanding
figure, placing emphasis on autonomy and independence.
She was excited at having this kind of image inside, for it
felt like a very helpful presence.

This patient had been confronted with the constant
pressure of an overloading of aggression through much of
her life, and her entire attitude was focused on preventing

any awareness of its magnitude. Through my abstaining from joining her in this defensive position she was able to express the anger she felt at being abandoned. The internal impression of this aspect of the therapeutic interaction was represented in the figure of the grandmother and was now available as a source of restraint and regulation. The qualities she had experienced in the relationship with me enabled her to stand on more separate ground and to begin to integrate the extreme hostility she had previously needed to ward off. The actual experience of feeling such intense rage was momentarily overwhelming. However, it resulted in a consolidation of her resources, supported by an internalization of the therapeutic interaction gradually becoming a part of her psychic structure. Initially, and on the surface, she thought of my refusal as an injustice. Underneath, however, my desisting from appeasing and infantilizing her helped her to discover that neither she nor I was destroyed by her aggression. Her defenses were designed to insure that she would not come in touch with the depth of her anger at the many injustices she had received. The consequence was in her moving into a more advanced level of psychic organization that carried with it a new way of looking at herself. She could then find the necessary resources to achieve a more complete and separate existence, since her extreme dependence on others for internal regulation was alleviated.

It is quite a different state of affairs when a patient is desperately seeking to gain a concrete experience of contact, which can provide the necessary groundwork for inaccessible, unspeakable, and inarticulable psychic content to enter the realm of mental representation and ultimately have access to expression. These are individuals for whom the only means of realizing psychic growth is through successfully engaging a therapist in what may reinforce a pathological defense, or even participate in the living out of an unconscious fantasy or infantile trauma. It usually involves very primitively organized and structurally deficient patients who have had little good self-experience in the developmental years. These sparse but valuable internal impressions then have to be split off from any attachment to an object in order to be preserved and protected. The resulting unrepresented, and hence unsymbolized, infantile experiences may only be reachable through the pathological structures built into the personality to guard them. Under such circumstances it is essential for a therapist to be alert for any hints of emergence of these vulnerable strivings for growth, so they can be given the support required to enable them to be experienced within a relationship.[7]

---

[7]**Robert Stolorow** and **Frank Lachman** approached the task of understanding the more severe forms of psychopathology and their treatment by conceptualizing the developmental lines leading to the differentiation, integration, and consolidation of self- and object-representations. Grasping the origins and consequences of interferences with, and arrests in this developmental progression provides a broader and more embracing view of psychopathology than was possible within the framework of classical conflict theory. In the process, they gave a penetrating developmental perspective on the effects of limitations in the therapist's ability to respond empathically, due to the constraints imposed by the usual conditions associated with psychoanalytic treatment. A theoretical comprehension of developmental deficits and arrests has crucial implications for the precise framing of analytic interventions and for conceptualizing the course and therapeutic action of psychoanalytic treatment. A variety of psychological products may not only express psychopathology but also signal the attainment of developmental steps in the structuralization of the representational world. In addition, the possibility of reversals to pre-stages, in which self- and object-images are merged and unintegrated, remains ever present. This may occur either as a regression or as a disintegration of newly acquired representational structure that is as yet insufficiently consolidated. The therapist must be

When a therapist's strict adherence to sound psychoanalytic principles is a product of defensiveness, it interferes with the flexibility needed to adapt these principles to the structural organization predominant in a patient's personality. A therapist may then recognize a patient's urgent appeal to be well contained but misinterpret the accompanying pressure to alter the framework as solely motivated by demands arising out of pathological defenses. The push may be fueled by a patient's reaction to the impossible limitations imposed by conditions unresponsive to what is essential for constructive growth to evolve and be exaggerated by an inability to overcome a therapist's unrecognized resistance. In this way a therapist may be coerced into behavior that ruptures the containing properties of the relationship, which may only be salvaged if it eventually leads to illuminating and clarifying what is lacking and must be supplied. A therapist therefore can be pressured into modifying the treatment framework, which might not have been necessary had there been an openness to receiving a patient's unconscious perceptions of what had been wrong.

It is important to make these various distinctions in order to become more discriminating in defining the specific thera-

---

attuned to these shifts, which may occur in consequence of minute failures in empathic understanding or in reaction to the arousal of intrapsychic conflict. Analytic exploration must not be complicated by a failure to recognize or acknowledge empathic lapses. The therapist's neutrality and consistent understanding of the patient's archaic states and needs not only contribute to the articulation of the patient's representational world, but also function as a holding environment. The therapeutic action of this environment is to provide a facilitating medium reinstating the developmental processes of representational differentiation and integration that had been traumatically aborted and arrested during the patient's formative years (Stolorow and Lachman 1980).

peutic experiences needed by a given patient.[8] Whenever the view of what constitutes a secure and effective treatment framework is obscure, there is a potential for entering into detrimental or destructive collusion with a patient. However, a therapist can be equally harmful and disruptive by responding to this difficult problem with the introduction of rigid rules. A secure therapeutic framework possesses containing and growth-promoting attributes. Therefore to alter this essential component unnecessarily would most certainly work against attaining a positive outcome. It may not always be possible, however, to identify clearly the exact features required, making it imperative to unearth any existing rigidities in a therapist's attitude.

---

[8]**John Gedo** did not believe the principles involved in addressing the therapeutic needs and curative influences in more severe disturbances were any different from those involved in treating less seriously disturbed patients, for psychological treatment in general consisted of a variety of interventions. If these interventions were classified in terms of the psychological changes they were designed to effect, a list of treatment modalities could be devised for whatever therapeutic measures were indicated. Thus, if the aim of an intervention was to bring some facet of a patient's mental life that was hitherto unconscious into explicit awareness, the therapeutic transaction could be classified as an interpretation. When the therapist lends himself as an empathic witness to organized aspects of a patient's efforts to achieve self-understanding, the operative therapeutic modality is the introspective activity itself. In addition, the nonverbal messages pertaining to a patient's limitations are equally relevant as communications to a therapist, and there are therapeutic realms beyond interpretation characterized by a set of noninterpretive measures that provide a holding environment for the patient. Psychoanalysis provides matchless conditions for a detailed study of early development, making it the optimal area for understanding and treating archaic personality disorders (Gedo 1984).

When confronted with obstacles to progress, for whatever reason, an exploration of new ways to effect constructive change has to be considered carefully. The task is to develop treatment principles that are sound because they are flexible enough to be adapted to the structural organization of a patient's personality. There is much to be discovered when a treatment process is unsuccessful, for therein lie the seeds of something that has gone awry. At the very least, a broader sense can be gained of what kinds of disturbances may not be amenable to psychological treatment as it is presently known.

A therapeutic failure almost always carries with it some painful awareness of a lack of knowledge or experience, an inability to have been sufficiently receptive to a patient's dilemma, or a vague sense of unseen, unconscious forces having been activated that interfere with ideal or even adequate therapeutic functioning. The fact that it is unrealistic to expect to function well in all situations at all times, or that the nature of a patient's disturbance was a major contributing factor offers little consolation. Whatever was responsible, a therapist's part in it, no matter how small, cannot be denied and must serve as a spur to new learning.[9,10]

---

[9]**Robert Stolorow** and colleagues adopted an intersubjective point of view, which they felt was especially important in treating patients whose archaic states often led to their being difficult to treat. These authors thought there was no such thing as a difficult patient, there are only difficulties that arise in the unique intersection of two subjectivities, which constitute the psychoanalytic situation. They were convinced that transference and countertransference, negative therapeutic reactions, psychopathology, and the therapeutic action of psychoanalysis could not be understood apart from the intersubjective context in which they took form (Stolorow et al. 1983).
[10]**Peter Giovacchini,** who has explored the role of a therapist's countertransference reactions in the problems encoun-

There are occasions when it does appear as though the failure is the consequence of unworkable qualities in a patient's psychological makeup, for whatever was required went beyond the limitations inherent in a psychotherapeutic undertaking. Whatever the circumstances, however, a lingering suspicion remains that there may have been more meaning to the experience than had thus far been unearthed, or that was capable of being known within our present grasp of psychological processes. It is relatively easy to search for and find rationalizations to explain why the result was inevitable. We may come to the conclusion that either the patient was too damaged to make use of a human relationship devoted to expanding self-awareness, or that the difficulty was simply not accessible to psychological influence. Nevertheless, there is great value in elucidating a therapist's role in that failure, no matter how large or small it may be. This was brought out in the treatment of a young adult man who was initially referred by a nonmedical therapist overwhelmed by the extent of the young man's illness. He was concerned that the patient might need more intensive psychotherapy and/or a hospital setting, and was worried that he might kill himself. He was also being seen concurrently by a physician in order to regulate his antipsychotic medication.

---

tered with more primitively organized patients, noted how the judgment as to whether a patient was treatable depended more upon the therapist's psychic integration than upon the patient's psychopathology. This did not mean that the therapist's psychic health was the sole determinant, since there are many technical factors that have to be learned and experienced. There is, however, a reciprocal relationship between the therapist's receptivity, which is a function of his integration, and the ability to incorporate certain principles and procedures and thereby make them inherent aspects of his analytic style (Giovacchini 1974).

The patient was a thin, stiff, soft-spoken young man with a fixed, forced smile. He walked like a robot and, though very nervous, spoke quite freely. He had not wanted to see me. He liked his therapist and was upset about the referral. He felt his therapist was helping him. After these introductory remarks he quickly switched to talking about his family. His parents had been divorced since he was 13. He described his mother as very emotional and unpredictable, going from outbursts of rage with no apparent provocation to enveloping him in a totally unpredictable fashion. He thought of his father as being much like himself—quiet, intimidated, and submissive. He had alternated living with each parent since the divorce, with a brief interlude when he tried to go away to college. He had a younger sister and a younger brother. As an adolescent, he was often called upon by his sister to sit with her when she felt suicidal. He was envious of his brother, who had escaped the family. He, however, had always felt responsible for his mother and sister and was terrified of being alone.

During his childhood he went through the motions of living, mostly feeling empty and isolated. As a young adolescent, he formed a homosexual love attachment and began to lose his sense of orientation. He experienced feelings of depersonalization and of fusing with those to whom he felt close. He panicked and "lost his mind." This period was blurry in his memory. The only clear recollection was the experience of feeling whole when he acknowledged that he was a homosexual. He could be close to someone, and no longer felt alone and isolated. There were numerous homosexual encounters in his adolescent years, making him feel loved and valued. He also felt engulfed by his family and incapable of managing on his own.

He went to college in an attempt to escape, and was cut off from any homosexual relationships. At first he became self-conscious and then increasingly paranoid. He felt attacked by everyone's eyes, withdrew, and was immobile. He began to hear voices through the walls and windows criticizing him, and to get away from them he returned home, feeling totally defeated. At that time he was hospitalized and given medication. Prior to the medication he had the idea that he would hurt someone if he moved and thus was almost paralyzed. He saw himself as the source of all evil and destructiveness in the world. With medication he could move, care for his body, work with numbers on a job, and be functional. He was worried, however, about the associated loss of his sexual drive.

The following session occurred after I received a telephone message from a local pharmacist requesting that I renew his prescription. Instead, I called my patient to let him know that I thought it was important for us to explore the meaning of this message. He sounded frantic on the telephone but then passively agreed and came to his session to explain. His prescription had run out, I was a physician, another one could easily be written, and I could then take over for the doctor who had been doing it. I remarked upon his assumption that I would simply prescribe medication without having much of an idea as to whether it was in his best interests. He looked surprised. He assumed that I would give him medication, since in the many contacts he had with doctors they had always done this. He knew there were a lot of different kinds and he wondered if that's what I was questioning. I must be uncertain as to which one I should prescribe. He also knew there were side effects and wondered if that's what concerned me. He could not grasp the idea that I was questioning the meaning of medication to him.

I said that if he could talk about the medicine I would listen and then maybe have a better idea as to how to answer. He was silent awhile before speaking of how his mother always did everything for him. He was troubled because he asked her to do things even though he knew it was bad for him. He often felt like a baby although he couldn't stop it. He gave many examples of getting up at night and going to his mother's room, pleading with her to give him reassurance. He knew she would always tell him everything was all right. He also knew that even though it made him feel better momentarily, it did not really help. He went on to describe what it was like to work for his father. His father was worried about him and felt that he should keep busy. He thought so too, for when he had nothing to do he was devastated. His father always took care of things for him, rather than encouraging him to do things on his own.

While he spoke I heard him expressing what medication meant to him, suggesting that it would be infantilizing and destructive for me to prescribe it. I also had a feeling that it would not be enough to simply say no, for the way he looked for help was certainly not in any way under his control. However it was not as yet clear to me what he needed or whether there was some irreversible self-damage. I wondered if he just did not have the where-withal to use a relationship as a means of gaining construc-tive change. I did say to him that he seemed to be answering the question about his medication. It looked as though my giving medication would support a way of being that he himself did not think was good for him, and I would then be of little use in helping him to grow. He listened, nodded his head, and reflected on how terrified he was at the thought of being without it. He wanted to be off medication but was afraid he'd be immobilized and totally unable to function. He feared having to go back into the hospital. As soon as he mentioned it, he frantically began to ask, "Do I have to go back to the hospital?" repeating the question over and over. I commented that it sounded like he could feel the need to have a hospital around him to make him feel secure, and he seemed to be questioning whether he and I could develop enough of a relationship to provide that for him instead. His frantic questioning shifted to, "Will I be okay?" and "Will I get well?" I remarked upon how he had let me know a little earlier that reassurance, though momentarily helpful, was not very good for him. He became silent again before softly saying that he had decided to stop his medication.

I understood the pressure of his demand as being motivated by defensive constellations that were maintaining his pathology. Although I had decided to refuse to collude and participate in reinforcing them, I still had no definite idea of what he would need from me to provide a proper "hospital." He was afraid that when the support system he had built was removed, there would either not be a sufficiently strong connection between us or that he would not have the capacity to use such a connection. At this point he started to phone me at home. He was desperate, felt like he could kill himself, and demanded reassurance. At times he described feeling like a baby, periodically stating that the calls and what he was asking for were really destructive. I reflected these words back to him and added that there must be something I was missing in our sessions. He would then get quiet and hang up.

Gradually he became increasingly immobile, intensely paranoid, fearful that he was destroying the world, and hallucinatory. His sexual feelings returned and he was convinced that he had fathered his younger brother. He was also terrified of being sexually aroused by his mother at home or by me in the office. He described it as his feelings pouring out of him like a sieve. Overtly he expressed a feeling that if I gave in and yielded to his pressure all hope was lost, but on the other hand if I didn't give in to his demands he would be destroyed by his internal chaos. I had many questions about his treatability and many doubts as to whether a psychotherapeutic process would be able to heal what seemed like extensive self-damage. My uncertainty was heightened by the absence of any indication that the relationship was offering a containing influence. It was becoming abundantly clear that the therapeutic relationship alone was not sufficient. However it was unclear as to whether there was a basic deficiency embodied in his illness, whether there had been too much self-damage already, whether my understanding was lacking, or whether possibly hospitalization was required as well. Furthermore, if round-the-clock care in a hospital was the missing ingredient, this did not mean it could be found in any given hospital.

Hospital facilities are often rigidly constructed and not able to adapt to the unique needs of a patient, or they are not flexible enough in their routines to support a profound regression. When an individual's attention is occupied with reacting to an unempathic environment, it works in opposition to what is involved in fostering a therapeutic symbiosis. Although a total treatment environment has the potential for being shaped to facilitate such regressions, it may also present an overall atmosphere that demands a defensive response. Under these conditions the extent of the necessary regression is obviated, and if it were to take place the patient would then be vulnerable to its destructive impact.

The task of building a relationship with the containing influences of a total environment is difficult at best, and may at times require the support of a hospital. With this patient, the therapeutic value of a regressive process was already in doubt, and it began to appear that he might need a hospital to evaluate fully his treatability by this approach. The absence of an adequate facility, however, added a further dimension of complexity. It looked unlikely that conditions of safety could be created with the therapeutic relationship as the only source of security.

He continued to make demands for medication and reassurance, always accompanied by some communication emphasizing that he couldn't be helped if I participated in that way. He also did not display any capacity to utilize interpretive interventions. There was much to suggest that his illness was so entrenched that a regressive treatment experience might not be either feasible or indicated. He posed a difficult dilemma. I could see no direction other than to continue to interpret the destructive effects were I to join him in reinforcing a pathological defense.

At this juncture he finally made a decision to see me no longer. He said that he couldn't tolerate the conditions of the relationship. He felt that he needed medication and was going to return to the doctor who prescribed it. It was much too overwhelming to him, too frightening, and he just couldn't go on. He stated, "You see right through me and I can't stand it." He then described how he could tell when he was understood and when he was not. "When you don't understand me I feel safer. It doesn't last long and I start to distrust you. Then you begin to understand me and your eyes are like laser beams that bore into me. I can't tolerate it when I call you in the middle of the night and ask you to treat me as my mother does, and you see that. It feels like you are cutting right into me. When I told you I thought I was my brother's father you were immediately aware that my sexual feelings were coming alive and I was aroused by my mother. I can't stand that vision of me. It's too painful and I'm too much of a baby. I've come to realize that when I tell you I'm afraid of going to the hospital I really have a very strong wish to go. I've been wanting you to put me in the hospital, where I once was, so that I can be totally taken care of." With this pronouncement he left, and I heard nothing from him for several weeks. Then he called for an appointment.

He came in looking energetic and alive, with animation in his voice. He was excited and couldn't wait to see me. After he had left his last appointment he had stopped and said to himself, "What am I doing?" Later he called the medicating doctor and ended that relationship. He stopped taking his medication and began to feel alive and like a person. His sexual feelings returned, as did his desire to find a homosexual partner. He was trying once again to recreate the conditions that had sustained him during his adolescent years. This time he wanted to be understood, and since he felt I understood him best, he returned. He thought he had been like a baby, too frightened, and had been running away from that understanding. He waited until he was free of the effects of the medication before he called.

On the surface it sounded as though he was accepting the conditions that he had previously rejected, which started when he left the office and I didn't stop him or object to his leaving. Although it hinted at some emerging potential for healing, and that I might have been on the right track, I was still concerned. The fantasy that motivated him was of a homosexual attachment with no suggestion of his seeking a healthy symbiosis. It seemed to represent his hunger for some kind of fusion in a pathological symbiotic relationship. In addition, there was still no indication of how he would respond in a regressed state. Regular appointments were scheduled and he proceeded to regress precipitously.

In each succeeding hour he became increasingly immobile, reaching a point where he was almost paralyzed and catatonic. He looked pale and developed a foul body odor that he spoke of as putrid. He appeared unwashed, disheveled, and nonfunctional. Speech slowly diminished until it was practically nonexistent. When he did speak his voice was quiet and stilted. Finally he spent each session sitting rigidly in one place with his head bowed. The only words he uttered referred to some attacking hallucinatory experience, or at times he mumbled that if he didn't remain silent he would injure me. The only occasion in which he spoke clearly was in response to his family's request to meet with me. He forcefully expressed his vigorous opposition to that idea. He was then given an ultimatum by his family either to become functional or go to a hospital. He told me to say nothing; it was his decision and he wanted it to occur in just that way. He wanted someone to hospitalize him rather than deciding for himself. He was making only one decision and that was to remain a baby. He knew he could become a baby with me, but that was only for the purpose of his growing up. He wanted to be put in the hospital where he could stay a baby. Shortly thereafter, the treatment ended when he was placed in a hospital by his family.

He had correctly perceived me as encouraging a regression in order to find the experiences that could provide him with the wherewithal to differentiate and separate himself. He sought reinforcement of compensatory, pathological defenses, and when I desisted, his regression became both malignant and out of control. He was totally unable to use me as an object onto whom he could project his psychic contents, a therapeutic symbiosis was not established, and he was only confronted with the severity of his damage and the extent of his limitations. The likelihood is that he may become periodically functional in severely restricted ways, in and out of a hospital, and supported by medication.

It is difficult to define exactly which factors were most influential in determining the negative outcome of this treatment venture. Whether it was my style and personality along with some unrecognized blind spots, or whether it was the patient's deficits was never completely clear. From the beginning, the depth of his disturbance was so great, and/or the absence of a containing influence so extreme, that an effective and workable therapeutic alliance was never formed. He had returned in a manner reminiscent of how he functioned in adolescence. The regression that ensued was malignant in nature, and it was not possible to provide anything that fostered growth.

Throughout the course of treatment, my understanding was a source of either pain or danger. The derivatives of what constituted pathological qualities in a relationship were abundant, but such relationships seemed to be valued rather than distrusted or rejected, and they were sought as a source of supply. Conversely, a relationship having growth-promoting attributes was seen as over-whelming or frightening and thus avoided. He consistently put pressure on me to collude with him in rein-forcing his pathology, but gave me no usable picture of what I could bring to help him progress. I was only able to offer my own concept, which he experienced as an impo-sition or demand. Either he didn't show it, I was blind to its presence, or there was so much damage that such a view was simply not available to him. His ability to function with medication, though narrow and depleted, gave some indication that it was the best therapeutic answer for him, at least in the present. Perhaps most importantly, he seemed to experience being understood as destructive, rather than offering hope in promoting growth.

Psychoanalytic treatment is based on a love of the truth and of understanding the resistances inherent in seeking it out. This is a process that has to be constantly fought for against what at times can be extremely strong opposition. The difficult and painful task of listening to the truth in our patients depends first on our ability to listen to the truth within ourselves. That task is fraught with so many dangers, and our natural inclination as human beings is so invested with the need to defend, that in order to maintain a proper listening attitude we need help. The process of self-analysis has to be an ongoing and active one, but we also need the help of our patients. Through listening carefully to a patient's unconscious perceptions we can gain validation of the accuracy of our interventions, and conversely, some idea of the obstacles that prevent us from seeing clearly. All of this must take place as we maintain our vigil and retain spontaneity.

The conditions of the treatment must be guided by a patient's unconscious communications on what is needed to promote growth. Yet such a pathway was not found with this particular patient. The patient himself felt that this lack was a product of the degree and nature of his disturbance, although an element of uncertainty remained in my mind as to whether there was something lacking in my ability to understand him well enough. Listening, responding to, and thereby encouraging unconscious communications was not enough, and interpretations had little influence. The offer of a sound therapeutic holding environment, which fostered positive introjects and allowed the emergence of the terrifying aspects of unconscious transference experience, was much too threatening. It suggested that some new actual experience may have had to be provided if treatment was to be successful, and if this was the case, its specific nature was not apparent to me at any time.

The Effect of Traumatic Preverbal Experiences on the Concept of Insight

The idea that psychological health was established through the solution of intrapsychic, primarily infantile, instinctual conflict was not tenable with more seriously disturbed individuals. In this earlier conception, cure was seen exclusively in terms of conflict resolution for the expansion of consciousness, which had little applicability to those individuals whose primitive level of psychic structuralization demanded a different view of the source of their pathology. Interpretation of unconscious mental content and of transference repetitions, together with what was thought of as the gaining of insight and working through, had previously all been considered essential elements in effecting therapeutic change. However, the particular factors that are curative in more serious disturbances tend to include other components that are different.[11-16] This information had

---

[11]**M. Sechehaye** was one of the early clinicians who attempted to utilize psychoanalytic methods in the treatment of profound psychic disorders. She considered it imperative for a therapist to find something other than the verbal method of psychoanalysis in order to be understood. The initial disturbance occurred before the development of spoken language, and the patient is regressed to the stage of magic, presymbolic participation. The mode of expression has to be more primitive and concrete and correspond to the stage at which the trauma took place. The transference is then the result and not the cause of the improvement (Sechehaye 1951).

[12]**Donald Winnicott** paid particular attention to the problem of extreme dependency in finding a cure for borderline and psychotic patients. The hope was to keep the dependency within the confines of the transference, the sessions, and the setting. However, there was no way to tell in advance, or even to make the sort of diagnosis concerned with the assessment of needs. Thus, when the patient is without parental mental nursing, the therapist doing psychoanalysis will find the patient is not only daydreaming of being taken over by the analyst and into his or her home, but also actually needing to be taken in (Winnicott 1963).

[13]**Edward Joseph** tried to explain the therapeutic action of psychoanalysis, especially in those instances where it seems to

to be taken into account, making it necessary to reassess the

_____

occur silently. He referred to analysis as a never-ending undertaking, since the tremendous realm of unconscious life is never exhausted. The therapeutic benefits of a variety of theoretical and technical approaches rest on the fact that each of these deals with some portion of the individual's unconscious life, although no one analysis deals with all aspects. Alteration of any one portion of the internal world leads to a readjustment of the relationships between other unconscious portions of the mind, a process that goes on silently. Patients frequently report the disappearance of difficulties that have never been analyzed during the course of treatment. Psychoanalysis itself has no unified theory and there is no one truth. There are a multitude of truths, behind which lie still more complex phenomena yet to be uncovered (Joseph 1979).

[14]**Robert Stolorow** and **Frank Lachman** presented a way of understanding the transference that could shed light on a crucial diagnostic distinction that must be made at any given moment in the treatment. Transferences in which the therapist is experienced as a whole object based upon displaced affects and conflictual wishes have to be distinguished from those in which he is experienced as an archaic prestructural self object based upon primitive representational configurations. There are those in whom self- and object-representations are insufficiently structured, and whose capacity for differentiation is so impaired that they require supplementation by specific interventions from the therapist. The therapist must provide a model for the defective discriminative and integrative functions by articulating these usually silent processes for the patient. At the very least, the therapist must take care that erroneous defense interpretations do not discourage any emerging structuralization (Stolorow and Lachman 1980).

[15]**Heinz Kohut** is widely known for introducing a self psychological approach to mental functioning, which is based on placing self-experience at the center of attention and is understood through introspection and empathy. He thus saw cure as the opening of the path of empathy between the self and self object on mature and adult levels. A self psychological perspec-

ingredients that go into the development and evolution of insight during the course of any approach to treatment.

The manner in which insight unfolds and the various components that are involved have implications for a therapist's

---

tive visualizes the self-structure as inherently healthy and able to realize its innate potential relatively conflict-free if not interfered with by excessive empathic failures. Increased self-knowledge and insight are then independent of the processes leading to increasing health. Preoedipal events and the role of the actual empathic environment are considered the primary agents of the cure. Defenses are thereby portrayed as miscarried attempts at repair in the effort of the self to realize its goals. Drive derivatives are the disintegration products of a self enfeebled by empathic failures (Kohut 1982a).

[16]**Sidney Blatt** and **Rebecca Behrends** thought progression in treatment took place through the same mechanisms involved in normal psychological development. Thus therapeutic change occurs as a developmental sequence of separation and individuation, including gratifying involvements, incompatibility, and internalization. It is clearly a relationship context that provides the patient with an opportunity to explore and change, and for that reason it is important to specify the way in which it creates a series of mutative experiences. A libidinal attachment can be an integrating and restructuring experience in and of itself. Infantile wishes are not merely resistances, but are essential for optimal use of the relationship. It is doubtful if anyone conducts a successful treatment without having done anything but interpret. Only a timely and appropriate attitude toward gratification, expressed in an internal state communicated unconsciously beyond a verbal level, can allow a patient to accept the need to love and be loved and express it without fear. The concerns about gratification seem to stem from concerns about the analyst's inappropriately using the relationship to manipulate or misusing the relationship to create a corrective experience. Theory and practice converge in the clinical situation, which is then reflected in the attitude of the therapist (Blatt and Behrends 1987).

conduct.[17] This continues to be a matter requiring greater clarification. In teasing out the multiplicity of curative factors encompassed within a given treatment process, the basic foundation of insight from which they emanate can sometimes be overlooked. This is particularly the case if insight is thought of in a narrow way, encompassing only intellectual and emotional perspectives on the meaning of experience. Insight must therefore be considered in any approach to understanding the changes leading to cure, but the concept must be expanded through observing how it evolves from the effects of positive identifications and new structure formation.[18]

---

[17]**Joseph Sandler** and colleagues attempted to clarify a number of frequently used psychoanalytic concepts whose meaning often became obscure when their original formulations were revised or expanded. They depicted the concept of insight as firmly rooted in any formulation regarding the processes of change that lead to cure. The concept of emotional insight, however, should be divorced from the concept of cure, for it did not follow that such insight would necessarily be followed by progressive therapeutic changes in the patient. These authors thought the most useful approach was to differentiate "intellectual insight" from those forms of insight that either release emotions or involve some aspect of a feeling state as part of the content of the insight itself. It appeared that therapeutic change as a consequence of analysis depended to a large degree both on the provision of a structured and organized conceptual and affective framework within which the patient could effectively place himself, and a subjective experience of self and others (Sandler et al. 1973).

[18]**Leo Rangell** considered it unnecessary for separate schools of thought to form over divergent theories of the oedipal and preoedipal years. He described the relative roles of castration anxiety and separation anxiety, sexual conflicts versus problems of self-differentiation, and the early mother relationship versus later triangular conflicts of the oedipal period. Reconstruction had always been pertinent to both the preoedipal and

An enlarging perspective on the many factors that possess curative value in a variety of patients has resulted in a reassessment of the concept of insight. Consequently, a more complete picture of what can be included within its definition has

---

oedipal period. Rangell questioned whether the research into narcissistic states had reached a new source of origins hitherto inaccessible, had sharpened instruments with which to make contact with such a period, or had added new and significant changes to psychoanalytic theory. The therapist moved between transference and nontransference, between phenomena stemming from early and later stages of development, and with conflicts in all patients presenting derivatives at all levels. Any fixation point is thus to be avoided and overcome; any repetitive pattern can serve a defensive purpose, and these are alerting signals for the therapist to step in. Necessary activity could be differentiated from manipulative role-playing, with the transference facilitating recall of the past, and the past illuminating the transference. Affect and cognition were both necessary, and neither was contradictory to or exclusive of the other.

The therapist combined humanistic and scientific concern, common sense and naturalness, and utilized affect and cognition, as does the patient. All four surfaces mesh and interact in the psychoanalytic situation, empathy is not to be confused with countertransference, and whatever material emerges is subordinated to rational understanding. Rangell also felt that an active role on the part of the patient was necessary and must be continuously enlisted, for every patient needs precisely that motivation in order to allow progress and the effects of analysis to take place. Emotional and intellectual insight together are effected by undoing unconscious structuralized conflicts, releasing energy for the pursuit of healthier activity. Along the way are a constant series of microidentifications with the analyzing function of the therapist, first partially and experimentally, then with more familiarity and security, and finally with autonomy. It is only in this way that an analytic cure can be achieved (Rangell 1979).

emerged.[19] Insight is the basic agent concerned with cure, though the means by which both insight and cure are achieved is conceived of quite differently by various clinicians, especially when dealing with more primitive personalities.

Insight is most clearly noticeable through the function of self-observation, to which it is intimately linked, whether it involves cognitive or affective elements or a combination of both. Thus if the structural foundation for self-observation has been formed during the developmental years, the capacity for achieving insight through emotional and intellectual understanding is facilitated almost solely by the influences of interpretations. For those individuals in whom the function of self-observation is on an unsteady foundation, insight requires the stabilizing effect of constructive identifications to be more firmly in place. Those in whom the function of self-observation is deficient or impaired need to have new experiences represented before there is enough of a structural underpinning for self-observation to be functional. This entire gamut of situations all comes under the umbrella of insight, although what would be necessary to attain it would be different in each case.

Approaching the definition in this way is quite consistent with the recognition that the role of the therapist in the treatment is that of a significant curative agent. It has also

---

[19]**Hanna Segal** placed insight as the precondition of any lasting personality change achieved in analysis, and indicated that all other facets were related to it. Psychoanalytic insight was a specific concept having to do with the acquisition of knowledge about one's unconscious, through consciously experiencing processes that were previously unconscious. In order for it to be of therapeutic value it must be correct, reach to the deeper layers of the unconscious, and illuminate those early processes in which the pattern of internal and external relations were laid down and in which the ego is structured (Segal 1981a).

become increasingly apparent that the effect of the interaction itself plays an essential role in eliciting positive changes. Combined with a discriminating view of a therapist's subjective responses as a tool for enlarging the grasp of a patient's preverbal developmental experiences, new light has been shed on the reconstructions that then become necessary. A number of preverbal and nonverbal experiences have become illuminated, since the way they are expressed in the transference relationship has become more recognizable. Interpretations can, therefore, be addressed to what is unspoken and repeated in behavior. This has the impact of being immediate and hence mutative, and adds to the accuracy of reconstructions of the original experience.[20] The result is filling the gaps created by

---

[20]**Harold Blum** paid particular attention to the value of reconstruction, underscoring how it assisted in the analytic restoration of the continuity and cohesion of the personality and how it was fundamental for the therapist. A therapist may not be explicitly aware of the use of these constructions, but will inevitably reconstruct aspects of a patient's infantile life in order to comprehend a personality disorder.

There is a synergism occurring between analysis of resistances and reconstruction, for reconstruction deals not only with content but with ego attributes, dysfunctions, affective states, and object relationships. It deals not only with conflict, but with developmental structure formation, with preoedipal influences, and with arrests and deficits. Reconstruction and recall reduce the transference to its origins and determinants. It attempts to take into account the different derivatives of disturbance that belong together in development, as well as the developmental changes that have taken place since the inception of a disturbance.

Reconstruction of both psychic and external reality is important in situations of denial or derealization, and also where reality has activated a fantasy or precipitated a dormant difficulty. There are significant differences between primal-scene fantasy and actual exposure, fantasy desertion and actual object

missing memories that have been incapable of being symbolized, and uncovering what would otherwise be an unreachable trauma. The traumatic experience can take shape in the therapeutic interaction, and with a new constructive outcome, can lead to the laying down of new structure, making it accessible to integrative functions.

Insight can only be experienced within the transference relationship, as the patient relives both past and present experiences, including real and fantasied aspects. Through the influences of the therapeutic framework and its management, a therapist's attitude and the experience of the ensuing interaction, within which interpretations play an important role, a patient's internal psychic contents undergo modification. Distortions are unraveled, allowing healthy movements toward growth to become more active and to flourish. Insight is curative because it results in the gaining and integration of all facets of the personality. The consequences are a more accurate perception of inner and outer reality, while increasing self-knowledge and awareness enable an individual to manage the internal and external worlds more effectively.

Insight certainly cannot emerge in an unempathic environment, and interpretations have to be much more than accurate

---

loss. The traumatic event may have to be identified and reconstructed to restore reality testing and judgment. If the delusion cannot be understood without the kernel of truth, neither can true identification be understood without the actual model from different phases of development.

Reconstruction goes beyond individual memory and fantasy, and is an integrative act. Childhood conflicts, dangers, and object world are fitted into a developmental context, establishing a new set of meanings, causes, consequences, and relationships. Transference analysis and reconstruction are mutually facilitating, leading to a reliving of the past in a way it was never experienced and could not be because of the child's developmental immaturity (Blum 1980).

or correct in their content. Therapeutic interventions must be presented in a way that allows them to be internalized without undue distortion by a patient, which requires that an effective holding environment have been established. Whenever that is disrupted, for whatever reason, there is a great deal to be learned so that it is not repeated again. Out of a number of such incidents a deeper understanding of a patient's unconscious communications can develop, thereby strengthening the therapeutic alliance. Such an alliance, though having a constructive and positive effect, is not curative in its own right. It does indicate, however, that there has been a change in a patient's ability to make use of a human relationship for whatever constructive input a therapist may have to offer. A freely flowing transference–countertransference interchange is essential for therapeutic success. This form of communication is also indicative of a holding environment and of a therapist's empathic responsiveness, which serves to encourage constructive identifications. Furthermore, if troubles occur in this kind of interchange, it may provide an opportunity to reconstruct what may have been crucial preverbal, infantile traumas.

A psychoanalytic point of view focuses particular attention on the unconscious determinants of psychic productions, with the therapist listening intently for the implied meaning of the patient's communications. It is only by being able to unravel the composition of this unconscious realm of mental activity that it becomes possible to comprehend fully the significance of those psychic contents that are finally observable. A psychoanalyst's total personality is the listening instrument, and the messages emanating from this hidden sector most clearly heard, deciphered, and understood will be those most resonant with a given psychoanalyst's unconscious world of experience. It is therefore likely that different therapists would hear and grasp a variety of meanings.[21] Psychoanalytic investigators have formulated concepts concerning mental functioning from disparate and often opposing points of view. These contradictory ideas, however, are offered from a basic theoretical position that places unconscious mental events as the most important force shaping human experience. Divergent opinions may at times appear irreconcilable and then serve as the grounds for

---

[21]**Fred Pine** believed it was necessary to synthesize the various psychoanalytic points of view if a more complete picture of human development was to be gained. He showed how drive psychology, ego psychology, object relations theory, and psychologies of the self each take a somewhat different perspective on psychological functioning, emphasizing different phenomena. In drive psychology the individual is seen in terms of struggles with lasting urges forged in the crucible of early bodily and family experience, taking shape as wishes embedded in actions and in conscious and unconscious fantasies. Psychic life is seen as organized around conflict and its resolution, signified by anxiety, guilt, shame, inhibitions, symptom formation, and pathological character traits. In a psychology of the ego the individual is seen in terms of capacities for adaptation, reality testing and defense, and their use in dealing with the inner world of urges, affects, and fantasies and the outer world of reality demands. Developmentally, these ego functions are slowly attained, can develop poorly or in aberrant ways, and can be viewed as ego defects. Conflict may have contributed to their going wrong developmentally, and they will enter into the individual's fantasy life and self-experience. In a psychology of object relations, the individual is seen in terms of internal images, loosely based upon childhood experience, which then put their stamp on new experience. The resulting memories are repeated, propelled by efforts at attachment, mastery, or both. In a psychology of self-experience the individual is seen in terms of the ongoing subjective state, particularly around issues of boundaries, continuity, and esteem, and the reactions to imbalances in that subjective state.

developing a separate school of thought. It is not surprising that in exploring unseen but powerful and regressive forces, a group of scientists with unique and individual experiences would yield insights sensitively attuned to a wide span of important factors determining human development and behavior. This blend challenges theoretical constructs, prevents them from becoming static, and furthers the expansion of knowledge. The attitude required to gain enlightenment when entering these dark areas of uncertainty in theory is similar to what is needed in understanding the undiscovered reaches of a patient's internal world. The unfolding of new information cannot be obstructed by a need to impose logic, unity, order, or meaning, and there must be an ability to sift through and filter out the distortions created by pathology in order to elicit the kernels of truth that must flourish for growth to occur. Memory and desire operate as a hindrance to new learning as well as to the

---

Each of these perspectives reflects different facets of the processes of change, for there are moments when one or the other dominates experience. The therapist in turn exhibits tendencies to organize a patient's material along lines of conflict, narcissistic transferences, or oedipal and preoedipal pathology, as each formulation has a different conception of an individual's essential tasks. Drive psychology emphasizes the taming, socialization, and gratification of the drives. Ego psychology emphasizes the development of defense with respect to the internal world, adaptation with respect to the external world, and reality testing with respect to both. Object relations theory focuses on the task of carrying within the self the history of significant relationships while simultaneously being free from the absolute constraints of those relationships, so that new experiences can be responded to on their own. Psychologies of the self focus on the diverse tasks of forming a differentiated and whole sense of self, of establishing the self as the center of initiative, and of developing an ongoing sense of subjective worth (Pine 1988).

emergence of vulnerable unconscious truths that have been carefully defended against. A therapeutic attitude consistently embodies the question, "How is the patient right?" rather than determining how the patient is wrong. Theoretical formulations must be approached in a similar manner, so that the valuable contributions of instinctual theory, object relations theory, self psychological theory, and ego psychology can all be taken into account, keeping the question of how they are right directly in the foreground (Mendelsohn 1987a).

A therapist must first understand as clearly as possible just why a patient's communications have the effect that they do, for whatever lies behind the particular material being expressed must be translated before a patient can be led into self-discovery. Often the sounds of distress originating in the preverbal period may only be heard through their impact upon a therapist, since they at least initially cannot be put into words. However, because they can be deciphered does not mean they can be treated, and the controversy is ongoing as to whether the distortions, deficits, or arrests they produce are reversible or whether they reflect the bedrock beyond which no therapeutic influence can be brought. It is frequently impossible to ascertain the extent to which their ultimate causation is a consequence of inherited factors or trauma, though when they appear to exhibit unyielding characteristics the tendency is to consider this as evidence of their unmodifiability and not to search for new avenues of approach. The assumption that constitutional characteristics have environmental determinants assumes great clinical significance, indicating the need to modify technique accordingly when confronted with the manifestations of these early disturbances.[22]

---

[22]**David Freedman** illustrated the interdependent relationship between inherited factors and environmental influences. Apparently the nervous system retains sufficient plasticity so that

Thus, when infantile and preverbal traumatic experiences accrete to more advanced intrapsychic structures and as a result are embedded in unconscious wishes, any modification of the therapist's interpretive posture within a well-contained therapeutic framework would serve to strengthen repressive forces and work in opposition to insight. Furthermore, any transformation of these psychic contents into action or behavior with the purpose of avoiding memories, living out unconscious fantasies, or reinforcing pathological defenses requires the containing, integrative influences of a firm framework with clearly defined boundaries and ground rules. Insight would not be forthcoming without it, for the information contained in these defensive maneuvers has to be processed by a therapist in order to be able to offer appropriate interpretive interventions. A therapeutic relationship, however, must also have room within it for innovations and creative interventions on those occasions when they seem called for and appropriate. Otherwise, insight would not evolve in less-well-organized and deficiently structured patients. In addition, a therapist may have to participate in achieving a new solution to an impossible early developmental dilemma, so as to gain the mental-representation foundation upon which symbolic processes can become functional and out of which insight can arise.

----

the effects of massive deprivation from the neonatal period can be reversed if correction of the environment is achieved by age 3. Also reversible are those in which the deprivation begins after a period of adequate mothering. The circumstances under which deprivation is imposed is a critical factor. Continuing investigation of the interaction between innate givens rooted in inheritance, which emerge according to a genetically determined timetable, and the effects of the experiential ambiance, in which the maturationally determined new potentialities become available, has yielded an increasingly complex picture of the developmental process (Freedman 1981).

6

The Role of Empathy
and Countertransference

The therapist's subjective responses have always played a crucial part in grasping the unconscious meaning of a patient's communications. Over time, however, clinicians have noted how important they are in maintaining the therapeutic properties of the treatment. Rycroft (1956), for example, observed how interpretations, in addition to their symbolic function of communicating ideas, also have the significant function of conveying to a patient the therapist's emotional attitude. These attitudes combine with the material setting to form an affective contribution to the relationship. With the growth of this recognition it becomes even more essential to examine in depth this aspect of a therapist's internal world. Greater precision could then be attained in determining the specific qualities that enhance a therapist's unconscious perceptiveness and those that are a hindrance to ideal therapeutic functioning.

A therapist's emotions might be a result of empathizing with a patient's internal experience, or be a response to how the patient was experienced in the interaction. In addition, the question of whether these affects furthered therapeutic progress or stood as an obstacle depended a great deal upon how they were understood and managed. Thus, making the distinction between empathy and countertransference, as well as developing more accuracy in discerning their positive and negative attributes, became a central concern.

Empathy

A therapist relies heavily upon the ability to be empathic in order to grasp the significance of intrapsychic phenomena. The place that empathy occupies in a treatment relationship therefore gradually moves into the forefront of attention, leading to a study of its manifestations and a search for its genetic origins. The need to explore the role of empathy is highlighted to an even greater degree in the treatment of more severe disturbances, since such psychic difficulties are often rooted in the empathic failures of early development. In these situations a relatively consistent empathic stance is required of a therapist in order to understand the impact of these developmental traumas and to prevent any repetition of them in the ongoing therapeutic interaction.

Many analytic investigators point to the origins of empathy within the earliest infantile period, while noting the maturational changes that have to take place before it can be functional in the mature forms essential for therapeutic understanding. Olden (1958) regarded the original mother–child fusion as the starting point of empathy, for the unity between mother and child is characterized by emotional interplay and by a mutual sensitivity to the other's feelings. Later, the mutual understanding is no longer the bodily sensual sensing that it was in the first few months, but it has become a part of the mind. It is from this background that other changes can then take place, eventually resulting in adult, mature empathy. Kohut (1959) underscored just how much our observations depend upon introspection and empathy, which were particularly important in treating more severely ill patients. He saw that the therapist as a transference figure was experienced within the framework of an archaic interpersonal relationship. The patient is trying to maintain contact and keep a separate identity, while at the same time attempting to derive a modicum of internal structure. The neurotic uses the therapist as a screen for the projection of existing psychological structure, whereas the non neurotic uses the therapist as a substitute for psychic structure.

Clinicians working with more primitively organized patients discovered that interpretations, no matter how correct, often had little influence, whereas empathizing with an individual's dilemma went far in advancing therapeutic progress. This positive influence, however, was fostered only by the more mature forms of empathy. It became apparent that an indispensable ingredient in a therapeutic interaction was mature empathy in the therapist's mode of functioning. It was therefore vital to identify as clearly as possible the indicators of its presence. Generally this means the ability to understand and actually experience in some fashion the feelings of another person. It includes both affective and cognitive elements, and requires making a temporary identification. Finally, the information obtained is used for the sole purpose of gaining a deeper appreciation of the unconscious significance of the other's experience. Mature empathy thus depends upon advanced levels of psychic functioning, as a consequence of which growth is promoted in both parties and in the interrelationship between them. Schafer (1959) used the term "generative empathy" for this more mature form. He described it as an experimental action in which the subject is above observation. It involves a conflict-free interplay of introjective and projective mechanisms, and it enlarges awareness, strengthens the controlling functions of the empathizer's ego, and potentially enhances communication with the object. It entails an expansion of ego boundaries with recognition of the object's separateness, and it has an altruistic aspect in that it is evoked for the sake of the object.

Although the therapist's emotional responses may be empathic, not all assume this more mature form. This kind of emotional knowing, whether silent or overt, can either advance or be an obstacle to therapeutic progress. Of course empathic responsiveness can also be defended against, in which case the therapist will tend to be insensitive to the effects of the relationship upon the patient. Conversely, the therapist may become so immersed in the empathic experience itself that instead of leading to understanding it can result in perpetuating feelings whose defensive purpose has to be uncovered before constructive movements can take place. Greenson (1960) referred to this problem in depicting the two major forms of the pathology of empathy within the therapist. The inhibited empathizer is afraid to act involved with the patient, while the uncontrolled empathizer becomes too intensely involved. Greenson believed that the maximum capacity for empathy required the therapist to be able to become both detached and involved, observer and participant, objective and subjective. Empathy leads to emotional contact with the patient, which alerts the analyzing ego to formulate what has occurred.

An empathic experience is initiated by making a transient identification with a patient. However, it is only through the memories, fantasies, and derivatives of unconscious perceptions, elicited by the identification, that the therapist's understanding of the unconscious significance of the relationship is increased. The therapist's unconscious resonates with the particular internal events most active in the patient. This has the potential of either enlarging what is known about the patient or of becoming enmeshed in the therapist's personal difficulties. Reich (1966) stressed how conflicts within the therapist can interfere with analytic understanding, which is based on the therapist's internal state of resonance. Thus what could otherwise be a useful signal for an immediate insight, spontaneous association, or visual image, becomes a form of positive or negative acting out or blocking and leads to a failure in understanding. In order to have direct access to the unconscious of the patient, the therapist must eliminate resistances through comprehension that takes the special form of empathic understanding.

The therapist's empathic responses are used to promote comprehension, but they also may reflect personal concerns or narcissistic needs, and it is vital to make the distinction. This is the fine line between empathy and unhelpful countertransference, which first must be recognized before the inappropriate elements can be eliminated. Once these potentially noxious components are filtered out, the therapist's empathic responses emerge as a critical feature of the growth-promoting properties of the relationship. Beres (1968) described the considerable degree of ego development that must be present before the cues that perception affords can lead to empathy. Empathy comprises more than an affective response, for to attribute one's feelings to another and then reidentify with them is far from empathy. In addition, the therapist must empathize with emotions and ideas that have not necessarily been experienced, and with affect, thoughts, and fantasies of which the patient is not aware. The sensitivity of one person to another can be called empathy only when it is not in the service of narcissistic needs but of mature object relations. There must be a balance between the therapist's empathic responses and knowledge of psychic function; the former without the restraint of the latter might lead to chaos, the latter without the former would be a drab intellectual recital. The final step is always the process of validation. Without validation empathy can offer no more than speculation. Empathy is thus a momentary response, based upon conscious and subliminal perceptions and unconscious identifications, which reaches conscious or preconscious awareness. Without the capacity to empathize, a therapist cannot set into action the process that goes on to intuition, interpretations, and insight.

Empathy is primarily an ego activity. Although an identification is made with a patient, it is transient in nature and accompanied by a clear separation between what is self and what is non-self. It is also associated with the use of memories, thoughts, fantasies, and intellectual activities, all meant to further the range of what can be observed about a patient. Olinick (1969) focused upon the momentary and reversible regressive nature of the identifications involved in empathy, which may even go to the point of fusing self- and object-images. The observing ego is subsequently brought into play in order for there to be awareness of what would otherwise be subliminal. The relevant affects are then employed as signals leading back to a reality-oriented appraisal, and it is out of this setting of mutuality that an effective, mutative transference interpretation may be made. Above all, the establishment of an empathic attitude is part of the groundwork that must be laid for engaging in a continuous process of identifying the signs of ideal therapeutic functioning.

A therapist's introspective and self-observational capacities have to be consistently attended to, so as to enlarge the scope of internal reactions accessible for a more penetrating understanding of how a patient's communications are being unconsciously received. Jacobs (1973) had this in mind by calling attention to those aspects of empathy intimately associated not only with feeling states but also with bodily reactions. These temporary reinvestments of the body are a means of empathizing and understanding, which can often provide clues inasmuch as they reverberate with the unconscious communications of the patient. Such body empathy may well be a primal and nuclear facet of the empathic experience, with the potential of enlarging the scope of awareness and of gaining access to attitudes and conflicts of which the therapist has been unaware.

Because the therapist places a great deal of reliance on subjective reactions, it is necessary to be discriminating as to their nature. Each therapist must become attuned to the internal signs and signals that indicate when empathic responses are unencumbered by interference from intrapsychic conflicts, narcissistic needs, or unrecognized regressive identifications. The unconscious meaning of a patient's input can then be perceived more clearly and accurately, and the messages received are relatively free of personal distortions. Shapiro (1974) showed how easy it is for empathic responses to serve as a vehicle for expressing narcissistic needs and as a false rationale for interventions, or they may serve defensively for the projection of affective reactions that are readily rationalized. Feelings that appear to be empathic should therefore be carefully explored, with the therapist always alert to the possibility that they may be skewed and lead one astray. Empathy may further the understanding of another's internal state, but first it must be subjected to validative processes, with a readiness to modify them on the basis of other available perceptions and information. Beres and Arlow (1974) described the therapist's empathizing as a mixture of affect and cognition, with the affect operating as a signal indicative of a momentary identification that enables the therapist to become aware of what the patient may be feeling. This empathic signal affect portends the emergence of an unconscious fantasy, and is appropriate to the nature of the fantasy. There is then a subsequent necessary rupture of the identification in order for the therapist to become aware of the inner experiences, even before the process of intuition can become operative, and it requires a set of cognitive operations to translate the fantasy into an interpretation. Empathic and intuitive responses should be subjected to disciplined validation, for when the therapist's associations precede or coincide with those of the patient, though it is suggestive of being on the right track, it is not confirmatory.

Most therapists agree that structural change is affected by mutative interpretations, which means that certain conditions must be met. The interpretation must be emotionally immediate, experienced by the patient as actual, directed to the point of urgency, and conveyed through a bond of affective relatedness so that the relevance can be perceived by the therapist's empathy. Modell (1976) thought that an entirely different theory of therapeutic action had to be developed when psychoanalytic treatment was utilized with individuals exhibiting disorders of ego development. However, it has become evident that it is the role of empathy that is especially relevant in addressing the treatment needs of these severe narcissistic disturbances. It is necessary first to distinguish between pathology that is the product of intrapsychic conflict and pathology that is the result of developmental deficits, arrests, and defects. A therapist has to be in touch with the impact of pathology emanating from the earliest stages of development in order to be empathic, for errors in interpreting them as the product of intrapsychic conflict can be quite hurtful. Stolorow and Lachman (1980) referred to the problems arising in extending psychoanalytic practice beyond the classical neuroses to the treatment of narcissistic, borderline, and psychotic disorders. They believed that many therapeutic stalemates were the consequence of specific failures in empathy, wherein the therapist misunderstands and misinterprets the meaning of the patient's archaic states by amalgamating them to his own more differentiated and integrated world of self- and object-representations. Such misunderstandings typically take the form of erroneously interpreting remnants of developmental arrests as if they were expressions of resistance against intrapsychic conflicts. A traumatic narcissistic injury is then inflicted that is similar in its impact to those which originally produced the developmental arrest.

The implications for what is curative in treatment, and consequently for technique, have undergone many changes as a result of work with more seriously disturbed patients. Expanded views of the function of interpretations, the significance of constructive identifications, the positive effect of a benign regression, and the place of providing new experiences have emerged as important factors. In all of these the role of empathy has stood out. Kohut (1977, 1982b), in formulating a psychology of the self, elaborated upon the significance of empathy. He believed that psychological health was achieved through the healing of a formerly fragmented self. Cure then had to be evaluated in terms of self-cohesion, particularly by the restitution of the self with the aid of a reestablished empathic closeness to responsive self objects. In this view, empathy was a neutral mode of observation, attuned to the inner life of man, just as extrospection is a mode of observation attuned to the outside world. Empathy is thus an information-gathering activity that can be right or wrong, in the service of compassion or hostility, or pursued slowly or intuitively. It is never by itself supportive or therapeutic. Kohut felt it was important to differentiate between empathy as a way of collecting data and as a powerful emotional bond between people, for the mere presence of empathy has a beneficial therapeutic effect.

These ideas were enormously evocative. Whether or not they are accepted in their entirety, they have given some important directions to follow in probing more deeply into the underlying forces at work in therapeutic failures. Through delineating more clearly the meaning and significance of unconsciously empathic responsiveness it has become possible to define more accurately what is required to promote growth. These qualities can then be discovered by looking for the specific evidences of how a patient's unconscious perceptions of the therapeutic environment are expressed. A means is thereby made available for a therapist's technique to be adapted as much as possible to whatever is needed, while identifying and correcting any empathic lapses, and a wider range of psychological difficulties can be reached. In this regard a more penetrating vision of the developmental line of empathy is helpful, for in tracing it back to maternal empathy, the reasons an empathic experience strengthens the healthy aspects of a patient's personality become evident. Post (1980) described maternal empathy in its primal form as a benevolent, integrated, and integrative attunement to whatever is the experiential state of the infant. This attunement requires more than an identification or a fusion with the infant; it also requires an ongoing awareness of separateness. The mother feels and thinks not only with but about her infant, which is essential to the empathic process. The mother's empathy involves a combination of feeling with and thinking about—both mutually informative in the process of progressive empathic attunement. This contribution of objectivity implies a widened conception of empathy beyond the sharing of sensory and affective experience. There is much to suggest that the representations of these early developmental experiences are at the foundation of unconscious perceptions (Mendelsohn 1985).

A therapist's empathic response utilizes all levels of consciousness, emphasizing the affective component as a way of emotionally knowing a patient. It is not an exact sharing of the experience, since it is impossible for two people to be identical. What it does, however, is give a sense of the broader implications of the experience by going beyond the amount of recognition that has thus far been obtained about a patient. Within the therapist the experience does not stay rooted in the emotional aspect. It goes on to higher-order intellectual and cognitive treatment. Empathy also means that the therapist repeatedly returns to the original affects, while progressively clarifying the state of the patient. Finally it requires validation from a host of ancillary information. It is probably inevitable for latent unconscious conflicts and narcissistic needs to be aroused in the therapist, and if these do not proceed to conscious recognition, the resulting countertransference can become a liability. This does not mean that the existence and meaning of these unconscious reverberations necessarily create countertransference interferences or stand in the way of empathy, for every therapist is going to have unconscious fantasies stimulated in the service of empathy even if they are also potential sources of distortion. Certainly any therapist will have significant regressive and conflictual unconscious constellations that continue to remain under repression, which can either contribute to an empathic response or elicit distortions of meaning and objectivity. This relationship between empathy and countertransference is activated by the therapist's sustained empathic immersion in the patient's experience, especially in response to primitive, narcissistic disturbances.

Emphasizing the value of empathy makes it imperative to be thoughtful about its limitations. Otherwise, many mistakes can arise from the assumption that more can be known by empathic means than the intrinsic nature of empathy allows. Buie (1981) defined three factors that limit how much one can understand of the inner experience of another person. First, it depends upon sensory perception of physically expressed cues. Inaccuracy or failure to provide cues limits, skews, or blocks the empathic process. In addition, primitive patients rely on defenses that keep painful memories and feelings rigidly preconscious. Second, there are inevitable inadequacies in the mind of the empathizer. Third, empathy ultimately depends upon inference, which is fallible. The impressions gained by empathy must therefore be verified by other means, for there is no absolute certainty that the patient's feelings, dreams, or defensive behavior may verify or invalidate empathy or give clues for its revision. Buie also categorized four kinds of referents employed by the ego to engage in empathic experience. Conceptual referents, are cognitive in nature and do not involve affect. Self-experience referents consist of memories, impulses, affects, bodily sensations, and superego pressures both past and present. An essential quality is their low intensity, and they reflect being in tune with the patient, making inner awareness and comprehension possible. Imaginative imitation referents use fantasy to imitate the patient by assuming all of the qualities of the patient's experience that can be deduced from perceptions. Usually the feelings generated bear a resemblance to the patient's intrapsychic state. Resonance referents, wherein strong affect is stimulated with no ideational component except for noticing the patient's words, seems more likely to correspond to the patient's actual state of mind, and if verified by the other referents, it is probably correct.

Empathy can only be used appropriately if its limitations are kept in mind, for above all a balanced perspective must be maintained. The therapist is then less likely to be led astray by overemphasizing the ability to be knowledgeable about another's internal experience. Ideally, an awareness of the many possible meanings of every piece of behavior should be present, so that information can fit into whatever framework to which it happens to apply. What and how best to respond to a patient is always a difficult and complex problem, and a more appropriate intervention may be made out of such an understanding. Generally speaking, a therapist's subjective responses, aided by introspection, are a highly significant part of grasping the unconscious meaning of a patient's productions. Unfortunately the level of self-awareness that is needed for a therapist to use subjective responses as a guide is not always available. There are many times when it is not easy to differentiate between emotions that are empathic and appropriate and those that come from inappropriate countertransference reactions. Gedo (1981) pointed out that empathy yields predictions that are based upon past experiences of human potentials including one's own, and that the tendency to equate it with kindness or human warmth or with the use of a particular set of psychoanalytic propositions, no matter how valuable, is a misuse of the concept. He believed that the less we rely on empathy in psychoanalytic work the fewer therapeutic errors we will make, for what has been commonly viewed as empathic performance is in actuality the outcome of a different set of mental operations. The therapist, in screening out personal responses, exercises a kind of self-restraint that deserves to be regarded as genuine altruism. When, as a consequence of such altruistic behavior, the patient achieves new insights, the psychological world of the therapist may expand into novel areas of experience. The therapist may then begin to understand aspects of humanity that were alien before, and subsequently utilize this new knowledge to achieve a broader range of empathic contact with patients in the future.

The idea of a therapist's unconscious being receptive to understanding the significance of a patient's unspoken, disguised, unconscious communications should not be taken as equivalent to an empathic process. Lichtenberg (1981) addressed this confusion concerning the role of empathy in a treatment situation and indicated there was a distinction to be made between empathy as a process and the empathic vantage point in analytic listening. The empathic vantage point does not overemphasize responsiveness to emotionality and underemphasize cognitive elements, either in the therapist's listening or interpreting. He felt that misunderstandings could be eliminated by a recognition that the processes utilized by a therapist who takes an empathic vantage point are those usually described as empathy, intuition, and secondary-process thought. Empathic perception never means having a direct view of what is happening inside another person's mind. More than anything else it is a considered judgment that there is some resonance with what a patient is experiencing consciously or unconsciously. In that sense empathy is not immediate, engaged in without careful consideration, or effortless. Empathic understanding requires a great deal of correction and refinement over a long period of time, and the accuracy of the information depends upon the processes a therapist has used to check on the validity of whatever conclusions are reached.

In essence, the degree of information that a therapist's subjective responses impart depends primarily on what is done with them, both associatively and cognitively. Basch (1983) brought greater clarity to both the definition of empathy and its use in treatment. He divided affective life into stages of affect, feeling, emotion, and empathic understanding on the basis of progressive development, with each stage encompassing and integrating what has gone before. Affect is an adaptive, somatic response that has come to have communicative value, for it is involuntary and initially not a psychological event. The conscious awareness of an affective event is then transformed into a subjective experience of feeling. Emotions are much more complex states in which feelings are experienced in a unity and in a relationship to the self and its goals. Affect is always unconscious, feelings and emotions always conscious, and empathy is the final potential transformation of affective communication. Empathy is a function capable of being performed and requiring a certain level of development, no more and no less. Mature empathy implies that one is neither threatened by the affective needs of another person nor tempted to confuse those needs with one's own. Empathy leads to knowledge—by itself it neither prescribes nor proscribes behavior. What one does with the insight provided by empathic understanding is determined by the nature of the relationship or the purpose for which empathy is used. A therapist employs empathic understanding in the service of furthering treatment.

Empathy is thus a special kind of identification, characterized by its transient, easily reversible nature, which blends into and utilizes other, more objective, intellectual and cognitive functions. It usually refers to the feeling responses aroused by the impact of a patient's experiences, which is then received with the sole purpose of understanding its meaning. Levy (1985) defined psychoanalytic empathy as a supraordinate term referring to a general attribute of the psychoanalytic situation. It involves a consistent focus on the patient's experiences, with empathic interpretations based on complicated affective, conceptual, and inferential processes. Empathy in the psychoanalytic situation is a synthetic term for the many different ways a therapist learns about and remains in contact with the patient's conscious and unconscious experiences and is guided by this knowledge in helping the patient to expand awareness and mastery of inner life.

Empathy and Countertransference

Whenever the process of empathy is given undue emphasis at the expense of other modes of reaching a therapeutic understanding, countertransference-based obstacles have to be considered. In addition, the potential for countertransference difficulty is ever present because of the tendency of subjective reactions to a patient to activate a therapist's infantile conflicts and narcissistic needs. Although directing attention to subjective responses leads to a broadened capacity for knowing and understanding the experience of a patient, it must be accompanied by respect for the limitations of that process and by a search for inappropriate components. A careful examination and assessment of the many interrelated factors involved is essential, with an awareness of the potential for self-deception.

Over the years there has been an ever-deepening appreciation of the differences between empathy and countertransference, along with a fuller realization of the significance of countertransference in both its helpful and harmful aspects. Berger (1987) underscored how the therapist's aim above all was to appreciate meaningful aspects of the patient's internal state, based on evenly focused attention as both participant and observer. Emotional and ideational, as well as conscious and unconscious factors, contribute to the process at every stage. The multiplicity of events, adding to the therapist's empathic understanding, does not occur in any particular order, and the greater the variety of modalities the richer and more complete the therapist's understanding. Various empathic experiences are then integrated into a conceptual model of the patient that becomes increasingly complex over time, and is shaped by the therapist's theoretical preferences. The likelihood of error and inexactness makes it necessary to check and recheck the accuracy of an empathic experience against the patient's experience and against what the therapist has already learned. The difference between a nondefensive state of empathy and a state of countertransference may be that in the latter state the therapist's appreciation of an inner experience is delayed. Some prefer to restrict the term empathy to nondefensively generated states characterized by emotional resonance. It needs to be stressed however, that the retrospective recognition of a countertransference state can also contribute a great deal to the therapist's understanding of the patient.

The fine discriminations between empathy and countertransference are more readily made when dealing with the advanced levels of psychic structuralization underlying the pathology exhibited in neurotic disorders. The transference relationship, though regressive and infantile in nature, is not infused with the primitive, disruptive qualities associated with non-neurotic disorders. Thus, in most instances there is both the time and opportunity for the therapist consistently to monitor internal reactions and expose them to a careful process of self-examination, which is then enhanced by the patient's primarily verbal associative material. Obstacles to therapeutic progress emanating from within the patient, the therapist, and the specific interaction between them, can then be explored at a more leisurely pace. The source of empathic lapses, or any opposition to constructive growth, has more room to be discovered and addressed effectively.

In applying psychoanalytic treatment across a broad spectrum of pathology, and in entering the realm of narcissistic difficulties, the resulting transference relationship is much more intense and primitive. Projective identifications are less differentiated, the demand for immediate responses is more pressing and urgent, and the therapeutic alliance more problematic and tenuous. All of these factors are behind the necessity to become more finely attuned to the impact of the therapeutic interaction upon the therapist's internal world. This is especially the case for the primitive facets of the therapist's subjective responses, since they must be accessible in order to grasp fully the unconscious significance of what the patient is expressing. In these treatment situations the transference–countertransference interchange has a quality of immediacy that many times cannot brook the delay involved for a therapist adequately to process subjective reactions. Therefore, the ability to effectively filter out those elements that are a product of inappropriate regressive identifications, remnants of narcissistic needs, or latent intrapsychic conflicts often may be somewhat compromised.

Additional complications come into play if the patient's sometimes frantic defensive efforts succeed in interfering with the therapist's ability to make these discriminations. At the same time, the therapist's emotional responses, especially those aroused in the here and now of the interaction, may very well be what is most required to maintain the therapeutic properties of the relationship. A problem is thereby created, because these subjective reactions also carry with them the potential of hindering or disrupting any constructive influences that are present. Thus, the circumstances encountered with primitively organized individuals have highlighted the need to identify the useful and obstructive facets of countertransference and have increased awareness of their more subtle manifestations in any treatment situation. Wolf (1983) discussed the significance of distinguishing between empathy and countertransference. Empathy is a method of collecting information and can be used for the patient's good as well as against it. Countertransference, by contrast, is not a method of data collection, but an expression of needs akin to transference. Empathy and countertransference thus mutually influence each other, for the regression in the therapist that is the counterpart of what is taking place in the patient implies an increased receptivity to introspectively organized perceptions. The therapist's regression, fostering this increased empathic "in-tuneness," is thereby accompanied by a mobilization of archaic needs. Sometimes countertransference can interfere with, inhibit, or derail the treatment process. This is the sense in which the term countertransference has usually been understood. However there has been a growing recognition of the inevitability of countertransference and of its potential usefulness in influencing a psychoanalytic process. Those countertransferences that can be used as signals to alert a therapist to a threatened derailment of the therapeutic process are helpful, whereas those that cannot be monitored are likely to interfere. These interferences can become the most fruitful points for investigation, however, and thus the most useful tools for moving the treatment forward.

Countertransference

In its broadest definition, countertransference refers to all of the feelings aroused in the therapist, while in its narrowest usage it refers to the therapist's specific unconscious transference reaction to the patient's transference strivings. It has been applied to untherapeutic, unconsciously determined neurotic attitudes and remnants of unresolved infantile conflicts and narcissistic needs. It has also been applied to the therapist's unconscious response to parallel unconscious processes in the patient, thereby providing clues to a more penetrating understanding of the patient. In this sense it has tended to be equated with unconscious perceptiveness, especially if it has occurred during times of troubled verbal communication. A balanced view of countertransference requires a grasp of the realistic consequences of primarily transference-based communications and behaviors of the patient, along with a recognition that they are designed to harm and help the therapist simultaneously. Winnicott (1949) referred to three components of countertransference. First, he described the abnormality in feeling, set relationships, and identifications under repression, which required further treatment on the part of the therapist. Second are the identifications and tendencies belonging to the therapist's personal experiences and development, which provide the positive setting for analytic work. Third is what Winnicott called the "objective countertransference," which is the therapist's love-and-hate reaction to the actual personality and behavior of the patient. He believed a successful outcome was impossible with psychotic patients unless the therapist's hate was well sorted out and conscious, so that the unavoidable hate and fear were not the motives that determined what was done.

Transferences and countertransferences are major sources of growth and disturbance, frustration and harm, and cure and motivation for psychotherapeutic work. The significant element is an appreciation not of the presence of feelings in the patient and their absence in the therapist, but rather the nature of the feelings that are experienced and the different uses made of them by each. Heimann (1950) thought of countertransference as covering all the feelings a therapist experiences toward a patient. She believed a therapist's emotional responses represented one of the most important tools of analytic work, and that countertransference was an instrument of research into the patient's unconscious. The image of a detached therapist who is not to feel anything but the most mild feelings toward a patient is inappropriate, but the open expression of feelings toward the patient so as to make the therapist seem more human is not helpful. The therapist must be capable of containing such feelings in place of discharging them and of using them in the task of gaining a better understanding of the overall significance and meaning of the patient's experience. This aspect is essential in order to comprehend more accurately the patient's emotional movements and the unconscious fantasies that underlie them.

The therapist is consistently engaged in assessing all feelings that are aroused, while comparing their meaning with the patient's associations and behavior. The purpose is to aid in determining whether the patient has been properly under-stood. Any conscious perception of the meaning of the thera-peutic interaction will almost always be preceded by the therapist's unconscious perception of what is taking place. Over time and stimulated by work with more seriously dis-turbed individuals, it has become apparent that the existence of countertransference-based reactions and feelings were not in themselves so much the problem, but rather their recognition and management. Racker (1957) considered countertransfer-ence to have three comparable meanings: it could constitute the greatest danger to the treatment, it could serve as an important tool for understanding and interpreting, and it could interfere with the therapist's action as an object of the patient's reexperience of something new in the analytic situation. The therapist's ability to understand transference will depend on the capacity to identify with the patient's impulses, defenses, and internal objects, and to be conscious of these identifica-tions. This ability depends upon the degree to which counter-transference is perceived and accepted, for repression of coun-tertransference leads to deficiencies in the analysis of transference, which in turn leads to repression and mishandling of countertransference.

The capacity of the therapist to listen to the patient's pro-ductions, with the purpose of both attaining validation of the understanding that has thus far emerged and gaining a deeper awareness of any countertransference-based obstacles to progress, possesses the potential of operating as a catalyst to healing and growth. Searles (1975) was convinced that when countertransference problems arose in the therapist it was particularly important to recognize the patient's attempts to help in their resolution. He speculated that no other determi-nant compared in etiological importance than the striving to heal, even though any neurotic or psychotic symptom was determined by a multiplicity of causes. In transference terms the patient's illness in some measure expressed an unconscious attempt to cure the doctor. It is only insofar as the patient can succeed in comparable strivings in the treatment, this time toward the therapist, that the patient can be sufficiently sure of his worth, so he can become more deeply a full individual. The crucial importance of the patient's input in identifying countertransference feelings was thus underscored, for whatever the motive, it could lead to new learning for the therapist and increased integration for the patient. Langs (1975c) noted that the development and resolution of sectors of the therapeutic alliance are aided by the patient's sensitivity to, and unconscious perception of, a therapist's errors. The patient's responses are designed to correct the therapist, assist in modifying countertransference difficulties, and reflect an effort to cure the therapist. Such curative efforts are not a primary goal of the patient, but occur in response to the therapist's difficulties, which must be resolved before the patient can be helped.

Countertransference-based troubles are especially noticeable in the treatment of structurally deficient, primitively organized patients because of the intensity and extremely regressive nature of the transference experience. Although the therapist must always be alert to those facets that reflect upon some specific psychic problem, they can also represent a reaction to the circumstances. Giovacchini (1974) discussed the special problems presented by psychotic patients, which, if left unrecognized, can be totally disruptive to analysis in the same way that their early development failed them. The feature deserving emphasis is the therapist's willingness to continue analyzing even though a professional role has temporarily been lost sight of because of countertransference difficulties. This type of countertransference problem is often ubiquitous and not necessarily indicative of specific psychopathology. The treatment of psychotic patients does not rely so much upon the content of the patient's productions as it does upon the therapist's sensitivities, and the awareness of these sensitivities is usually referred to as countertransference. Their recognition can only broaden the range of treatable patients.

A great deal of controversy continues to persist around the meaning and use of countertransference feelings. It ranges from viewing countertransference as a function of a patient's personality to contending that ideally it should be eliminated. Countertransference nevertheless is now widely seen as a vital part of the treatment, and as changes take place in the concept of transference, they are equally reflected in the changing views on countertransference. Originally, a therapist was portrayed as a mirror onto which a patient projected internal figures, an idea that has long been abandoned. The concept of projective identification has opened the doors to a deepening understanding of the impact of the therapeutic interaction itself upon the transference, so that a patient is now thought of as projecting into a therapist. Segal (1981b) called attention to how a patient is not only perceiving the therapist in a distorted way, reacting to the distorted view and communicating the reactions, but is also doing things to the therapist's mind—projecting into the therapist in a way that affects the therapist. Countertransference now is also clearly recognized as a part of every therapeutic interaction, so it must be identified, clarified, and acknowledged in order to maintain the constructive attributes of the relationship. Little (1981) went a step further by pointing out that not to refer to countertransference is tantamount to denying its existence or forbidding the patient to know or speak about it. Honest recognition of such feeling is essential to the analytic process, since a patient is naturally sensitive to any insincerity and will inevitably respond to it with hostility. The patient will identify with the therapist as a means of denying feelings, and will exploit the situation in every possible way to the detriment of the treatment. Should a countertransference interpretation from the patient for the therapist not be accepted, repression with strengthened resistance follows, with consequent interruption or prolongation of the treatment.

The implication that a process similar to the patient's transference is operative in a therapist's countertransference is probably one of the major reasons for concern about utilizing its manifestations within the context of the therapeutic interaction. In those situations where this is the case, and similar processes are operative in both parties, there is justifiable cause for considering it as a detrimental factor. Countertransference, although aroused in response to a patient's input, is not the exact counterpart of the transference. This is primarily because the therapist works hard to contain the feelings so they can be a source of information, instead of acting upon them, which would be the case if they were projectively identified. It is this internal posture that enables the therapist to provide and regulate the conditions required for a therapeutic regression. Baranger and colleagues (1983) had this in mind when they directed attention to the structural reasons that countertransference was not the inverse of transference. The therapist is committed to truth and abstinence from anything acted out with the patient, which implies that countertransference is limited in its expression and maintained within an internal unfolding. This structural position makes it erroneous to define countertransference as including projective identification (in contrast to transference, which depends upon this mechanism). When projective identifications of the therapist toward the patient occur, they provoke a pathological restructuring of the field, require a second look, and demand priority in interpretive management. Reliving a trauma is useless if not complemented by working through, if the trauma is not reintegrated into the course of an individual's life history and if initial traumatic situations are not differentiated from the historic myths of their origin.

A major impetus to the study of countertransference

phenomena and their various nuances has been derived from applying psychoanalytic principles to the treatment of profoundly disturbed individuals. The resulting narcissistic and archaic transferences have confronted therapists with the confusing task of simultaneously utilizing emotional responses, which are essential for maintaining an effective therapeutic alliance, and filtering out those that emanate from intrapsychic conflict, narcissistic needs, and regressive identifications. Often this has to be accomplished without the necessary room and time to do so with a measure of certainty and accuracy. Tyson (1986) discussed the countertransference problems of working with grossly disturbed patients. These are not treatment situations in which one gradually becomes aware of feeling something about a patient other than benevolent neutrality; rather, conscious feelings of this sort often arise quite soon, and they must be dealt with or there is no treatment. These affects, and the situations engendering them, are frequently so dramatic that it may be easy to lose sight of the fact that the therapist's conscious feelings are a superstructure resting on an unconscious foundation. The implication is that countertransference is of the greatest importance in work with severely disturbed patients, in contrast to its lesser role with neurotics. Under these circumstances it is crucial to discern the interrelationship between empathy and countertransference, so as to determine adequately what is required for therapeutic work to result in constructive structural change. Any therapeutic stalemate, impasse, or negative reaction must then be carefully examined to unearth the therapist's contribution and to use that knowledge to alleviate any barrier to ongoing progress. Loewald (1986) stressed that by being aware of how transference–countertransference operates in patient and therapist, their interplay can be monitored, the behavior of both parties can be understood, and the understanding can be utilized for the content, form, and timing of interventions.

Empathy, Countertransference, and Ideal Therapeutic Functioning

When the nature of the therapist's total response to the input of the patient is empathic with its unconscious significance, this factor consistently emerges as a major determinant for insuring the growth-promoting properties of the relationship. Conversely, when the therapist's total response is infused with projections, defensiveness, or narcissistic needs, it seriously undermines an effective therapeutic alliance and feeds pathological forces to an excessive degree. The important matter is how the therapist's countertransferences operate within the interaction, how they are used or handled to further therapeutic work, and how it is determined under what conditions these feelings interfere. There has to be resonance between the patient's and the therapist's unconscious communications before any meaningful understanding can emerge, although the therapist may unknowingly repress the very affects and their derivatives that would yield the deepest, most penetrating grasp of what is taking place in both parties. At such moments there is a collusion with the patient's defenses and until it can be recognized and dissolved, the work of integration cannot go forward.

It has long been evident that the effectiveness of treatment relies heavily on the nature and quality of the therapist's subjective responses, making it mandatory that their form, content, intensity, and attributes be as clearly identifiable as possible. Those subjective responses having features that involve intrapsychic infantile conflict, regressive identifications, or the arousal of unsettled narcissistic needs must be exposed to a process of self-examination and integration, leading to a fuller grasp of the elements in the patient's input that evoked them. In this way the potential for projecting personal meaning onto a patient's experience can be filtered out, so it is not incorporated in the motive for intervening or in the specific content or form that an intervention may take. The therapist's subjective responses can then further the task of decoding a patient's unconscious messages and eliminating defensive distortions, and not serve as the basis for feeding an unconscious fantasy or colluding in the reinforcement of a pathological defense.

When a narrow view of countertransference is adopted, it encompasses the distorted or defensive reactions that operate to the detriment of therapeutic progress. The other aspects of the therapist's unconscious, preconscious, and conscious emotional responses then tend to be embraced within the realm of what is considered empathic resonance. When a broader view of countertransference is taken, empathy is included, but a distinction is then made between countertransference reactions enhancing the therapist's unconscious and conscious perceptiveness and the process of empathy, in which more advanced intrapsychic functions are utilized and in which transient identifications play a part. Countertransference is thus seen as including instinctual components, whereas empathy involves a deinstinctualized process of introspection.

In this presentation, the totality of the therapist's subjective reactions that flow freely, unencumbered by internal states of conflict and regressive narcissistic needs, are a reflection of ideal therapeutic functioning. Any obstruction must then be identified, so as to facilitate an ongoing transference–countertransference interchange. In the more structured individual this ebb and flow can be facilitated more readily, as any interference is relatively quickly observable. At such moments a therapist's self-analytic task is easier, since there is little pressure or demand for some immediate response or active involvement. The signs and symptoms of any disturbance within the therapist, or of the loss of ideal functioning, can then be identified and understood in a gradual manner. This introspective task is aided by the derivatives of the patient's unconscious perceptions. The therapist's empathy and the facet of countertransference-enhancing unconscious perceptiveness tend to blend together, thereby deepening the appreciation of the patient's unconscious communications.

It is in addressing the treatment needs of primitively organized individuals exhibiting archaic narcissistic transferences, that the finer nuances in discerning the differences between empathy and countertransference become both more confusing and more important. The projective identifications fueling the transference relationship are more primitive and undifferentiated, eliciting more regressive experiences within the therapist. This creates a heightened need for sensitive management of the treatment framework. These are frequently situations in which interpretive interventions have little influence, so that the behavior and emotional responsiveness of the therapist is a predominant feature of the interaction. Unless a broader view of countertransference is taken, there will be a tendency to introduce more rigid and inflexible procedures, thereby either re-creating the traumas of early development or not allowing an opportunity for a new solution to an early infantile dilemma to be achieved and represented. If anything, in these circumstances, it is even more essential for a therapist to be successful in filtering out idiosyncratic, conflicted, narcissistic, and defensive reactions, often under conditions of great intensity and urgency.

7

The Role of Acting Out and Reenacting Infantile and Preverbal Traumatic Experiences

When action and behavior are predominant in a therapeutic interaction, it is particularly crucial for the therapist's interventions to be introduced from an empathic stance. What is paramount and called for from the therapist will not be evident until an unobstructed view is available of what is required to foster constructive growth. This is partly provided by the derivatives of a patient's unconscious perceptions, but they may be so distorted as to be highly unreliable or even completely unavailable. Therefore, a therapist must, in addition, become adept at determining the underlying structure and significance of a patient's productions. This is especially true if the most meaningful communications are expressed through behavior. Identifying the differences between behaviors that are a reflection of some form of destructive acting out, and hence in need of containment, and behaviors that are a constructive attempt at communicating or a reenactment of early traumatic experiences, and hence in need of encouragement, can be an imposing task. The implications for the treatment, however, make it mandatory to discern whether the underlying motivation comes from powerful unconscious fantasies or archaic needs that seek inappropriate gratification or reinforcement of a pathological defense, or whether the motive grows out of the fact that no other avenue for expression exists, an effort to find some new experience to bridge a gap in psychic functioning, or a search for mastery.

Acting Out

The concept of acting out has undergone considerable revision and alteration since it was first formulated by Freud (1914). Originally it was conceived of as a way of repeating forgotten memories, without realizing they were being repeated. In not remembering what had been repressed the patient reproduced it not as a memory but by acting it out. Furthermore, this compulsion to repeat could not be escaped and was therefore best understood as a way of remembering. Acting out was thus equated with the transference, which also was a piece of repetition. The greater the resistance, the more extensively would acting out replace remembering. Freud cautioned about dangerous activities outside of analysis, threatening either the treatment or even the patient's safety. The entire transference was thereby essentially viewed as an acting out.

It soon became apparent that there were many patients for whom action and discharge were a predominant characteristic of their mode of adaptation, and though the unconscious determinants of the behavior were obviously a significant factor, they did not always respond well to interpretive influence. Greenacre (1950) described patients who had major propensities to act out in their lives and in connection with their analyses. She observed that they tended to have experienced early emotional disturbances accompanied by increased orality, diminished frustration tolerance, and heightened narcissism. She found this habitual acting out difficult to analyze and felt uncertain as to what extent the contents of the preverbal period could be converted into verbal expressiveness, which seemed to vary with each patient.

Unfortunately, the concern that acting out would render unconscious strivings inaccessible to therapeutic modification was exaggerated and then perpetuated by the idea of its being a way of avoiding remembering. Although it was to some extent true, it also tended to obscure the communicative facets of the behavior. Generally speaking, acting out was seen as an often unwelcome repetition, with interpretations being the vehicle by which it could be averted. Much thought was given to try to explain those instances wherein this approach was not successful. Silverberg (1955) speculated that when seemingly valid interpretations failed to prevent these repetitions, the unaltered acting out was based on an unverbalized memory of a traumatic experience. One component was the attempt to rectify the helplessness of the original event. Therefore, the therapist's interpretations were a blow to the patient's narcissism and omnipotence and were experienced as a subtle manipulation. It is seen within the transference as an effort by the therapist to discipline the patient and demand conformity. In a similar vein, Bird (1957) believed that acting out, when unaffected by interpretations, was a response to stimulation by another person whom the acting out individual aims to please or influence. Its most important cause, in addition to the emergence of disturbing material, is the unconscious influence of the therapist. The danger signs for this kind of unconscious interaction included the patient's trapping the therapist, the therapist's feeling pleased, angered, or hurt by the patient, an absence of feeling, or any bursts of acting out by the patient.

Concomitantly, the concept of acting out was gradually expanded to encompass a wide variety of behavioral manifestations, with a subtle shift in emphasis toward focusing more intently on its defensive aspects. This development created problems in treating a number of patients, particularly those whose capacity to function in a symbolic mode was compromised. Insufficient attention was paid to the unconscious conflicts and hidden messages contained in the behaviors themselves. Ekstein (1965) addressed this issue by stressing the communicative value of acting out and explaining how it was a form of recollection and a kind of trial thinking. He pointed out that most therapists think of acting out merely as a resistance, and it is then seen as an undesirable feature that should be stopped because it stands in the way of psychotherapeutic technique. The discovery of transference, the use of resistance, and the utilization of countertransference reactions were all at first perceived as a hindrance to the cure, but instead they became an essential part of the treatment. The same holds true for acting out, which is a form of playing with thoughts and an attempt at resolution of conflict. It should be treated as such rather than met with regret and prohibition. The difficult technical problems it creates can be anxiety-arousing for the therapist who overlooks the fact that acting out can be future-directed, representing the beginning of a new spontaneity rather than the repetition of a paralyzing compulsivity.

It is essential to keep the communicative functions of acting out clearly in mind, for only then does it become possible to gain a discriminating picture of the specific meanings that various actions and behaviors contain as they emerge during the course of treatment. Robertiello (1965) discussed the way in which repressed childhood impulses begin to break out of the unconscious in treatment. Acting out occurs when a patient sees the present as similar to the past and then tries to gratify the unconscious wish in the present situation. An important element is that the action, though it may be inappropriate, is ego syntonic and rationalized as appropriate. The past events are not remembered, there is no insight gained, and it is merely a repetition in the present of the past emotions. This is expected to occur in the transference prior to interpretation. However, it is valuable only if the patient is amenable to uncovering the nature of the childhood situation that is being repeated. Working through consists of demonstrating the unconscious impulse in all its different forms of expression. In the process, the impulse becomes conscious, the defenses against it are diminished, and it falls under control of the ego. Working through is therefore an essential part of growth and change. Deutsch (1966) went even further by indicating that everyone acts out to some degree, because no one is free of regressive trends, repressed strivings, and the burdens of more or less conscious fantasies. She was interested in how the concept of acting out had been widened from its original clinical meaning to apply to a vast array of psychological events. Thus artists create in acting out, neurotics use their symptoms to act out, psychotics do so with hallucinations and delusions, and delinquents in their asocial behavior.

One important consequence of looking more deeply into the significance of behavior is that preverbal aspects of the patient's developmental experiences come more clearly into view, since they can only be recovered through reliving. Rexford (1966) placed the manifestations of acting out on a continuum. There was transient, highly specific acting out in the transference, pervasive acting out within or outside of analysis in persons so disposed, and finally the chronic acting out pattern of daily living. She ascribed the evolution of the acting-out character structure to faulty development during the first two years of life, early and repeated traumata, and disharmony in the maturational sequence of the motor system and speech. Acting out was thus rooted in oral conflicts, heightened narcissism, intolerance for drive frustration, and an inadequate grasp of reality. The therapeutic rewards accompanying the recognition that in certain instances a given piece of behavior turned out to be the most satisfactory mode of adaptation to an impossible infantile dilemma or an intolerable life situation were immense. These were patients for whom early traumas were the source of their pathology and who had no other recourse than to communicate through behavior.

In conjunction with the increase in interest in the preverbal period, a more penetrating grasp of the role of aggression has emerged. Aggressive impulses are always closely linked with action, and when they are poorly regulated they are more likely to be acted out than remembered. Widening the concept of acting out, however, has created some confusion as to exactly how it should be defined and how its varied manifestations can be understood and responded to in the treatment. A. Freud (1971) reviewed the implications for treatment that go along with expanding the concept of acting out. She felt there were some specific dangers created by the change in usage of the term. It is often associated with an increased tolerance for extreme forms of acting out that bypass the analytic situation, invade the patient's external life, and only secondarily are drawn back into and interpreted in the transference. The concept of acting out has also been extended beyond behavior directed toward the therapist within the analytic situation and is used to describe the impulsive patient both within and outside of analysis. There are significant differences in the impaired ego controls of these individuals, as compared to the non–acting-out patient who develops limited tendencies in this direction within the treatment. The intactness of the ego's synthetic functions is critical in this regard.

Accompanying this greater understanding of how preverbal experiences are expressed has been a shift toward looking more closely at the development of specific ego functions. Kanzer (1961) referred to acting out as being important not only in terms of substituting one ego function for another, memory expressed through action rather than conscious recall, but also in terms of the entire structure of a personality. Acting out assumes forms and meanings related to defensive and adaptive mechanisms that have become incorporated into the ego's alterations. It may constitute an impulsive search for distorted objects in order to maintain a precarious equilibrium of self and ego organization. Often the degree of acting out will serve as a criterion for the extent of ego alteration. The need to achieve more advanced ego organization has only recently been recognized clearly. From the structural viewpoint, acting out of the transference relationship is not simply an alternative to verbal recall but is part of the total reorganization of a hierarchy of personality functions and structures during treatment, including beneficial as well as resistant aspects. Thus, through utilizing psychoanalytic principles and methods in addressing the treatment needs of more serious disturbances, the significance of dealing more effectively with behavioral expressions of underlying ego distortions, deficits, and arrests has been underscored. Consequently, the way in which the patient behaves has become a vital source of information, providing material to aid in directing the therapist's interventions.

In looking for the structural underpinnings of a patient's behavior, important distinctions were made between acting out, which is an exclusive form of resistance, especially against the transference, and actions as a first indication of new material emerging from the unconscious. Rangell (1968) described actions as overdetermined end products of complex, intrapsychic processes with a wide range of motives and structural determinants in a variety of forms. In his opinion, acting out should be seen as occurring only in those situations that impose upon the individual both the hope and the challenge of undoing repression, and should therefore be viewed as a specific type of neurotic action directed toward interrupting processes involved with achieving insight. The behaviors should not be prohibited because of an inappropriate application of the rule of abstinence, as they contain important elements of both resistance and communication. At times the actions are an expression of the transference itself, and any restrictions deemed necessary should not be taken as a prohibition against effective actions by patients so inclined for internal reasons.

Gradually it has become apparent that what is most significant is to grasp fully the dynamics of utilizing action in place of verbal communication. Through unearthing the motives directing a given piece of behavior, a better understanding of the impact it has upon the therapeutic interaction is also achieved. Otherwise there is a tendency to consider transference and acting out as separate and actually opposed to one another, which would be almost the opposite of the original definition. Sandler and colleagues (1973), for instance, noted that in applying psychoanalytic treatment to patients with severe personality disorders, to psychotics, to adolescents, and to children, new technical problems arose and this resulted in a widening of the concept of acting out. Because of the similarities between the impulsive aspects of the behavior of patients in these groups and the acting out of neurotic patients under the pressure of analysis, the temptation to label all behavior as "acting out" was very strong. They thought it was unfortunate that a term such as "enactment" was not used to distinguish the general tendency to impulsive or irrational actions from acting out, which is linked with the treatment process.

A patient's actions are in fact expressing the psychic reality of the transference relationship, which is then best understood by getting as clear a picture as possible of its structural determinants. Stein (1973) regarded the tendency to act out as a universal human characteristic, which in some individuals was sufficiently marked to be seen as a character trait of pathological significance. In these individuals, acting out in the transference occurs as an irresistible shift of a previously well-established pattern of pathological behavior, and is a signal of the development of a transference neurosis. Similarly, Joseph (1975) felt that acting out in the transference, which is a prerequisite of true understanding, was where the alive, immediate, emotional contact between patient and therapist resided. She also believed that a lot of what patients communicate is not expressed in the representational content of words but through the use of words to carry out actions: to do something to the therapist, or to put subtle pressure on the therapist to do something to the patient. This acting out in the transference is usually designed to obstruct real understanding, and the therapeutic task is to accept the pressure, reflect on the fact that one is being subjected to it, and make a limited and precise interpretation only about the immediate action. In regard to the same issue, Boesky (1982) pointed out how both transference and workable levels of acting out were essential and how the definition of working through was anchored to acting out. Acting out might occur without working through if the transference was not judiciously interpreted, but working through could not occur without acting out because the entire transference was an acting out. Thus acting out is best viewed as inseparable from a transference neurosis, and what becomes relevant is the fate of the unconscious transference fantasy. Making this distinction frees us from the insoluble contradiction of a descriptive definition of acting out.

The expanding appreciation of the role of projective identification in fueling a transference relationship has been of inestimable value in therapeutic work with all patients, but especially with those exhibiting narcissistic transferences and primitive levels of psychic organization. Having a clearer picture of just how less-differentiated psychic contents are expressed by exerting pressure on a therapist either to behave in particular ways, or to at least feel the impact of the interaction, has also brought the process of acting out in the transference more sharply into focus. Bott-Spillius (1983) depicted the clinical usefulness of extending the concept of projective identification to include its use for communication. The patient gets the therapist to understand a feeling by subjecting him to the experience the patient undergoes. Of course the demand is for a therapist to join in this acting out, but if it can be understood instead of acted upon, the potential for positive therapeutic influence is increased. It allows primitive, unverbalized, and even unsymbolized psychic content to be grasped from the effects they have upon the therapist's subjective responses. De Folch and colleagues (1987) outlined this consequence with patients having recourse principally to splitting and projective identification. The technical problem of analyzing a patient locked into this paranoid-schizoid position is one of understanding the relationship established with the therapist through acting out. The patient tries to provoke reactions in the therapist, who must be prepared to experience the reactions and take notice of emotional responses. Countertransference and even momentary collusions were considered to be serious obstacles in the past, but now can be regarded, along with introspection into their source, as important factors in comprehending a patient's psychical world. The therapist's capacity to be affected by and experience feelings the patient is unable to assume and to verbalize them and turn them into a shared experience can help a patient be secure enough to feel. It is an important instrument that clarifies the patient's intrapsychic functioning and helps reintegrate the parts previously projected.

The Continuum of Acting Out and the Implications for Treatment

The structural composition of the various manifestations of behavior that are encompassed within the concept of acting out must be specifically identified as accurately as possible. Depending upon the underlying significance of a given piece of behavior, there are differing implications as to how therapeutic influence can be effective. Thus it is certainly relevant to consider the transference as an acting out, in that early developmental experiences are being relived in place of being remembered, but it is the structural basis for the way it is ultimately expressed that determines what is required of the therapist to further therapeutic progress.

When acting out is primarily used to defend against repressed and painful memories, as is often the case in the neurotically structured personality, the therapeutic task involves the use of interpretive interventions designed to call attention to and elicit what has previously been repressed. When acting out primarily has communicative value, giving expression to psychic contents that have no other avenue for expression, as is often the case in situations where infantile traumas are a major factor in the pathology, the initial treatment endeavor is one of translating the unconscious communication embedded in the behavior. Afterward it may be called for to offer either specific concrete experiences or appropriate interpretations within a well-managed treatment framework, in order to open a pathway toward symbolization, verbalization, and finally, integration. When acting out is a reflection of a developmental deficit, arrest, or gap in psychic functioning, created by early preverbal and traumatic experiences, the therapeutic task is one of presenting a new solution in the current interaction. This is accompanied by a reconstruction of the impossible infantile dilemma embodied in the original event. The introduction of modifications in the conditions of the treatment may be required until interpretative interventions can be established as the primary therapeutic instrument.

A patient's acting out may be instigated by, and mirror, a therapist's pathological attributes or lapses in empathy. In this case it can be received as a source of information, aiding the therapist in the process of self-examination, which is essential in exploring any obstacle to ongoing therapeutic advancement. The identification of a countertransference-based barrier is the first step in alleviating the problem. In a similar vein, acting out may primarily function as a response to a therapeutic misalliance or to a collusion with a patient's pathological defenses. It can then illuminate the process of recognizing and unearthing the forces that have been at work in forming this unhelpful interaction. In this fashion a potentially disruptive experience can be turned to therapeutic advantage, serving as a catalyst to increase self-knowledge on the part of both patient and therapist.

Finally, after all these factors have been taken into consideration, what could be and has been called acting out may also represent a desperate effort to create conditions vital to a patient's growth. It points to the need for examining the unconscious significance of the conditions of the treatment, in order to ascertain whether they are too restrictive and limiting for the necessary transferences to evolve and unfold. This is an area in which new avenues for introducing therapeutic influence are explored. In most instances it concerns an impending therapeutic failure with the most seriously disturbed and structurally deficient patients.

Extending the concept of acting out beyond its original and narrow definition is relevant because of the special problems presented by individuals who could communicate only in this way. A deeper understanding of the unconscious determinants of behavior and action must therefore be gained in order to discover more effective ways of treating their manifestations. Acting out is clearly an aspect of the transference, taking the form of reliving instead of remembering, but it is not always amenable to interpretive interventions, no matter how accurate. Additionally, it does appear to be a necessary component for the full unfolding of a regressive transference experience. The distinction between those aspects of behavior that have to be encouraged within a flexible, modifiable treatment framework, so as to further constructive growth, and those aspects that need to be received as input to be processed and interpreted while maintaining a firm and unyielding therapeutic stance to accomplish the same aim, is often confused and confusing.

Reenacting Infantile and Preverbal Traumatic Experiences

Psychoanalytic investigators have long been aware that the primary preverbal attitude of an individual could be revived under circumstances involving a complete regression of the ego and have presented discrete clinical evidence to demonstrate its manifestations. Isakower (1938) described a group of phenomena often occurring at the point of falling asleep, with the individual in a recumbent posture. What was striking was a blurring of the distinction between different regions of the body, and of the body and the outside world. Usually there was a shadowy, round impression coming nearer and nearer, swelling to gigantic size and threatening to crush the individual, after which it became smaller and shrank to nothing. A sensation of something present in the mouth was experienced, and at the same time the skin felt sandy or dry. Thus the body ego appeared to have reverted to an archaic stage of development, eliciting this hallucinatory revival of long-abandoned and lost objects. Another example was given by Lewin (1953), who noted how the dream screen and its associated qualities resided as early memory traces very near perception. He thought that along with the Isakower phenomena, it was reproducing some of the impressions that the smallest baby has at the breast.

Identifying the existence of these preverbal experiences and observing that they have an ongoing impact upon mental functioning instigated a search for their appearance within the context of a regressive transference relationship. Their positive growth-producing elements had long been speculated to be an aspect of the silent background underlying positive transferences, and their traumatic elements had been thought of as the basis of otherwise inexplicable disruptions in a therapeutic alliance. It was especially suspected to be a factor with seriously disturbed individuals, particularly those who received interpretive interventions as a narcissistic insult even when the content did not appear to be threatening, noxious, or unempathic. Nacht and Viderman (1960) referred to those times when words from a therapist were treated as an incurable wound. They felt such patients were searching for a primitive relationship to the mother in global, undifferentiated terms, more like a biological than an object link, and the task of responding therapeutically to these manifestations of preverbal traumatic experiences was an imposing one. Often, they did not emerge as the consequence of some specific traumatic event that could lend itself to being reconstructed and integrated within the fabric of the personality. Instead, there was a powerful anticipation of ongoing traumatic disruptions in the internal sense of containment and stability, accompanied by an exquisite sensitivity to even the slightest nuances of an empathic lapse. In an attempt to explain this phenomena, Khan (1963) developed the concept of cumulative trauma. This was a type of partial breakdown of the mother's role as a protective shield, which becomes visible as a disturbance only in retrospect. These breaches are in the nature of a maladaptation to the infant's anaclitic needs. They occur over the course of time, and through the developmental process accumulate silently and invisibly. Most importantly, they affect the vicissitudes of body ego development and the gradual integration of a sense of self.

The realization that early preverbal traumas were being re-created when a regression was encouraged with seriously disturbed individuals raised important concerns as to how or whether they could be healed. Lipin (1963) noticed how with some patients, recurrent experiential replicas of stressful past experiences were produced whose essentials were unrecallable. Consequently, it became imperative to examine therapeutic methods to discriminate the effects they were having on these deepest layers of the personality. A reliance upon an exclusively verbal mode of communication was brought into question, as well as the need to look more closely at the impact the other conditions comprising a treatment situation were having on the evolving transference relationship. Many clinicians struggled with this problem, and over the years a greater understanding of what made the treatment process flourish and what stood in the way slowly began to be evident.

One critical aspect grew out of the awareness that any lack of communication or even minimal empathic failure had an extremely disruptive effect, reflecting how much the therapist was functioning as a regulator of the patient's internal world. This meant that for the patient to find help at such primitive levels of regression the therapist also had to be both willing and able to operate effectively on a similar regressive level. Loewald (1970) showed how analytic work with many primitive patients led to a deeper insight into the genesis of the psychic substructures at the root of deformations and defects in the ego and superego. Transference and resistance were again the guiding light, but on much more primitive levels and with less differentiation. Communication then tended to approximate the kind of deep mutual empathy seen in the early mother–child relationship. By the same token, lack of communication tended to approximate an event of annihilation, insofar as the insufficiently differentiated matrix was disrupted.

A great deal of controversy was generated as to whether the evidences of preverbal trauma appearing in a transference relationship could be treated effectively within a psychoanalytic framework, or whether they had left an imprint that was in essence irreversible. A. Freud (1971) defined the problem, and expressed doubts and uncertainty as to the efficacy of a psychoanalytic process in bringing therapeutic influence to bear. She believed that in spite of the knowledge and conviction that preverbal experiences exert an influence that threatens to be lasting, there has been little evidence that it is possible to deal with them therapeutically. Many analysts nevertheless pinned their faith on the analysis of the first year of life, with the purpose of therapeutically modifying the impact of these earliest happenings. Any attempt to carry analysis from the verbal to the preverbal period of development brings with it practical innovations as well as theoretical implications, many of which are controversial. It means going beyond the area of intrapsychic conflict and into the darker area of interaction between innate endowment and environmental influence. The implied aim is to undo or counteract the impact of the very forces on which the rudiments of personality development are based. Analysts who work for this aim assure us that it can be achieved. It is obvious that different methods are needed for the approach to the earliest rather than later phases, since remembering yields its place to repetition, and verbal communication to reenactment.

Many clinicians recognized that early development could be reconstructed through an analytic process, since it was expressed in the transference and was often validated in a patient's responses. Such situations demanded more of a therapist's intuitive and empathic understanding of a patient's signs and signals, which were primarily expressed through action and behavior. Finding a solution was quite a different matter, because neither memory nor verbal recall were capable of reaching into the depth of these preverbal experiences. Most thought that early conflicts were essentially immutable and could not be analyzed. Blum (1977), for instance, had similar doubts about the reversibility of the impact of early preverbal traumas. He observed that reconstructions include archaic ego states and object relations reaction patterns. These reconstructions were particularly relevant to the origins of structuralization and to their later reactivation or persisting influence. He believed that historical reconstruction of real experience and real traumatic episodes remained significant because they can reorder the misinterpretation of internal and external reality. The assessment of preoedipal influences may be especially noted in the transference, therapeutic alliance, attunement to reality, and quality of object relationships. He warned, however, that our expanding preoedipal knowledge should not be misunderstood to mean that initial psychic development and differentiation are accessible to psychoanalytic treatment, that there are no limits or ambiguities to reconstruction, or that the earliest ego disturbances are reversible.

Some clinicians were convinced that the primary obstacle to alleviating the destructive effects of preverbal traumas was a result of intense and powerful countertransferences, which were elicited by the primitive nature of the therapeutic interaction and not adequately understood. McDougall (1979) described in depth the primitive communications and the ways a therapist's countertransference must be utilized if they are to be understood correctly and responded to therapeutically. For certain individuals, fusion and communion, rather than separateness and communication, are the only authentic means of relating to another person. Developmental experiences of patients who live out this inarticulate drama were marked by incoherent relationships with the earliest objects and in a context in which the inevitable frustrations of human growing were not tempered with sufficient gratifications to make them bearable. Therefore, the supreme reward of individuation and subjective identity was not acquired with pleasure, but instead continues to be relived as a rejection and an insult. The demand to be understood without words implies a terror of facing disappointment or refusal of any kind. This is felt as an unbearable pain that cannot be contained and psychically elaborated and thus can destroy one. To the extent that areas of experience have been repudiated from the psychic world, these extruded fragments of experience are expressed in behavior or constantly enacted in a primitive exchange. Words function as weapons, as camouflage, as a cry of rage, or of any other emotional state of which a patient is only dimly aware. At certain moments we can at least "hear" a distress signal, come to know it as an indication of profound pain that cannot yet be fully recognized as personal suffering, and recognize this as the basic message. This way of communicating and relating is rooted in early psychic suffering, and the countertransference phenomena to which it gives rise is the key to its understanding. However, in order to formulate an interpretation, the therapist must first understand why the patient's discourse creates the effect it does, for to lead the patient into self-discovery, the sounds of distress that lie behind the angry or confused associations must be decoded.

The question as to whether the ego distortions, deficits, and arrests emanating from the earliest stages of development reflect the bedrock beyond which no therapeutic influence can be brought is ongoing. In addition, it is frequently impossible to ascertain the extent to which their ultimate causation is a consequence of inherited factors or trauma. When they appear to exhibit unyielding characteristics, the tendency is to consider this as evidence of their unmodifiability and thus not search for new avenues of approach. However, a great deal of evidence has accumulated suggesting that whatever constitutional characteristics are present do have environmental determinants, a fact that takes on important clinical significance. Freedman (1981) called attention to how heavy emphasis is placed upon the role of "constitutional" factors in explaining failures of the analytic method. He wondered if it would be necessary to be so pessimistic if what appeared to be fixed constitutional traits turned out to be the products of early developmental events. He went on to explain that the most rudimentary aspects of self-awareness, such as the ability to differentiate self from non-self, to enter into relations with other selves, or to establish representations of others, all emerge in intimate relation with one another and as a result of ongoing maturational and developmental processes. Dramatic changes occur in the structure and potential function of the brain throughout the first two or three years of postpartum life and, while these changes are predominantly genetically determined to begin with, as maturation proceeds the ambiance in which it is occurring plays an increasingly important role.

Traumatic disruptions of the preverbal phases of development produce gaps in psychic functioning, so that continuity of experience is lacking in the personality, and symbolic processes are also severely impaired. Consequently, if treatment is to be effective, these deficits and the distortions they create become a primary focus of attention. A means must be discovered to adapt the principles of psychoanalytic treatment to the unique therapeutic needs of each individual, without being bound to procedures having relevance for more structured disorders. Gaddini (1982) had this in mind in discussing the differences between nonintegration and disintegration. A primitive fantasy expressed in the body can hardly be further elaborated in the course of development. It is the result of a gap in the process of integration, not of a splitting mechanism, and is representative of mental functioning preceding the integrative process. When reactivated, it is fragmenting and prevents integration. In treatment, the reconstruction of the level of integration that was broken and damaged by splitting is different from that occurring for the first time. Now there is an integration of parts never previously integrated. The anxiety of integration is the true pathology, for it is stronger, prevents the natural developmental process, and contributes to maintaining the nonintegrated state as an extreme defense. In the suffering of nonintegration there is no place for conflict, since for the fragmentary self no object can exist as an object. Thus it cannot give way to wishes and drives but instead must obey only necessity and need.

The work of a number of clinicians has shown that it is possible to provide effective therapeutic input even with the most regressive psychic states displaying profound disturbances in ego functioning. In order to do so, however, the proper conditions have to be present, enabling a regression sufficiently extensive to reach the deepest layers of the personality. This is an area in which the experiences growing out of the preverbal period are activated, and in some instances unusual measures may be called for. Kinston and Coen (1986) addressed this issue by pointing out that from a developmental viewpoint, needs must be met before mental representations in the form of wishes can be elaborated. A failure in need-mediation results in a persistent absence of associated wishes, and thus a gap in emotional understanding (psychic structure). The reemergence of a traumatic state in treatment is conveyed by prerepresentational experience, including sensory impressions, stereotyped actions, physiological reactions, and isolated images or affects. Action is a precursor of understanding in the absence of representation. A person is forced to express needs and inner states through action, and through provoking the therapist to act. This special type of self-transformative action in relation to symbolization is termed developmental acting out. It refers to action, which by virtue of the absence of wishes, is the only means available for achieving some perspective, some awareness of needs and experiences, or for affirming identity and separateness. Rather than interpret, the therapist may need to cooperate with requests or explain a failure to cooperate in ways not appropriate in other stages of the treatment. There are many examples of creative work, apparently overriding the rules and norms of psychoanalytic treatment, with three unifying similarities: a meeting of the patient's needs, action by the therapist playing a crucial role in the cure, and providing the patient with a new experience. Such an approach will be benefited and encouraged by a theory that enables these interventions to take their place as a new norm, for a therapist's responses will then be seen to be requisite rather than improper or irregular.

Reenacting Early Trauma and the Conditions of the Treatment

Individuals showing evidence of preverbal trauma are often impelled to express their needs and internal states either through action or by forcing the therapist to act, since this is the only avenue available to them. Therefore, the therapist's ability to understand the unconscious significance of this behavior and, in addition, to respond to it constructively is essential, since in the absence of mental representation it may be the only way to maintain emotional contact in the relationship. In one sense it can be seen as a form of acting out, although quite different from the acting out that is defensive, impulsive, or inappropriately gratifying. The therapist may very well have to participate in order to provide the necessary concrete experience of attachment, or at least be able to explain why it is not possible. The resulting interventions may in all outward appearances seem to be out of the realm of the usual rules and procedures of the treatment, but in this case they are required if a positive outcome is to be attained. The conditions are designed to provide the patient with an opportunity to internalize a new experience, which establishes the mental representational foundation necessary for processes of symbolization to become functional or which echoes with the split-off experiences in such a way that they can be included in the transference relationship. Only then can an interpretive mode of communication be effective and support the growth-promoting forces in a patient's personality. Once this is achieved, the reasons for altering the framework of the treatment can be subjected to exploration (Mendelsohn 1991).

A therapist's selection of what is considered to be an appropriate intervention depends entirely upon making an accurate assessment of its suitability for furthering therapeutic progress. This, of course, can be extremely difficult and is always open to question. Of the many factors used to arrive at that determination, one vital aspect is the nature and quality of a patient's affective responses, which often serve as a reliable guide in the midst of confusion. Emde (1988) underscored the extreme importance of positive emotions in development from earliest infancy. The most sensitive indicator of emotional availability is the presence or absence of positive affects, and pleasure and interest are major signs of affect attunement. He went on to state that affective life gives continuity to experience in spite of change, because its central organization is biological and its vital relations are unchanging. This affective core insures that we are able to understand others who are human, and because it touches upon those aspects of experience that are most important, it organizes both meaning and motivation. The emotional availability of the caregiver in infancy seems to be the most central growth-promoting feature of the early rearing experience, and by implication, there is no reason to suspect that it would be any different when dealing with the infantile emotions aroused in a psychoanalytically conducted therapeutic interaction.

In many instances, early experiences of trauma have no other way to gain access to expression except through behavior. These usually involve psychic events that have either been totally split off or are otherwise inaccessible to processes of symbolization. They then have to be reenacted if they are ultimately to be integrated within the fabric of the personality. The particular form the action takes may not only express the impact of an infantile trauma but may also be seeking to establish the specific conditions necessary to represent a new experience before developmental progression can be reinstituted. These are special circumstances in which the therapeutic relationship, as we have come to know it in our present state of knowledge, is not sufficiently receptive to the idea of introducing unusual conditions to facilitate growth. When it is called for and appropriate, a therapeutic relationship must have room for innovations and creative interventions, in order to enable the full reenactment of an early trauma and to achieve a new solution in the present to what was an impossible infantile dilemma in the developmental past.

8

Summary

"How can talking help me?" An anxious 6-year-old girl was protesting to her parents as she resisted the whole idea of going to see a psychiatrist. They did not quite know what to tell her; they only knew how concerned they were about her extreme tension and unhappiness. It was compounded when her school teachers were worried about her attitude and poor performance, in spite of what seemed like her great potential. She appeared to be extremely bright but was unable to do well and was constantly frustrated in accomplishing things. Her parents described her as driven and perfectionistic. When she recently had developed an eye tic they no longer listened to her objections and insisted that she seek psychological help. She was constantly overstriving yet underachieving, and an ever-present feeling of tension filled the air whenever they were with her. The slightest frustration would end up in an angry outburst or in berating herself and saying she wished she were dead. Although she fought with her parents about coming to see me, she did reluctantly comply when they stood firm.

To the first appointment she came in looking prim and proper, picked out a chair, and sat immobile as she talked. She spoke in an overly mature fashion about herself, her relationships with her parents, sister, and friends, and about her involvement in school and outside activities, while periodically displaying an eye-blinking tic. She worked hard to present a picture of herself as a competent, adequate little girl who was perfectly content with her life. My impression as I listened, however, was of a tightly wound spring, and I eventually expressed this to her. She responded by starting to giggle and then said, "That's silly, people can't be like springs." She added that she thought I was awfully weird. Her reaction made me feel that I had made some kind of empathic connection to an inner longing inside of her that had to be held tightly in check. At the end of the session I told her I thought she had given me a picture of her outside appearance, but it might be important to meet regularly to learn what was going on inside her. Again she giggled, stating that too was very silly. All that people had inside of them was a heart and lungs. Now, however, her entire demeanor became more relaxed. Her movements were more spontaneous and she agreed, almost eagerly, to the idea of regular meetings.

During the beginning sessions she looked forward to coming and was enthusiastic in the way she greeted me. Her behavior and verbal expressions were gradually less constricted and she was full of vitality. Her overly mature facade slowly dissolved as she revealed a wide range of emotional reactions. Initially they centered around her descriptions of school, extracurricular activities, and interactions with peers. She voiced her hatred, envy, or admiration of a number of children, and put emphasis on her intense dislike of school, especially the effort and concentration that was demanded. She longed to just sit in front of the TV, watch cartoons, and be free of any expectations. She saw her teachers as the source of much pressure and visualized them silently looking at her in intensely disapproving ways. This triggered a series of associations concerning children who were out of control, which led them into positions of great danger. I thought of how frightened she was both of her instinctual drives and of the harsh prohibitions they evoked that so controlled her.

Periodically a hunger to be nurtured and comforted would surface, as she sought relief from her internally conflicted state. This was poignantly expressed as she described her inability to fall asleep. It began with her feeling restless and frustrated, like having an itch she needed to scratch but couldn't reach. It reminded her of the movie, *Lord of the Flies.* It was scary to think of situations where there was no structure and no rules. I related her concern to the experience she was having with me. The atmosphere of implicit encouragement seemed to make her feel overstimulated, which mobilized power- fully strict and disapproving prohibitions. It looked like she was asking me to give her some kind of rules and structure that could protect her. Her immediate response was to talk about her wish to be just like her father. He always seemed able to handle everything and had an answer to every problem. The following session occurred shortly afterward.

She started out by telling me how much she knew and how capable she was. She had brought an advanced book to show me just how well she could read, and wrote several complicated words on a piece of paper to prove how well she could spell. While she was doing this it was evident that she both misread and misspelled several words. Her attitude was emphatically self-righteous as she challenged me to try to find any mistakes. I said to her that she seemed to be questioning whether I would tell her things that I could see were wrong and help her to face her own uncertainty. First she got angry, proclaiming that she was right and she knew it. Then she put the book down to demonstrate her skill at doing gymnastic tricks. She put special emphasis on how much more adept she was than her sister, even though her sister was several years older. Suddenly she became embarrassed and, speaking softly, referred to the envy and admiration she felt for her sister. She hesitantly admitted that she was always fighting hard to beat her and was never able to do it. She felt driven to show everyone that she could do everything well and when she couldn't, it made her very frustrated and she began to hate herself.

Her attitude toward me shifted as she teasingly asked if I could do the gymnastic feats she had just done. She proceeded to do some more, commenting on how impossible it would be for me to repeat them. She thought I was much too clumsy and awkward and was convinced that I felt very envious of her ability. She just knew I was disappointed in myself as I watched her and was wishing I could be more agile. I noted how she was now attributing feelings to me that she had experienced shortly before, and I thought she was telling me that I had missed the significance of what she was talking about. It seemed to me that she must want me to see how she didn't quite feel complete and was disappointed in me when I couldn't help her see where that feeling came from. She became pensive before suddenly remembering a dream. She was in her bedroom with her mother and father, a monster threatened to break into the room, and she felt she had to protect her mother, who was very awkward and inept. Her father disappeared but she knew he was okay.

The dream made her think of her mother and of how much she missed her after school. She then fantasied sitting on her mother's lap watching TV. In a soft voice she spoke of being disappointed in her mother, becoming contemptuous as she described her mother's ineptness. I said that I was reminded of her feeling about my being inept and how it barely covered another feeling about me that made me think of the monster in the dream. Her attitude became very secretive. Hesitantly she told me she was thinking about a lot of things but felt very embarrassed. She didn't know if she could say them out loud. Slowly she revealed her fantasies concerning sexual activities, interspersed with comments concerning the bad words she was both using and thinking about. She recalled giggling with her friends as they used bad words and felt excited in doing so. She went on to elaborate upon her wish to have a boyfriend and of her interest in various boys. She stopped, felt embarrassed again, and then alluded to her curiosity concerning male genitals.

At the outset of the treatment she had worked hard to picture herself as competent and capable, yet the defensive meaning of this effort was apparent in the rigidity of her movements, her overcontrolled words and tone of voice, and the almost total focus on conscious mental content and immediate perceptions. There was little overt evidence of instinctual activity, for her ego was almost totally organized toward keeping any such strivings repressed. The relative absence of fantasy and instinctual derivatives or of any sublimated expressions of instinctual impulses were all indicative of a highly conflicted internal state. Her superego organization was immature, possessing inordinately harsh, punitive, and restrictive qualities. My initial metaphorical comments concerning her tense appearance and referring to the introspective act of looking inside were consciously taken literally and rejected. They seemed, however, to give her a sense of being unconsciously understood, since her entire demeanor indicated she felt more securely held. Evidences that a therapeutic regression was being initiated followed almost immediately.

Subsequently she became more relaxed and spontaneous, but also more frightened of the forces mobilized internally that were pushing for expression. She displayed a very active fantasy life, as derivatives of unconscious mental activity slowly began to be abundant. The underlying instinctual conflicts became more evident, facilitated by my interpretations of her defensive posture and of the underlying content, so that communication between her unconscious and preconscious systems was increased. At the same time, disturbing infantile instinctual wishes were exposed to more advanced integrative functions, while her self-knowledge and awareness were expanded. A wider range of emotions and an ability to represent a larger variety of experiences were also manifested. Concomitantly, she was able to use her intellectual functions more effectively, for they were not so bound up in sustaining repression, and she was becoming more adept at symbolically expressing her internal experiences.

Her intense disappointment in, and rivalry with, her mother alternated with contempt and envy, which came to life through their appearance in the transference relationship. They were barely disguising a negative oedipal attachment. This defensive transference attitude was addressed interpretively, which allowed more threatening positive oedipal drive derivatives gradually to emerge. The intensity of her genital instinctual demands, in conjunction with the inhibiting effects of her defensive reactions, was interfering with the resolution of her oedipal conflict and with the consolidation of her developing superego. The process of instinctual integration was made possible with the help of my interpretations, and the fixed, unyielding defensive attitudes that caused her so much trouble were slowly relinquished.

A readiness to continue the thrust for developmental progression and to attain a resolution of her oedipal conflict now occupied her mind and became the central focus of the treatment. This child had developed a neurotically structured personality and as such her treatment needs were for a well-managed therapeutic framework within which interpretive interventions could be the exclusive modality of communication. A benign therapeutic regression could then unfold, so that the integrative forces within her personality gained access to psychic contents that were previously too conflicted and had to be repressed. My therapeutic attitude also encouraged and evoked constructive positive identifications, which alleviated the harshness of the infantile prohibitions built into her evolving superego. A freer flow of unconscious mental activity was thus enabled. Derivatives proliferated, making instinctual energy more available for expanding the range of her ego interests. There was no indication of early developmental deficits or arrests so that her pathology was primarily in the realm of the fantasy distortions created by her infantile instinctual conflicts. Any modification in the boundaries, ground rules, or conditions of a psychoanalytically conducted treatment framework would only have supported her pathological defenses and have been infantilizing.

The determination of the specific conditions of the treatment, the management of ground rules and boundaries, the timing, depth, and content of interpretations, and, if indicated, the consideration of noninterpretive interventions, should emanate from a patient's unconscious communications rather than from the authority of a therapist. In general, a patient's healthy strivings for growth are constantly in search of a relationship in which they can be realized, in spite of equally intense efforts to defend against them or even to deny their existence. Perceiving any particular disturbance as being a spontaneous attempt at finding a cure focuses therapeutic attention upon the growth-producing factors reaching for expression. With this in mind, the directions necessary to enable progressive structural change are embedded within a patient's personality and primarily expressed through derivatives of unconscious perceptions. The basic psychoanalytic principles, guiding the conditions and conduct of the treatment, can then be applied so as to be consonant with them.

The various ground rules, including fee, length and frequency of sessions, and the position of patient and therapist, are all evocative of the patient's unconscious perception of what is growth-promoting and are filled with potential unconscious meaning. Lesser frequency and face-to-face contact often diminish the sense of intimacy, establish clearer boundaries, and present more distinct impressions of reality. They do not exclude these elements, nor do they exclude the communication of distortions. Increased frequency and the use of the couch fosters regression and facilitates a greater availability of deeper derivatives of core unconscious fantasies. The stimuli of the external world are decreased, the position is an impetus for sexual and aggressive fantasies to surface, the potential for a wider range and intensity of transference experiences is expanded, and the possibility of a blurring of boundaries is increased. The use of the couch also intensifies the potential for arousing the therapist's countertransference-based responses, and the reaction to a profound regression and ego dysfunctions may elicit too great a readiness for introducing modifications. However, it is balanced by enhancing the therapist's capacity for processing psychic content, yielding a more penetrating grasp of unconscious meaning, and solidifying the ability to maintain an interpretive attitude when necessary.

The attention given to discriminating between those conditions that elicit the containing, growth-promoting mental representations in a patient's personality, those that make impossible demands by virtue of depending upon the existence of psychic functions that are either absent or defective, and those that reinforce pathological defenses, is an integral facet of developing the proper imbalance in the relationship required for establishing a well-defined boundary. A clear sense of the most optimal emotional distance in the relationship can thereby be discovered jointly. A therapist's ability to introduce features operating in the best interests of a patient, combined with those required to support the therapist's appropriate needs, establishes the groundwork for forthright, direct, and honest communication. From the initial moment of therapeutic contact, the conditions of the relationship are gradually constructed to produce an emotional climate in which an individual's most intimate, vulnerable, infantile, regressive experiences can be unveiled for the purpose of expanding self-awareness and self-knowledge. Attending to the fixed ground rules thus presents a powerful stimulus and gives expression to the therapist's mode of functioning.

The setting of a fee, which may or may not have room for adjustment, conveys a great deal of information, both conscious and unconscious, about a therapist's motivations. The attitude with which it is presented may have a lot to do with how much freedom the patient may experience in being able to discuss it and thereby open a door to discovering its unconscious meaning. Third-party involvements may come into play, having important unconscious meaning, and the therapist's awareness of the importance of listening to that meaning before accepting it can be a vital message about the way the treatment will be conducted. Insurance, payment by others, and arrangements concerning cancellations and vacations can all be matters that support pathological defenses, increase the internal dangers associated with a regression, and intensify separation anxieties. Conversely, they may foster the use of latent resources, strengthen the containing influences of the relationship, or address a much-needed acknowledgment of existing deficits in psychic functioning.

The length of a given session is most frequently designed for the therapist's convenience, since ideally this varies from patient to patient and with a given patient at different times. It is just one of a body of factors that is a part of creating the proper imbalance that gives impetus to the regressive experiences encompassed in the transference. A therapist's confidence in this fact and honesty in acknowledging the inequity can go far toward enabling the patient's feelings to be expressed without introducing an adversarial atmosphere. The most desirable frequency of sessions can also be a difficult matter to discern. During the early sessions, when the ground rules are laid down, the optimal pace for furthering a therapeutic regression may not be evident. In addition, a patient may adopt a submissive posture, looking to the therapist for an agenda to be followed, or take on a rigid, oppositional stance rationalized by pointing to existing realities as the reason for limiting the number of sessions. At the beginning there may not be enough material available for a view of the unconscious meaning of these attitudes. Therefore, it might be most helpful to delay a decision about frequency until an avenue is opened for a deeper understanding of what is facilitating to constructive growth, even though this temporarily leaves a sector of the framework not fully secured. The patient is thus implicitly encouraged to become an active participant in the therapeutic work, primarily through the production of usable derivatives, diminishing the aura of unwarranted authority that can so easily permeate the relationship.

There are many analysts who consider the conditions of psychoanalytic treatment to include daily sessions, and in many instances this unconscious direction is given by a patient. However, there are those for whom too great a frequency may reinforce a pathological defense or unnecessarily amplify defensively constructed, submissive attitudes. Similarly, the patient's position of either sitting up in face-to-face contact with the therapist or utilizing the couch, out of direct view, is best determined through a sensitive reading of its unconscious significance. When it is presented as a condition that must be adhered to, an important dimension of the therapeutic framework becomes infused with a defense-inducing attitude. The ultimate decision concerning these fixed components of the therapeutic framework depends upon a blending of, what is required by the therapist to support ideal functioning and the guidelines emanating from the patient's unconscious perceptions of what is growth-promoting in a relationship.

Therapeutic communication is grounded upon principles designed to support healthy processes in an interaction, and to foster the undoing of pathological distortions of internal experience. The behavior and actions of a therapist are usually not regarded as significant, unless they are utilized consciously and purposefully or are reacted to in some overt manner. Communication is generally considered to transpire primarily through words, and at times this is specifically stated as a direction. On those occasions when behavior and action are the predominant mode of communication, it is predicated on the patient's inability to use or understand words. The more primitively organized the personality, the more clearly the ingredients that comprise a holding experience must be identified and provided, and as developmental advancement is manifested, whatever has been necessary can gradually be presented in a more symbolic form. In the more organized personality the mental representations at the foundation of experiences of holding and containment are capable of being symbolized and hence can be evoked through a verbal interchange. There are structurally deficient patients, however, for whom only direct emotional or physical contact can bring the much-needed experience of being held and contained. In such situations, it may be vital for a therapist at least to entertain the possibility of introducing this form of participation.

There are some narcissistic individuals for whom the task of establishing the proper conditions of a well-contained therapeutic framework and a clear set of ground rules and boundaries is extremely confusing. With these more primitively organized personalities the activity of unconscious perceptions emanates from a realm of psychological experience that has been split off and is excessively vulnerable. It is then dangerous to express the contents of this split-off realm, because the act of communicating elicits a regression resulting in destruction if the proper conditions are not present. The therapist's primary beacon for guidance is thereby protected and guarded by a defensive force working to obscure the nature of these required conditions. Therefore, a picture may emerge that is both inaccurate and destructive, as an effort is exerted to enlist the therapist's participation in the destruction of the meaning of the relationship. The therapist must first be able to receive and see what lies behind these defensive distortions before a pathway to the proper conditions can be located.

Defensiveness in a therapist may create "blind spots," which stand in the way of identifying the specific interpersonal qualities that are essential for enabling a benign regression. Often the same attributes that make it possible for a therapist to be receptive to primitive projective identifications expose the relationship to a blurring of boundaries and destructive deviations, and it may be a fine line from one to the other. When this dilemma is responded to by withdrawal, it obviates against effective therapeutic influence. In not being open to internalize the patient's primitive productions the therapist may construct a firm but rigid and inflexible therapeutic framework. With some patients this may be disruptive and even life-threatening. With others it may lead to more solidly entrenching an adaptive style based on conformity. Years may then be spent strengthening an empty, depleted, advanced realm of functioning, thus deepening the despair of finding life-giving new solutions.

If the therapist presents an unyielding obstacle to the experiences needed for healing to take place, the patient may have to go to extremes in trying to penetrate the therapist's defensiveness in order to make contact in a way that has the potential for growth. Thus the therapist has to engage in a continuous process of self-exploration in order to maintain a clear focus on the patient's therapeutic needs. With more primitively organized individuals, the application of the basic psychoanalytic principles is gradually shaped from the concrete to the symbolic and verbal, as the patient's personality becomes more consolidated, coalesced, and integrated. Verbal interpretations can become a primary therapeutic instrument only when there is sufficient psychic structuralization for words to elicit body ego experiences.

Interpretations are the ultimate therapeutic instrument. They are designed to intervene with the distortions produced by pathological defenses, to facilitate the expression of psychic contents in the deeper layers of the personality, and to strengthen the foundation upon which healthy integrative functions operate. They convey the manner in which the patient's input has been unconsciously understood and indicate the degree to which the therapist's unhelpful, idiosyncratic, or countertransference-based responses have been filtered out. In being empathic with unconscious communications, they amplify containment and the experience of feeling held, cement a therapeutic alliance, foster positive identifications, and solidify the groundwork on which the transference unfolds. Interpretations serve the combined purpose of enabling the movement toward a benign regression as defensive structures are clarified, and thereby undoing distortions. This very act aids in integrating the previously inaccessible psychic contents that are reached. One consequence is in a freer interplay between the varied systems of consciousness. At the same time, effective management of the treatment framework and the therapeutic attitude required to do so enhance constructive identifications. All of these factors combine to support the patient's move toward more advanced levels of psychic organization and structural change.

It is quite a different matter when dealing with individuals manifesting narcissistic and prestructural transferences, because global, unformed unconscious fantasies are expressed in the direct interaction with the therapist, often in the form of immediate needs. The ground rules, boundaries, and conditions of the treatment therefore assume the utmost significance, since holding and containment must be provided if a useful benign regression is to occur. At certain moments, attention is also drawn to the ineffectiveness and sometimes harmful effects of seemingly innocuous and even accurate interpretations, while the importance of grasping the unconscious meaning of nonverbal communications is underscored. An alteration or break in the treatment framework, or a modification of the ground rules, can interfere in major ways with the stability and support they have to offer. Thus, if some behavioral involvement or direct emotional contact appears to be called for, or some condition of the treatment has to be changed, the potential dangers inherent in this kind of situation must be kept in mind. There are some circumstances, however, especially with primitively organized and structurally deficient patients, where new experiences have to be provided in order to bridge gaps in psychic functioning that are a result of developmental defects, deficits, or arrests. In that case, a therapist may introduce interventions involving concrete actions or direct emotional contact, but it is important that they follow the guidelines laid down by the basic psychoanalytic principles as closely as possible.

Effective therapist–patient boundaries must be maintained if the goal is to be reached of enabling the constructive influences of interpretive interventions to rise to the forefront. Bringing the conditions of a psychoanalytically conducted relationship into the treatment of patients who show disturbances emanating from the preverbal period of development carries with it the need to find new ways of exerting a positive influence, many of which may be controversial. The therapist's task shifts from exploring the nature of conflict within a structured personality to unearthing the experiences required to strengthen or even build deficient psychic structure. In the process, the destructive forces that have had an impact on the very foundations of a patient's personality are counteracted or undone.

In the primitively organized patient, projective identifications are less differentiated. The transference relationship therefore becomes an arena for expressing psychic contents through demands for gratification of regressive cravings or by other forms of discharge through action. The resulting pressure placed upon the therapist to participate may lead to momentary collusions, which at one time were considered to be a serious obstacle. Although in fact it may become a problem, this kind of interchange may very well be vital if the makeup and significance of a patient's internal world are to be fully understood. The therapist must be open to be affected by, and experience, the feelings a patient is unable to assume for this interchange to take place. Once their source is understood, they can then be put into meaningful words. Along with a flexible management of the treatment framework, the end result is to provide a secure and safe holding environment, in the context of which the patient's primitive mode of functioning can be clarified as previously split-off psychic contents are reintegrated. This means that the therapist has been capable of facing personal regressive and potentially anxiety-arousing experiences, a necessity for attaining this goal, and through understanding has avoided acting out in turn.

Whenever a treatment process is obstructed or halted, the forces that have stood in the way have to be identified. Sometimes this can be an imposing task that begins by examining the therapist's subjective responses. They must be as clearly understood as possible, at least distinguishing between those that are empathic and those that are countertransference-based, either interfering or enhancing unconscious perceptiveness.

Empathy involves everything the therapist knows about the patient, including conceptions based upon theoretical knowledge and clinical experience, information gleaned through derivatives concerning unconscious processes, and his own perceptions as to the person's unused potential. It requires a controlled and reversible regression, allowing trial identifications along with the use of advanced functions to synthesize the objective and subjective sources of data.

Countertransference was first conceived of as a troublesome, usually neurotic disturbance in the therapist, which obviated against a clear and objective view of the patient. Gradually these subjective reactions have been recognized as a crucial source of information about a patient, as well as a major contributor to the helpful or harmful features of a therapeutic interaction. Whenever the therapist's emotional responses are unobstructed by infantile conflicts or narcissistic needs, unconscious perceptiveness is enhanced and the resulting interventions tend to be unconsciously empathic and to further therapeutic progress. The therapist must therefore simultaneously utilize emotions and subjective reactions of all kinds to support and strengthen a therapeutic alliance, while filtering out those that are a product of personal difficulties and antithetical to growth.

In addition, the therapist must become adept at making accurate assessments of the structural organization of the patient's personality. In doing so, the therapist can make crucial distinctions between the various destructive forms of acting out and behavior that represents a striving for growth. Over the years the concept of acting out has undergone many changes. It no longer refers exclusively to behavior aroused by the conditions of the treatment that are motivated by psychic contents pushing for expression but transformed into action to avoid remembering. Acting out has also come to refer to behavior that is the consequence of ego deficits. Under these circumstances infantile experiences are repeated, often utilizing the therapeutic relationship and other external objects as well, either to master the trauma or to seek a new solution to an impossible infantile dilemma.

The unconscious meaning of psychic contents expressed through behavior can be difficult to read. Furthermore, because such movements tend to be impulsive, have a propensity for seeking inappropriate gratifications, and expose a patient to potential dangerous consequences, it puts the therapist into an awkward and uncomfortable position. Although some behavior may represent a way of remembering, not all acting out is past-oriented. On occasion, it reflects the activity of defenses designed to avoid such recall, but it may be a means of finding a new resolution. The distinctions are vital to make, for to foster growth they are handled differently. Much depends on an accurate appraisal of the patient's personality as well as an empathic appreciation of the unconscious communications that a given act is expressing.

There is much yet to be learned as to how a psychotherapeutic relationship can best be put in the service of easing human suffering. Fortunately, there is much knowledge available to provide a foundation from which we can continue to explore. It is essential to live with a degree of ambiguity and uncertainty if meaningful answers are to be found, especially when problems arise. Otherwise theories are applied either inappropriately or with an unwarranted authority that stands in opposition to further investigation and new learning. An overly rigid idea of the meaning of behavior and mental functioning results in a distorted picture of what it is to be human. Access to as many of the ways as possible an understanding of human development has been conceptualized, in conjunction with a sensitivity and alertness to the uniqueness of individual experience, helps to deepen a grasp of what can be curative.

An interpretation must be addressed to experiences that are urgent and pressing in the transference relationship if it is to be properly received. It must also be in tune with the patient's psychic capabilities, and rest on the background of an effective therapeutic alliance if it is to be mutative. Interpretations, however, do not always lead to change. The therapist must be guided by the patient's unconscious perceptions of what is required to promote growth and must be prepared to try to offer whatever is possible. This means careful management of the treatment framework, which must be flexible enough to adapt to the structural organization of the patient's personality. Within that context, different things may be done at appropriate times.

Management considerations take priority with individuals showing developmental defects, deficits, and arrests, for interpretations alone do not take into account the lack of capacity to utilize symbolic modes of communication. The subsequent emotional distance in the relationship and unawareness of the depth and nature of the disturbance only serve to intensify underlying feelings of despair and helplessness. Including interpretive reconstructions of the infantile experiences responsible for the deficiencies, however, along with careful provision of the necessary conditions in the relationship, does present a positive influence.

An ideal therapeutic attitude focuses attention upon receiving unconscious communications, with the sole purpose of understanding their meaning and significance, as the therapist's entire being is devoted to that task. Consequently, personal elements are filtered out so that inappropriate emotional responses are not directed into the relationship, having the effect of ameliorating the harshness of prohibitive forces in the patient's personality. In the process, constructive identifications become more viable, thereby enhancing an self-esteem. Finally, the act of being able to represent an internal event, put it into words, and communicate it in a search for its meaning, gives form to previously unformed experience.

All of these factors combine to further an integrative process leading to structural change and more advanced levels of psychic organization. Thus the question posed by the child mentioned at the beginning of this chapter, and the title of this book, *How Can Talking Help?* can be answered quite succinctly: it depends entirely upon who you talk to, what you say, the way in which you say it, and most important of all, the response that you receive.

References

Alexander, F. (1954). Some quantitative aspects of psychoanalytic technique. *Journal of the American Psychoanalytic Association* 2:685–701.

Anthony, E. J. (1977). Non-verbal and verbal systems of communication: a study in complementarity. *Psychoanalytic study of the child* 32:307–326. New Haven: Yale University Press.

Balint, M. (1968). *The Basic Fault: Therapeutic Aspects of Regression.* London: Tavistock.

Baranger, M., Baranger, W., and Mom, J. (1983). Process and non-process in analytic work. *International Journal of Psycho-Analysis* 64:1–15.

Basch, M. F. (1983). Empathic understanding: a review of the concept and some theoretical considerations. *Journal of the American Psychoanalytic Association* 31:101–125.

Beres, D. (1968). The role of empathy in psychotherapy and psychoanalysis. *Journal of Hillside Hospital* 17:362–369.

Beres, D., and Arlow, J. A. (1974). Fantasy and identification in empathy. *Psychoanalytic Quarterly* 43:26–50.

Berger, D. (1987). *Clinical Empathy.* New York: Jason Aronson.

Bettelheim, B. (1974). *A Home for the Heart.* New York: Knopf.

Bird, B. (1957). A specific peculiarity of acting out. *Journal of the American Psychoanalytic Association* 5:630–647.

Blatt, S. J., and Behrends, R. S. (1987). Internalization, separation-individuation, and the nature of therapeutic action. *International Journal of Psycho-Analysis* 68:279–294.

Blum, H. P. (1977). The prototype of preoedipal reconstruction.

Journal of the American Psychoanalytic Association 25:757–785.

———— (1980). The value of reconstruction in adult psychoanalysis. *International Journal of Psycho-Analysis* 61:39–52.

Boesky, D. (1982). Acting out: a reconsideration of the concept. *International Journal of Psycho-Analysis* 63:39–55.

Bott-Spillius, E. (1983). Some developments from the work of Melanie Klein. *International Journal of Psycho-Analysis* 64:321–332.

Boyer, B. L. (1979). Countertransference with severely regressed patients. In *Countertransference*, ed. L. Epstein and A. H. Feiner, pp. 347–374. New York: Jason Aronson.

Buie, D. H. (1981). Empathy: its nature and limitations. *Journal of the American Psychoanalytic Association* 29:281–307.

de Folch, T. E. (1987). The obstacles to analytic cure: comments on analysis terminable and interminable. In *International Psychoanalytic Association Educational Monographs,* no. 1, chap. 5, pp. 89–111.

Deutsch, H. (1966). Discussion remarks. In a Developmental Approach to Problems of Acting Out, ed. E. Rexford, pp. 173–219. New York: International Universities Press.

Dickes, R. (1967). Severe regressive disruptions of the therapeutic alliance. *Journal of the American Psychoanalytic Association* 15:508–533.

Dorpat, T. L. (1974). Internalization of the patient–analyst relationship in patients with narcissistic disorders. *International Journal of Psycho-Analysis* 55:183–188.

Ekstein, R. (1965). A general treatment philosophy concerning acting out. In *Acting Out,* ed. L. E. Abt and S. L. Weissman. New York: Grune and Stratton.

Emde, R. N. (1988). Development terminable and interminable. *International Journal of Psycho-Analysis* 69:23–39.

Fairbairn, W. R. D. (1957). Freud, the psychoanalytic method and mental health. *British Journal of Medical Psychology* 30:53–62.

———— (1958). On the nature and aims of psychoanalytic treatment. *International Journal of Psycho-Analysis* 39:374–385.

Frank, A. (1969). The unrememberable and the unforgettable: passive primal repression. *Psychoanalytic Study of The Child* 24:48–78. New York: International Universities Press.

Freedman, D. A. (1981). The effect of sensory and other deficits in children on their experience with people. *Journal of the American Psychoanalytic Association* 29:831–867.

Freud, A. (1968). Acting out. *International Journal of Psycho-Analysis* 49:165–170.

_____ (1971). Difficulties in the path of psychoanalysis: a confrontation of past with present views (1969 [1968]). *The Writings of Anna Freud,* vol. 3, pp. 124–156. New York: International Universities Press.

Freud, S. (1914). *Remembering, repeating, and working through. Standard Edition* 12:145–156.

Gaddini, E. (1982). Early defensive fantasies and the psychoanalytic process. *International Journal of Psycho-Analysis* 63:379–388.

Gedo, J. (1981). On the use and abuse of empathy in psychoanalysis. In *Advances in Clinical Psychoanalysis,* pp. 160–184. New York: International Universities Press.

_____ (1984). *Psychoanalysis and Its Discontents.* New York: The Guilford Press.

Giovacchini, P. L. (1974). Countertransference with primitive mental states. In *Countertransference,* ed. L. Epstein and A. H. Feiner, pp. 235–265. New York: Jason Aronson.

Gitelson, M. (1962). The curative factors in psychoanalysis. I: The first phase in psychoanalysis. *International Journal of Psycho-Analysis* 43:194–206, 232–233.

Green, A. (1975). The analyst, symbolization and absence in the analytic setting (on changes in analytic practice and analytic experience). *International Journal of Psycho-Analysis* 56:1–22.

Greenson, R. R. (1960). Empathy and its vicissitudes. *International Journal of Psycho-Analysis* 41:418–424.

_____ (1972). Beyond transference and interpretation. *International Journal of Psycho-Analysis* 53:213–217.

Greenacre, P. (1950). General problems of acting out. *Psychoanalytic Quarterly* 19:455–467.

Grinberg, L. (1968). On acting out and its role in the psychoanalytic process. *International Journal of Psycho-Analysis* 49:171–178.

Heimann, P. (1950). On countertransference. *International Journal of Psycho-Analysis* 31:81–84.

Hurwitz, M. R. (1986). The analyst, his theory, and the psychoanalytic process. *Psychoanalytic Study of the Child* 41:439–466. New Haven: Yale University Press.

Isakower, O. (1938). Contribution to the psychopathology of phenomena associated with falling asleep. *International Journal of Psycho-Analysis* 19:331–345.

Jacobs, T. J. (1973). Posture, gesture, the movement in the analyst: cues to interpretation and countertransference. *Journal of the American Psychoanalytic Association* 21:77–92.

Joseph, B. (1975). The patient who is difficult to reach. In *Tactics and Techniques in Psychoanalytic Therapy,* vol. 2, *Countertransference,* ed. P. Giovacchini, pp. 205–216. New York: Jason Aronson.

Joseph, E. (1979). Comments on the therapeutic action of psychoanalysis. *Journal of the American Psychoanalytic Association* 27(suppl.):71–79.

Kanzer, M. (1961). Verbal and non-verbal aspects of free association. *Psychoanalytic Quarterly* 30:327–350.

_____ (1968). Ego alteration and acting out. *International Journal of Psycho-Analysis* 49:431–435.

Khan, M. M. R. (1963). The concept of cumulative trauma. *Psychoanalytic Study of the Child* 18:286–306. New York: International Universities Press.

Kinston, W., and Coen, J. (1986). Primal repression: clinical and theoretical aspects. *International Journal of Psycho-Analysis* 67:337–355.

Kohut, H. (1959). Introspection, empathy and psychoanalysis. *Journal of the American Psychoanalytic Association* 7:459–483.

_____ (1977). *The Restoration of the Self.* New York: International Universities Press.

_____ (1982a). Introspection, empathy, and the semi-circle of mental health. *International Journal of Psycho-Analysis* 63:395–407.

_____ (1982b). *How Does Analysis Cure?* Ed. A. Goldberg and P. Stepansky. Chicago: University of Chicago Press.

Kuiper, P., Garma, A., King, P., and Heimann, P. (1962). The curative factors in psychoanalysis: contributions to symposium discussion. *International Journal of Psycho-Analysis* 43:218–231.

Langs, R. (1975a). The therapeutic relationship and deviations in technique. *International Journal of Psychoanalytic Psychotherapy* 4:106–141.

_____ (1975b). Therapeutic misalliances. *International Journal of Psychoanalytic Psychotherapy* 4:77–105.

_____ (1975c). The patient's unconscious perception of the therapist's errors. In *Tactics and Techniques in Psychoanalytic*

Therapy, ed. P. Giovacchini, pp. 239–251. New York: Jason Aronson.

_____ (1981). Modes of "cure" in psychoanalysis and psychoanalytic psychotherapy. *International Journal of Psycho-Analysis* 62:199–214.

Levy, S. T. (1985). Empathy and psychoanalytic technique. *Journal of the American Psychoanalytic Association* 33:353–377.

Lewin, B. D. (1953). Reconsideration of the dream screen. *Psychoanalytic Quarterly* 22:174–199.

Lichtenberg, J. D. (1981). The empathic mode of perception and alternative vantage points for psychoanalytic work. *Psychoanalytic Inquiry* 1:329–355.

Lipin, T. (1963). The repetition compulsion and "maturational drive representatives." *International Journal of Psycho-Analysis* 44:389–406.

Little, M. (1981). *Transference Neurosis and Transference Psychosis.* New York: Jason Aronson.

Loewald, H. W. (1960). The therapeutic action of psychoanalysis. *International Journal of Psycho-Analysis* 41:16–33.

_____ (1970). Psychoanalytic theory and the psychoanalytic process. *Psychoanalytic Study of the Child* 25:45–67. New York: International Universities Press.

_____ (1986). Transference–countertransference. *International Journal of Psycho-Analysis* 34:275–287.

McDougall, J. (1979). Primitive communication and the use of countertransference. In *Countertransference,* ed. L. Epstein and A. H. Feiner, pp. 267–304. New York: Jason Aronson.

McLaughlin, J. J. (1987). The play of transference: some reflections on enactment in the psychoanalytic situations. *Journal of the American Psychoanalytic Association* 35:557–582.

Mendelsohn, R. (1985). The onset of unconscious perceptions. *The Yearbook of Psychoanalytic Psychotherapy,* vol. I, ed. R. Langs, pp. 209–240. Emerson, NJ: New Concept Press, Inc.

_____ (1987a). *The Synthesis of Self, vol. I The I of Consciousness.* New York: Plenum.

_____ (1987b). *The Synthesis of Self, vol. IV The Principles that Guide the Ideal Therapist.* New York: Plenum.

_____ (1991). *Leaps: Risks in Offering a Constructive Therapeutic Response When Unusual Measures Are Necessary.* Northvale, NJ: Jason Aronson.

Milner, M. (1952). Aspects of symbolism in comprehension of the not self. *International Journal of Psycho-Analysis* 33:181–195.

Modell, A. H. (1976). "The holding environment" and the therapeutic action of psychoanalysis. *Journal of the American Psychoanalytic Association* 24:285–308.

Nacht, S., and Viderman, S. (1960). The pre-object universe in the transference situation. *International Journal of Psycho-Analysis* 41:385–388.

Olden, C. (1958). Notes on the development of empathy. *Psychoanalytic Study of the Child* 13:505–518. New York: International Universities Press.

Olinick, S. (1969). On empathy and regression in the service of the other. *British Journal of Medical Psychology* 42:41–49.

Pine, F. (1988). The four psychologies of psychoanalysis and their place in clinical work. *Journal of the American Psychoanalytic Association* 36:571–595.

Post, S. (1980). Origins, elements, and functions of therapeutic empathy. *International Journal of Psycho-Analysis* 61:277–293.

Racker, H. (1957). The meaning and uses of countertransference. *Psychoanalytic Quarterly* 26:303–357.

Rangell, L. (1968). Symposium: a point of view on acting out. *International Journal of Psycho-Analysis* 49:195–201.

———— (1979). Contemporary issues in the theory of therapy. *Journal of the American Psychoanalytic Association* 27(suppl.):81–112.

Reich, A. (1966). Empathy and countertransference. In *Annie Reich, Psychoanalytic Contributions,* pp. 344–360, (1973). New York: International Universities Press.

Rexford, E. N. (1966). *A Developmental Approach to Problems of Acting Out.* New York: International Universities Press.

Robertiello, R. C. (1965). "Acting out" or "working through." In *Acting Out,* ed. L. E. Abt, and S. L. Weissman, pp. 247–275. New York: Grune and Stratton.

Rycroft, C. (1956). The nature and function of the analyst's communication to the patient. *International Journal of Psycho-Analysis* 37:469–472.

Sandler, J., Dare, C., and Holder, A. (1973). *The Patient and the Analyst.* London: Allen and Unwin.

Schafer, R. (1959). Generative empathy in the treatment situation. *Psychoanalytic Quarterly* 28:342–373.

Searles, H. F. (1975). The patient as therapist to his analyst. In *Tactics and Techniques in Psychoanalytic Therapy,* vol. 2, *Countertransference,* ed. P. Giovacchini, pp. 95–151. New York: Jason Aronson.

Sechehaye, M. A. (1951). *Symbolic Realization.* New York: International Universities Press.

Segal, H. (1981a). The curative factors in psychoanalysis. In *The Work of Hanna Segal,* pp. 69–80. New York: Jason Aronson.

_____ (1981b). Countertransference. In *The Work of Hanna Segal,* pp. 81–87. New York: Jason Aronson.

Shapiro, Theodore. (1974). The development and distortions of empathy. *Psychoanalytic Quarterly* 43:4–24.

Silverberg, W. V. (1955). Acting versus insight: a problem in psychoanalytic technique. *Psychoanalytic Quarterly* 24:527–544.

Stein, M. (1973). Acting out as a character trait. *Psychoanalytic Study of the Child* 28:347–364. New Haven: Yale University Press.

Stern, D. N. (1984). *The Interpersonal World of the Infant.* New York: Basic Books.

Stolorow, R. D., Brandchaft, B., and Atwood, G. (1983). Intersubjectivity in psychoanalytic treatment with special reference to archaic states. *Bulletin of the Menninger Clinic* 47:117–128.

Stolorow, R. D., and Lachman, F. M. (1980). *Psychoanalysis of Developmental Arrests.* New York: International Universities Press.

Strachey, J. (1934). The nature of the therapeutic action of psychoanalysis. *International Journal of Psycho-Analysis* 15:127–129. Reprinted in *International Journal of Psycho-Analysis* 50:275–292.

Tyson, R. L. (1986). Countertransference evolution in theory and practice. *Journal of the American Psychoanalytic Association* 34:251–274.

Wallerstein, R. S. (1967). Reconstruction and mastery in the transference psychosis. *Journal of the American Psychoanalytic Association* 15:551–583.

Weigert, E. (1954). The importance of flexibility in psychoanalytic technique. *Journal of the American Psychoanalytic Association* 2:702–710.

Weill, A. P. (1985). Thoughts about early pathology. *Journal of the American Psychoanalytic Association* 33:335–352.

Winnicott, D. W. (1949). Hate in the countertransference. *International Journal of Psycho-Analysis* 30:69–74.

_____ (1954). Metapsychological and clinical aspects of regression within the psychoanalytic setup. *International Journal of Psycho-Analysis* 36:16–26.

_____ (1960). The theory of the parent–infant relationship. *International Journal of Psycho-Analysis* 41:585–595.

_____ (1963). Dependence in infant-care, in child-care, and in the psychoanalytic setting. In *The Maturational Processes and the Facilitating Environment,* pp. 83–92. London: Hogarth Press, 1965.

Wolf, E. S. (1983). Empathy and countertransference. In *The Future of Psychoanalysis,* ed. A. Goldberg, pp. 309–327. New York: International Universities Press.

Index